BATTLE
FOR GROUND ZERO

BATTLE
FOR GROUND ZERO

INSIDE THE POLITICAL
STRUGGLE TO REBUILD THE
WORLD TRADE CENTER

ELIZABETH GREENSPAN

First published in 2013 by PALGRAVE MACMILLAN® in the
United States—a division of St. Martin's Press LLC, 175 Fifth Avenue,
New York, NY 10010.

Where this book is distributed in the UK, Europe and the rest of the world,
this is by Palgrave Macmillan, a division of Macmillan Publishers Limited,
registered in England, company number 785998, of Houndmills,
Basingstoke, Hampshire RG21 6XS.

Palgrave Macmillan is the global academic imprint of the above companies
and has companies and representatives throughout the world.

Palgrave® and Macmillan® are registered trademarks in the United States,
the United Kingdom, Europe and other countries.

All photographs were taken by the author and are reproduced with
permission.

ISBN 978–0–230–34138–8

Library of Congress Cataloging-in-Publication Data is available from the
Library of Congress.

A catalogue record of the book is available from the British Library.

Design by Newgen Knowledge Works (P) Ltd., Chennai, India.

First edition: August 2013

10 9 8 7 6 5 4 3 2 1

Printed in the United States of America.

For Stanley

CONTENTS

ACT III   DEALMAKERS: 2008–2011

*Eight pages of photographs appear
between pp. 144 and 145.*

ACKNOWLEDGMENTS

I AM MOST GRATEFUL TO THE MANY PEOPLE WHO SHARED THEIR stories. To those who interrupted their visits at Ground Zero to answer my questions; to the downtown residents, rescue workers, architects, and victims' family members who told me about experiences; to the architects at New York New Visions who welcomed me into their meetings; and to the members of the Philadelphia Families Group who so graciously invited me to attend their group. Thank you.

I am also indebted to Michael Arad, Rick Bell, Janno Leiber, Daniel Libeskind, George Pataki, Larry Silverstein, Chris Ward, and the staff of the 9/11 Memorial Museum, including Alice Greenwald and Lynn Rasic, for their time, thoughts, and participation. To Paul Goldberger and Edward Linenthal, both of whom helped me further understand the complexities of the rebuilding. To Rachel Branwen, who transcribed tirelessly. And to Christina Davis, Azra Hromadzic, Genevra Murray, and Marlon Kuzmick, for talk, brainstorming, and friendship.

Jon Sternfeld believed passionately in the project, and led me to my smart, thoughtful editors at Palgrave, Emily Carleton and Laura Lancaster. Years earlier, my mentors at the University of Pennsylvania—Bob Preucel, Kathy Hall, Asif Agha, Elaine Simon, and Setha Low at the City University of New York—provided insight, guidance, and support.

Without Christina Thompson and Greg Harris, who read every chapter, some multiple times, there would be no book at all. My parents, Nancy and Stanley, encouraged and believed in me. And my husband Mike was the wisest reader and greatest supporter I could have hoped for. This book is dedicated to my father, who taught me not to be afraid of big battles.

PREFACE

AMERICA THE RE-BUILD-IFUL

IN THE FIRST MONTHS AFTER 9/11, THOUSANDS OF PEOPLE DESCENDED upon the World Trade Center site in Lower Manhattan to see the destruction and, while they were there, many wrote comments on nearby walls, emergency railings, and streets signs. The graffiti was usually written in ink or marker, not spray paint, and included everything from simple signatures to original poems to increasingly political exchanges between passersby. ("Blame Bush!" "Who did the damage? Not Bush. Thank <u>God</u> for Bush!") One refrain, in particular, caught my eye: "America the Re-build-iful."

It was scrawled on a boarded-up bank entrance across from the wreckage (though after that first sighting, I spotted the refrain all over the site's temporary architecture). It was catchier and more playful than "United We Stand" or "God Bless America," and it seemed to capture the idealistic, unifying spirit of the times. It also expressed the idea that prompted me to pick up and head to Ground Zero in the first place: the idea that the identity of the country was inextricably tied to the rebuilding of the World Trade Center site. It was the idea that whatever we decided to build here would reveal nothing less than what makes us American. The catchy little refrain, in other words, expressed the very big stakes of the rebuilding—and presaged the battles to come.

I was a 24-year-old graduate student then, in anthropology and urban studies. I was interested in the rebuilding partly because 9/11 felt so monumental, but also because I had always been intrigued by how cities worked, in particular, how people shaped and fought over space, and, after 9/11, the space everyone was talking about was Ground Zero. Once I arrived in New York, I learned that there was more than one process to examine. I went to civic group meetings and public hearings, where I met area residents, city architects, victims' families, and rescue workers. I also went to the WTC site regularly to follow progress and conflicts on the ground, and photographed the spontaneous memorials and graffiti, and then the construction work, the protests, and the annual anniversary ceremonies. I collected reports, press releases, newspaper articles, and talked to more people. By the end of my research, I had interviewed more than 300 people at the World Trade Center site, more than 150 downtown residents, victims' family members, rescue workers, and architects, and nearly 50 city and state officials involved in rebuilding, including the politicians, architects, and developers making key decisions.

The battles over what and how to rebuild were heated from the beginning, so much so that at times they reminded me of some of the most entrenched struggles over territory, like the Israeli-Palestinian conflict. Of course, people didn't resort to violence to determine who owned the WTC site, a sixteen-acre parcel that is considerably smaller than, say, Jerusalem. But sixteen acres in the heart of New York City is not unlike vast, rolling tracts of property elsewhere; it certainly costs as much. And people felt very strongly about Ground Zero. Most of all, the questions that defined the battles downtown were the same ones that have triggered land conflicts everywhere. Who does it belong to? And, as importantly, how will we decide?

At the WTC site, the question of ownership appeared relatively simple: the Port Authority of New York and New Jersey owned the land, and developer Larry Silverstein owned the lease to the office space. But these were merely the legal answers, and for many people legality wasn't the only or even the most appropriate framework to employ. Nearly three thousand people were killed at the World Trade Center, in the deadliest foreign attack on American soil in the country's history. Was the land really owned by one individual and one institution? A lot of people didn't think so, at least not in the aftermath of the attacks. Victims' families and neighborhood residents believed they had legitimate claims to the WTC site, as did many New Yorkers, as did many of the thousands and then millions of people coming to see the destruction. The question of ownership proved so big and open-ended it often felt rhetorical. *Everyone* owned Ground Zero—or, at the very least, they believed they owned a piece of it. So, they fought for their piece. For years. Some are still fighting for it.

This book tells the story of these battles. It begins in the fall of 2001, when the debates about what and how to rebuild commenced, and it ends in the fall of 2011, when the memorial opened to the public and many, though not quite all, of the major decisions had been made. It doesn't document every conflict or participant; instead, it tells the story of the multiple forces that remade the World Trade Center site. This means that it is partly a story about owners and politicians sitting around tables in conference rooms, but it also means it is a story about people in streets, public hearings, and living rooms voicing desires, demands, concerns, and beliefs—and occasionally garnering the attention of the influential men. It is a story about capitalism and democracy. It's a story about those who built the walls and those who wrote on them.

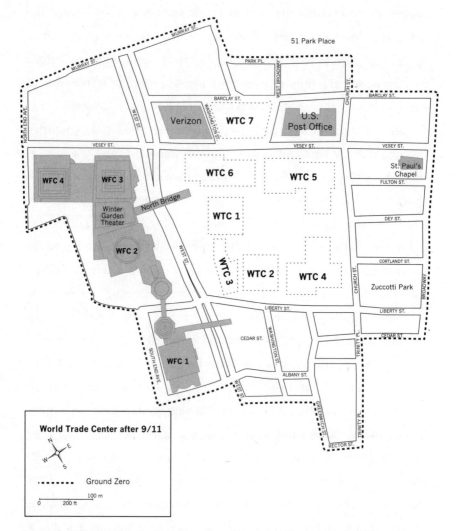

Soon after the attacks, the city erected temporary walls around the destruction, marked by the dotted line, blocking off an area much larger than the sixteen acre World Trade Center. As the years passed, the city gradually moved the walls closer to the hole. Outlined inside the site are the footprints of the original WTC buildings.

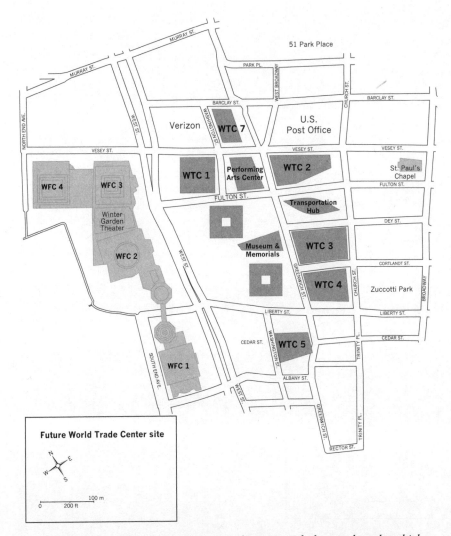

At the reconstructed World Trade Center, the memorial plaza and pools, which occupy eight acres, are surrounded by commercial skyscrapers and a transit hub. Greenwich and Fulton Streets run through the complex again, further separating the commercial and commemorative quadrants. 1 WTC/Freedom Tower stands in the northwest corner.

ACT I

VISIONS AND VISIONARIES
2001–2003

CHAPTER 1

PEOPLE COME

ARK LIVED THREE BLOCKS FROM THE WORLD TRADE Center, on Church Street. He was a twenty-seven-year-old screenplay writer, and on the Tuesday morning of September 11, he was at home, as usual, working on his computer. When the first plane hit the North Tower, the impact jolted him from his desk chair and threw him onto the floor. He rushed outside, where he saw people screaming and running away from the towers. Soon ambulances raced toward them, driving down the wrong side of the road. When the second plane hit the South Tower, a piece of the plane's engine, "larger than the size of a keg of beer," as he put it, landed on his street corner.

Mark did not flee his apartment immediately. He had a friend who worked in the South Tower and an ex-girlfriend who also worked in the area. "I thought one of them might come by," he said. "The guy was my best friend. They were close people." Mark decided it was time to leave his apartment after both towers collapsed, but unlike the thousands of neighbors evacuating, he instinctively wanted to stay as close to home as possible.

He headed to a friend's place in SoHo, the next neighborhood up, and then went to his favorite bar near his apartment building to look for his friend. He did not find him. That night, he tried to get back into his apartment, but the police had padlocked it. So, instead, he climbed the stairs leading to the roof of his five-story building and sat alone, watching as teams of rescue workers covered with gray dust maneuvered on top of twisted steel beams. Angled spotlights lit up the mounds of craggy, fiery wreckage.

Earlier that day, National Guard troops armed with machine guns had filed onto 14th Street, about a mile north of the wreckage, to control the flow of people into Lower Manhattan. No one could cross below the militarized line without official permission. This is why thousands of New Yorkers congregated in Union Square that afternoon; it was the closest any of them could get. The guards left 14th Street a few days after the attacks, but, for Mark, the boundary had been set. Fourteenth Street was his line, the temporary edge to his new New York. His sister lived uptown, on 86th Street, but he refused to visit her. "My sister kept telling me to come up there," he said. "But that was like a different city."

Mark found Lower Manhattan weird and unsettling—"There were cops everywhere, people in streets, people stapling up memorial signs," Mark said—but this was precisely why he wanted to stay. "Downtown was the only place that felt normal," he said. "It was the only place that felt like you did. Completely fucked up." For weeks, 14th Street was the farthest Mark would go before turning around and heading back toward Ground Zero.

Almost everyone I spoke to in those first weeks and months after 9/11 had their own sense of this line, the invisible boundary that separated the destruction from the rest of New York City. Most in Manhattan lived north of their line, outside the disaster zone, and the question they faced was how close to travel to it. Some kept their distance, observing the line from afar, while others made regular pilgrimages, spending a few minutes each day at their chosen boundary marker to reflect on the violence and destruction. As time passed, people's lines shifted and moved closer to the site.

Two months after 9/11, I walked to Ground Zero from Midtown to see where I would first notice something akin to a line. When I mentioned my plans to a friend who lived in New York, he said two words: "Canal Street." Canal Street was south of 14th Street, about three-quarters of a mile from the wreckage. I wouldn't see the destruction, he said, but this is where I would smell it. For him, this was the de facto border: the place where the smell began.

When I arrived at Mark's line, at 14th Street, Union Square was back to normal. The only traces of the thousands of people who had gathered here in early September were spots of colored wax, speckled with an occasional burnt wick, stuck to concrete walkways. Police had cleared the thousands of bouquets, candles, and handwritten notes weeks earlier. Likewise, at Canal Street, the odor had already disappeared. The sidewalks were filled with customers walking in and out of electronics shops and looking over street vendors' designer knockoffs. It wasn't until Chambers Street, about six blocks away from the sixteen-acre site, that I first noticed a smell of stale dust filling the air and heard the constant, heavy hum of machinery and high-pitched jackhammers.

Most of the streets within this six-block radius were closed to car traffic and packed with people. Rescue workers in full fire gear, covered in ash, walked slowly from the site, taking breaks from their shifts. Downtown workers in suits carried briefcases and often wore white face masks to filter the air as they maneuvered around slower movers. The vendors were the most ubiquitous. Some wandered corner to corner selling American flags and patriotic banners from black trays hanging around their necks, while others hawked a greater assortment of goods, including full-color books on the Twin Towers and hats and T-shirts branded with "FDNY" (Fire Department, New York), from rickety card tables. Handfuls of tourists, some with American-flag bandannas tied around foreheads and biceps, encircled their tables negotiating for better prices.

The wreckage was surrounded by a series of tarp-covered, chain-link fences and plywood walls. The ad hoc structure blocked nearly all ground-level views of the destruction; all you could see from street level were the pieces of jagged facade, a bit distant, that rose up from the center of the sixteen-acre hole. But people wanted to see more. Some bent down on hands and knees, necks twisted, cheeks against the sidewalk, to look through slivers of space where the tarps were not quite long enough to touch the ground. Others stood on tiptoes or balanced on top of emergency railings, necks arched, to peer over. And some went to even greater lengths. Later in the afternoon, I came upon a man shimmying his way up a streetlight just outside the walls. We were at the intersection of Fulton Street and Broadway, which featured a large break in the fencing and a close, unobstructed view of the serrated remnants of the North Tower. At least fifty people stood shoulder to shoulder in silence. Meanwhile, the climber inched his way up the streetlight, a camera bumping against his chest. When he reached the top, he teetered and cautiously extended an arm to take a few snapshots. It was impossible not to watch him, and soon a series of flashes popped below him, which prompted the man to smile and wave his camera-filled hand in recognition.

It was a little shocking to watch and be a part of such a spectacle: rescue workers were still searching for bodies. But I instinctively began to take a picture of the teetering man too. The only reason I didn't was because I had already filled the exposures on my quickly purchased disposable camera.

I was a graduate student from Philadelphia, and the year before I had become interested in cities and how they rebuilt in the wake of violence and war. I had read books about Berlin and Hiroshima and Oklahoma City and the contentious reconstruction efforts that went on for years, sometimes decades. The books nominally concerned architecture, but they were really books about politics and history—and, of course, real estate. Time and again, fierce battles broke out among every imaginable constituency—architects, developers, residents, politicians, tourists, victims' families—as they vied to control land and the narratives being told about it. There was a sense of urgency behind the battles; people were anxious to repair the cityscape and to determine what the historic events meant. In every instance, a stretch of land or an iconic building suddenly belonged to an array of groups and, for better or worse, brought everyone together to talk about it.

After 9/11, these same struggles began to unfold on op-ed pages and in press conferences about the WTC site, so I took a break from my books and went to New York. The questions people were debating were both extremely straightforward and incredibly open-ended. Questions like, what should be rebuilt? How should we decide? And, most contentiously, what will different choices say about us, about America?

THE TALK IN THOSE EARLY DAYS WAS mostly metaphorical. Few people were discussing specific plans or buildings—it was too soon for that. On September 18, *Daily Dish* blogger extraordinaire Andrew Sullivan posted this: "Someone sent me this small quote from a book on architecture. It's from Minoru Yamasaki, the designer of the World Trade Center. Yamasaki wrote: 'The World Trade Center should, because of its importance, become a living representation of man's belief in humanity, his need for individual dignity, his belief in the co-operation of men, and through this co-operation his ability to find greatness.' No wonder these demons destroyed it. I want Bush tomorrow to say that we will rebuild it—taller, bigger, stronger."

A few days later, the *Philadelphia Inquirer* published a rejoinder to Sullivan on its op-ed page. "Yamasaki's claim that the WTC represented individual dignity is laughable," philosopher Crispin Sartwell wrote. "The gleaming glass and steel rectangles were objects of a kind of unimaginable ferocity, a human imagination so dedicated to its own annihilation that it was the opposite of anything mammalian, a kind of refutation of the human body.... Let's build something human," he declared. "Not a symbol, a real place; not a place to die, a place to live."

The rhetoric was epic, practically biblical. There were "demons" on one side and, on the other, "a human imagination dedicated to its own annihilation." (And this was in the mainstream *Philadelphia Inquirer*, not some little-known alt weekly.)

Non-pundits were weighing in too. Americans were calling television stations like CNN and describing visions for memorials, parks, plazas, and buildings. Larry Silverstein, the developer who owned the lease to the Twin Towers, received nearly three thousand letters in the first month after the attacks, telling him how and what he should rebuild. It wasn't long before the list of things for Ground Zero to house reflected a host of irreconcilable desires: revenge, rebirth, peace, power, empathy, the latest in green design, a park, commercial space, and last but not least, affordable housing.

The conversations weren't limited to Americans. In his book *Watching the World Change*, David Friend reports that more than two billion people watched the 9/11 attacks in real time or saw images of them that same day. CNN's coverage of the attacks was seen in 170 million households in more than two hundred countries; ABC, CBS, and NBC also aired original broadcasting all day long. Altogether, media analysts believe that over a third of the earth's population watched the events of 9/11 that very same day. In the current Twitter and Facebook era, the international viewing of the attacks is perhaps a bit less remarkable, but the timing was still uncanny. Robert Pledge, head of Contact Press Images, told Friend that the timing of the attack on the Trade Center in particular—just before 9 a.m. EST—was precisely when the largest percentage of the earth's people are awake. "It never happens with the Olympics or the World Cup," Pledge said. "During all major events in the recent past—Tiananmen Square, the Gulf War, the Iraq Invasion—there's always a part of the world that's in the dark. But this could be seen at once, anywhere, in both hemispheres, any latitude...live—something that we've never had happen before."

It was the most watchable moment, unfolding in the one of the world's most filmed locales. This was the other reason, of course, that so many saw the Twin Towers collapse: the city housed an incredible concentration of media outlets ready to transmit images around the globe. In addition, New York City is home to millions of immigrants and travelers, whose families wanted information too. Of the 2,980 who died in the three sites of attack, 329 were determined to be foreign nationals, and initially the numbers were believed to be much higher. Just as names and photographs filled American newscasts, names of non-Americans feared dead scrolled down television screens in their home countries. They were bankers and consultants, students, cooks, security guards, and janitors. Some lived in New York, others were passing through, and some were undocumented.

On the evening of the eleventh, thousands congregated outside the American embassy in Berlin with candles, flowers, and peace signs. In one photograph, a teenager holds a sign that reads, "No World War 3." On Friday, September 14, forty-three cities across Europe held a coordinated moment of silence.

Some celebrated the violence. In Peshawar, Pakistan, thousands filled streets holding signs and banners honoring Osama bin Laden. And some tried to define a third option, something between total allegiance and total opposition. A few hours before President Bush addressed a joint session of Congress on September 20 to announce the beginning of the War on Terror, in which he declared that "either you are with us, or you are with the terrorists," a few thousand marched through Rome behind a large white banner that read, "NO al terrorismo alle guerre. Un altro mondo è possibile." ("No to terrorism and no to war. Another world is possible.") Three days later, students in Santiago, Chile, demonstrated behind a sign that read, "George & Osama: you are not the owners of the world."

At the center of this unfolding public expression was Ground Zero, a walled-off piece of real estate where rescue workers were laboring twenty-four hours a day, seven days a week, searching for bodies and loading tons of twisted steel beams onto trucks headed for Fresh Kills Landfill, the unfortunately named Staten Island site receiving WTC wreckage. (In Dutch, *kille* means stream, and the landfill, which dates back to the late 1940s, sits on the banks of a freshwater estuary, also named Fresh Kills.) At first, practically everyone commented from afar, but people began to travel to New York again a few weeks after the attacks, and slowly but steadily, they congregated on the streets and sidewalks around the site.

"I just wanted to come see it," said Steve, a middle-aged business-man from Michigan, standing on Broadway in mid-November. He had come downtown during the lunch break from his dental conference. Sarah, from North Carolina, stood next to Steve. "To pay respects," she said when I asked her why she had come. Sarah had short, wispy brown hair and wore a windbreaker. She added, "I fly every day. These are my fellow travelers. It could have been me."

THE MOST CROWDED SPOT AT GROUND ZERO was St. Paul's Chapel, which stood next to the intersection of Fulton Street and Broadway, and its striking sightline of the destruction. St. Paul's was one of the few build-ings close to the WTC to remain undamaged after the towers' collapse, and volunteers quickly transformed it into a resting place for firefight-ers and rescue workers taking breaks from their shifts. Soon, everyone else transformed its fence into the area's largest grassroots memorial.

One sliver of fence displayed more than seventy pieces. There were six worn T-shirts filled with messages from California, Texas, and

Florida, and eight baseball caps, including a red one with the French message "avec toute notre amité" ("with our affection"). It looked as if, in some instances, visitors and passersby, unexpectedly moved to contribute, had taken off the hats they were wearing or the T-shirts on their backs. Some even refashioned trash: one person left behind an empty Nesquik bottle sporting a miniature American flag in place of a straw. There were dozens of handmade posters, quilts, and cloth banners. A handwritten poem from Samantha, age ten, was titled "we will overcome." There were three bouquets of flowers, four teddy bears (one of which featured a black question mark drawn on its belly), and ten laminated newspaper clippings and obituaries of victims. There were twelve American flags, three British flags, and one flag of Ireland. A pair of worn, white ballet toe shoes lay on the ground with the words "Now you are really dancing" handwritten on one slipper. And someone, a Sesame Street–loving child, perhaps, contributed a small Ernie figurine (without Bert).

Explicit politics, like those expressed in some of the international outpourings, were largely missing from Ground Zero, at least at first. People expressed sadness, hope, and curiosity about what it all looked like, and this was true of those coming from outside the United States too. One afternoon I met Sam, who wore a long, dark gray overcoat and steadily removed handfuls of purple and blue origami cranes from a stuffed duffel bag and hung them on a series of iron fence posts. Sam was originally from Kansas, he told me, but was in New York during a brief vacation from Japan, where he taught English in a small town of seven thousand residents outside Nagasaki. The schools' two hundred seventh, eighth, and ninth graders had folded four thousand cranes for him to deliver. "The kids wanted them brought to New York," he said. "They wanted to give them to city hall, but I said I would bring them here."

Folding cranes is an ancient Japanese tradition—one thousand cranes bestow a wish or a charm upon the folder—but origami cranes took on added significance in the aftermath of Hiroshima and Nagasaki, when Sadako Sasaki, a young girl who developed leukemia from the bomb's radiation, folded cranes as she lay dying in her hospital bed. A statue of Sadako stands at the original ground zero in Hiroshima, now called the Peace Memorial and Atom Bomb Dome, where Japanese children continue to fold and deliver cranes. Each of Sam's cranes contained the message "keep your dreams" handwritten in Japanese characters.

Amidst the calls for peace and hope, however, an occasional angry, more aggressive response dotted the landscape too. Across from the bouquets and teddy bears hanging in front of St. Paul's Chapel was an emergency railing that contained, in big, black, handwritten letters, "Bomb Afghanisthan [sic]." I wasn't sure which was more eye-catching, the layers of multicolored paper espousing love, or the singular call for revenge. Around the corner from St. Paul's, a couple of people had engaged in a charged, but nonetheless poetic exchange on a temporary, wooden sign. One visitor wrote the antiwar slogan: "Our grief is not a cry of war." To which another responded, "Fuck you, you left-wing coward piece of shit."

One winter afternoon, I met an Israeli couple, Lev and Naomi, who were visiting the WTC site with French and Croatian friends who lived in Las Vegas. I asked why they wanted to come, and Naomi said it was mostly out of curiosity. After a pause she added that being here "is a reason to hate them more." "Who?" I asked. "Arabs," she said matter-of-factly.

Anti-Arab commentary wasn't difficult to find after 9/11, but no one else at Ground Zero had made such a remark to me and for a moment I didn't know what to say. Naomi filled in the silence. She said that she thought New York had a different tone—a new quietness. "My town, [between Tel Aviv and Haifa] it's all bombings lately," she said. "It's scary to see here. Tel Aviv is dangerous, and here too. There is no safe place." Naomi paused and then continued. "I am not *glad*, but I am glad it happened in the States. Now Americans will under-stand what we go through."

Her French friend from Las Vegas nodded and then offered a clari-fication. "I wish they attacked the buildings, not people," she said.

It was difficult to imagine Americans walking around the site and saying they were glad it happened, or, for that matter, making a dis-tinction between the buildings and the people. The destruction of the towers sometimes seemed as great an affront as the killing. But even though the comments were not typical, they captured a certain truth about the WTC site: it was becoming a place—*the* place, in fact—where people spoke out about post-9/11 America.

Graffiti, that infamous target of the Giuliani administration, was everywhere. Thousands of messages and signatures slowly crept up and over every structure still standing. The collection of boards sealing up the entrance of a bank on Greenwich Street was one of the area's most popular graffiti spots. Some areas were illegible, there were so many layers of text:

"No Fear to be Happy Everywhere," "Rio de Janeiro, Brasil," "We will pull through America," "United We Stand," "All my tears + prayers 2 those lost."

And, my favorite, repeated on numerous surfaces: "America the Re-build-iful."

Of course, the most powerful statement was not written on any wall; it was the one people made simply by showing up and taking over more and more space. By mid-fall, much of the city had been swept clean. In Union Square, at 14th Street, cops cleared the can-dles and bouquets after one week. But at the WTC site, where more police officers roamed the streets than anywhere else in New York, the public increasingly filled surrounding sidewalks with stuff. On West Street, a six-foot-high mound of pastel-colored teddy bears sat under a white tent. There must have been a few hundred of them. On Broadway, by Liberty Street, a whole block was slowly consumed by flowers, flags, and banners, tripping up pedestrians as they tried to make their way.

One morning, I asked the police officer standing guard at a utility entrance on Greenwich Street if he knew who was maintaining the memorials on the opposite corner where, every couple of days, a new piece of empty chain-link fence would mysteriously appear and quickly fill with banners, flags, flowers, and notes. The officer shrugged. "Maybe Salvation Army volunteers?" he said, as if he were asking me the question. No, he had never seen anyone attend to the surprisingly neat arrangement of objects or bring new pieces of fence. They were just, always, there.

"Do you ever help with them?"

He tilted his head and narrowed his eyes. "I'd love to," he said. "But, you know, I've got other things to do. Pruning flowers isn't my forte."

He was tending to more important tasks, like guarding the still-fiery wreckage and making sure that those of us outside the walls did not disturb the people and work inside. Still, I was a little surprised he was so uninterested. The memorials and graffiti—what anthropologist Miles Richardson has described as "gifts of presence"—were not only innocuous expressions of grief. With each bear, banner, and handwritten signature, people were expressing sympathy but they were also making claims upon the land. Walking around the site, you would see no more than a few hundred people observing, reading, photographing, but a glance at all the stuff revealed a far larger collective. One that wasn't going away on its own.

ONE GROUP WAS NOTICEABLY ABSENT FROM THE bustling streets and sidewalks around the sixteen-acre site: New Yorkers. Almost all the city residents I spoke to disliked the crowds; the more that tourists filled the streets around Ground Zero, the more many city residents avoided the area. Some never went to the site, while others went once or twice in the first days after. Screenwriter Mark, who refused to cross 14th Street, also refused to walk the three blocks from his building to the perimeter of the wreckage. "I don't need to go and make it more real," Mark said. "I lived it. I went to funerals." When Mark's brother visited him in November and asked to go to the site, Mark walked with him for half a block before turning around. "There's nothing to see but a hole and a lot of gawking," he said.

Many New Yorkers had other ways of grappling with 9/11. The city's first major exhibit after the attacks was a grassroots production titled "here is new york: A Democracy of Photographs." Michael Shulan, a longtime New Yorker, and two colleagues retrofitted two storefronts in SoHo to artfully display and sell hundreds of original photographs of the attacks donated by amateur and professional photographers: the towers collapsing, the engulfing cloud of dust and debris, the eerie smoking rubble, the dangerous rescue and recovery work. The exhibit was located just north of Canal Street but well south of 14th Street; it brought people close to the wreckage, but not too close. And "democracy," not "loss" or "trauma" or "New York," was the production's key word. There were no labels or bylines accompanying the images, which meant that no one knew if they were paying twenty-five dollars for a picture by a world-famous photographer or the consulting firm employee who happened to take a striking shot with his handheld. The line between expert and novice was erased. There was also no explanatory text, no interpretation. The crowds of people decided what it all meant.

The exhibit opened in October, and Shulan estimated that over 100,000 people visited during its initial two-month run. Through a combination of in-house and online sales, as well as a book, he sold 78,000 prints and raised over $2 million, which he donated to charities for victims' families. Meanwhile, the exhibit quickly became a temporary community hub, open at all hours, hosting events, readings, and meetings for victims' families. Shulan attributed the interest to people's desire to collectively face the violence in a space that was a bit removed and also a bit curated. He believed that people wanted to be part of something social and creative, something emotional. During a time that lacked clear explanations and understandings, art was flourishing. "New York City was an incredibly exciting place," he said of those early months. Shulan said the time reminded him of a college professor's descriptions of the years preceding the American Revolution, when "Everybody would go down together and they would have arguments, they'd have discussions, they would write things and that's really what New York felt like in the aftermath of 9/11," he said. "It was pretty terrific...because these ideas which are ingrained in America came to the fore and popped into daily life."

Shulan's exhibition was a sort of cousin, then, to the outpouring at the WTC site. In both instances, thousands of people traveled to confront the destruction and walk away with photographs of it. They came to make a piece of Ground Zero their own. But the outpouring at the WTC site *was* different, mostly because people were taking over streets and sidewalks instead of store fronts. Graffiti, sidewalk occupations, spontaneous memorial/street art installations: these activities were banned on all other city streets, but at the site, they proliferated, under the semi-watchful eyes of the city's police force, no less. With little fanfare, Ground Zero had become the country's newest public square. The people were setting the rules of the recovery.

CHAPTER 2

THE LEASEHOLDER AND THE LANDOWNER

I N JULY 2001, DEVELOPER LARRY SILVERSTEIN COMPLETED THE BIGGEST deal of his career, and the largest real estate deal in New York City's history. He paid $3.2 billion to the Port Authority of New York and New Jersey for a ninety-nine-year lease on the Twin Towers. Six weeks later, the buildings were destroyed in the deadliest foreign attack on American soil.

In that brief window after Silverstein bought the lease but before the Twin Towers collapsed, many in the city wondered how the deal would change Lower Manhattan. The Port Authority, a vast bistate agency dedicated primarily to transit, had built the trade center and owned it for nearly thirty years. Though the Port Authority was always an unlikely developer, it had settled into something of a familiar rhythm with the property. Silverstein promised to bring change—he wanted to modernize the Twin Towers' office space—and people wondered what kind of impact a new World Trade Center would have on the commercial landscape downtown. After 9/11, the questions multiplied, of course, but not only because Lower Manhattan was in chaos. The brand new public-private partnership added an additional layer of uncertainty to the unprecedented rebuilding effort. How would the partners work together? Who was in charge? Did Silverstein's lease still stand?

While the questions lingered for some time, Larry Silverstein, a short man with striking green eyes and a full head of once-blond hair, provided a few answers early on. Silverstein speaks calmly, assuredly, in staccato bursts, and always meets your gaze directly. He wears dark tailored suits and throws in accents of color—golds, reds, and oranges—with thoughtfully selected ties and handkerchiefs. In his frequent interviews after the attacks, he told one story in particular. It was late January 2001, and Silverstein was walking across Madison Avenue, heading to his apartment on Park Avenue, when a drunk driver ran a red light. Silverstein, sixty-nine at the time, was rushed to the hospital, where he was treated for a crushed pelvis. Doctors estimated that he would stay in the hospital for four or five days, at which point Silverstein made one demand: "Take me off the morphine!" It was five days before Silverstein needed to submit his proposal to buy the Twin Towers, and the morphine, he told his doctors, was clouding his thinking and interfering with his work. His doctors discouraged the move; the pain would be substantial without the drugs, they said. But Silverstein insisted. He had the World Trade Center to purchase.

"I ended up with a broken pelvis, smashed in a number of places, the most excruciating pain of my life, ended up in the hospital, of course, and I remember thinking to myself, how much time do I have? It's the twenty-fifth of January and the bid is due on the thirtieth," Silverstein told Charlie Rose. "I said, 'Doc, cut my morphine, I've got to be able to think,'" he told *The New York Times*. "So they let the morphine run down, the pain was terrible," he said in an interview with the television station NY1. "But I brought everyone together and that's when we framed our best and final bid."

There are probably many reasons Silverstein liked this story. It's dramatic, and it speaks to Silverstein's many admirable characteristics, including his ambition, dedication, his ability to tolerate significant discomfort, and, last but not least, his persistence. Indeed, not even a near-death experience and severe pain kept him from seeing his commitment to the Trade Center through to the end. For those wondering about Silverstein's future at the WTC site, this was the most important part. There were a lot of unknowns regarding the rebuilding effort, but Larry Silverstein wasn't going anywhere.

Silverstein's life contains many remarkable stories. On the morning of September 11, he was supposed to be at the World Trade Center, having breakfast in the Windows on the World restaurant with employees. But a coincidental dermatologist appointment kept him from his daily routine. It was one of those flukes that dotted news articles in the aftermath—tales of lucky people kept for one reason or another from being where they should have been.

Born and raised in Brooklyn, Larry started Silverstein Properties in 1957, when he was twenty-six years old, with his father, Harry. The two purchased a few properties in the Garment District, but then Harry died in 1966, leaving Larry to take over the business. A few buildings on Fifth Avenue followed, but it wasn't until the 1980s, when Silverstein bought the last, undeveloped parcel of the World Trade Center from the Port Authority, a piece of land adjacent to the primary campus, that he broke into the world of major corporate real estate. Silverstein quickly built WTC 7, a plain forty-seven-story skyscraper that fueled his desire for the Twin Towers. As Silverstein tells it, on the morning of his press conference to unveil the building, he looked out, proud as could be, only to realize that his skyscraper was teeny-tiny compared to the 110-story Twin Towers next door. "Wouldn't it be something," he said he thought to himself, "to own these too?" Amazingly, fourteen years later, he did.

At times, though, Silverstein's overconfidence has hurt his cause, as it did in the immediate aftermath of 9/11. Silverstein mobilized very quickly. As soon as two days after the attacks, he instructed his lawyers to develop an insurance strategy to maximize his payout—a strategy designed around the argument that the two planes that flew into the towers twenty-six minutes apart constituted two separate attacks rather than one. For two attacks he would win twice the cash: $7.2 billion versus $3.6 billion. Silverstein also contacted his architect, David Childs, at the firm Skidmore, Owings & Merrill, and hired him to begin drafting designs for new buildings. These were reasonable, regular things for a real estate developer to be doing, but the weeks after 9/11 were not regular times, and the WTC site was no longer a regular piece of real estate. As thousands of men and women were signing up to go to war, thousands of rescue workers were searching for bodies atop the smoking wreckage, and millions of Americans were trying to make sense of what happened, Silverstein moved to consolidate his control.

Then Silverstein held a press conference on September 20 to announce his rebuilding plans. Standing in his Midtown headquarters, Silverstein said that he would build four fifty-story buildings at Ground Zero, basically cutting each 110-story Twin Tower in half. He reasoned that the shorter heights would avoid creating a new target for terrorists. He also embraced the idea of a memorial on the property. But Silverstein devoted considerable time with the press to justifying the need to rebuild all his destroyed office space, something that planners and critics had already begun to question. It had taken decades to fill the Twin Towers to occupancy, and now there were hints of a recession. Plus, many of the companies with offices in the Trade Center and in nearby buildings were relocating to Midtown and

New Jersey. Critics contended that the last thing downtown needed was office space, but Silverstein disagreed. The market would return, he said, and moreover, it was his right and obligation to America to rebuild. "The people who have inflicted this upon us are clearly out to destroy our way of life," he said. "It would be a tragedy to allow them their victory."

It was a sentiment that many Americans likely agreed with, at least in the abstract—building "bigger, taller, stronger," as writer Andrew Sullivan had put it. But it wasn't because they believed in the supremacy of office space or in something modest that topped out at fifty stories. When it came to buying the Twin Towers, Silverstein was a visionary, but when it came to rebuilding them his initial vision felt small and out of touch, and risked generating a backlash. While it made sense to Silverstein to announce his plans early—he could establish himself as the guy in charge and reassure people that he was committed to the rebuilding effort—the announcement risked alienating everyone else grappling with the more immediate, and human, aspects of the attacks.

Not long after Silverstein held his press conference, I spoke to Tracy, a WTC site volunteer at St. Paul's Chapel from South Carolina. Tracy stood by the chapel's entrance and handed out markers for people to write notes on the fence's homemade shrines. People streamed by us, knocking shoulders as they passed through the crowded sidewalk, trying not to disturb those reading the banners. Acquiring her post was not easy, Tracy said. She spent months making phone calls and networking within her local Episcopal parish to get her name to the top of the list. Tracy told me that the competition was so stiff that some volunteers, once they arrived in New York, had come up with a little aphorism about volunteering at the site. "Yup," she said, "it's harder than getting tickets to *The Producers*!"

We both laughed. It seemed about right to liken securing a volunteer post at Ground Zero with snagging a seat at Broadway's hottest, always-sold-out show. With thousands of people straining to see the wreckage or catch a glimpse of a real-life rescue worker, the WTC site often felt like something of a performance. But the comparison made me uneasy too. The WTC site wasn't supposed to be like a Broadway show, was it? Volunteers weren't supposed to be elbowing each other out of the way to garner a post, were they?

After the attacks, everyone was mobilizing around selfless desires to give and to help; everyone was realizing their inner goodness. Few talked about the other motives at play, like power and status and competition. For the times, Tracy was, perhaps, a little *too* honest. Larry Silverstein was too.

WHILE LARRY SILVERSTEIN CONSTITUTED THE PRIVATE half of the new partnership downtown, the Port Authority of New York and New Jersey constituted the public half. But the Port Authority isn't a typical public institution. On the one hand, it is overseen by the governors of the two states, who appoint the executive director. On the other hand, it has its own board and budget and functions independently.

After 9/11, New York governor George Pataki held considerably more sway over the Port Authority's role in rebuilding than New Jersey governor Jim McGreevey, partly because the WTC was in New York, and partly because Pataki had big ambitions, for himself and downtown. Pataki was eyeing national office—a 2008 run for the presidency, perhaps—and he wanted to spearhead a swift rebuilding effort to position himself politically as well as to shore up confidence in New York's marketplace. "The economic risks in the weeks after the attacks were enormous," he told me, years later. "I can't tell you the number of companies that said, 'We're going to go to Connecticut, and by the way, we're going to go right away, and we don't think we're going to come back.'" For Pataki, the disappearing market was the *reason* to rebuild commercial space, to lure back uncertain companies, and he worked with the Port Authority to prioritize Silverstein's space.

But, of course, the Port Authority isn't the same as the governor's office. Ever since it was established in 1921 to oversee the regional port district, the Port Authority has enjoyed no direct public oversight. Scholar Marshall Berman, writing about the New York of the 1950s and '60s, the Robert Moses years (and also the World Trade Center years), put it perhaps most succinctly when he wrote that the Port Authority is "capable of raising virtually unlimited sums of money to build with and accountable to no executive, legislative or judicial power." Pataki, like all New York governors, had influence over the Port Authority, but it was far from absolute.

The Port Authority's unique powers stem from its status as a public authority, or public corporation, designed to intertwine public works with private enterprise. Back in the 1920s, this was a brand-new type of institution. When New York and New Jersey created the Port Authority, they decided to allot it limited annual resources, enough to pay some employees. But because they did not want to be responsible for the large amount of debt that bridge and tunnel projects accrued, they also granted the Port Authority the unique power to raise capital by selling bonds. It was a publicly backed corporation in the truest sense. Through the bonds, the Port Authority acquired private investors, which made it like a corporation. But because the debt was underwritten by both states, investors were afforded a level of security in Port Authority projects that the corporate world could not provide. Moreover, the Port Authority had direct help from taxpayers because it used revenue from bridge tolls to pay off interest on the bonds.

At its best, such a public-private partnership generated incredible funds for public works, particularly during the years of the Great Depression, when public authorities proliferated. The government guarantee freed investors to participate in projects that they may have otherwise deemed too risky, and the public enjoyed the use of new services and roadways. The most famous of the Port Authority's earliest projects was the George Washington Bridge, begun in 1927. Until the Port

Authority, no bridges or tunnels connected the two states. Everything, and everybody, moved across the Hudson River on ferries.

At its worst, however, the partnership exploited the public to enrich the private. The public has no direct say in what projects the Port Authority pursues in its name, with its tax dollars. The Port Authority's is a sly, unnerving sort of control. Unnoticed when channeled toward a bridge that everyone wants, its power appears to pop out of nowhere when directed toward its own financial interests. Or those of the businessman in tow.

In the 1960s, that businessman was David Rockefeller. Grandson of oil tycoon John D., and brother of soon-to-be New York governor Nelson, David was president of Chase Manhattan Bank, and he had recently taken interest in an idea that had been floating around for some time: a New York–based World Trade Center. The name and concept first appeared during the 1939 World's Fair, in Flushing Meadows, Queens, when the Chamber of Commerce hosted an exhibit dedicated to "world peace through trade" called the World Trade Center. Every few years or so after the World's Fair, political and business leaders explored the idea of a World Trade Center as a way for New York to build upon the growing importance of international finance, but they always decided that the project was too expensive or too uncertain or both. Rockefeller, however, had a different point of view.

Rockefeller had recently broken ground on a new headquarters in the Financial District, One Chase Plaza. It was a risky move. At the time, almost all businessmen were buying real estate and setting up headquarters in Midtown; Rockefeller's was the first downtown construction of a skyscraper in years. To help support his investment, he created the Downtown-Lower Manhattan Association, an agency designed to mobilize downtown's financial elite around high-profile development projects. In 1959, the association's records mention for the first time a "World Trade and Finance Center...where the United States and foreign business and financial interests can meet to do business." The report said that "such a center might accelerate the development of international business and act as a symbol of this country's growing world leadership in the international business community." Rockefeller imagined five million square feet of office space in a series of buildings styled after Midtown's United Nations consortium. It would be the second-largest office complex in the country; only the Pentagon, at six million square feet, was bigger.

Rockefeller knew that he would need government assistance to fund such an unprecedented endeavor (particularly since most businesses were heading uptown) and the Port Authority, with its bonds and toll revenues, political independence, and institutional power, was the only viable option. The big challenge was how to convince everyone that it made sense for an agency dedicated to regional port development to take on a massive, speculative commercial real estate project.

Rockefeller's first move was to commission the consulting firm McKinsey & Company to study the potential benefits of such a complex, which he also hoped would generate some advance buzz. After months of study, however, McKinsey concluded that a downtown World Trade Center would likely be an enormous failure—there were few prospective tenants, and downtown was a dying business hub. Rockefeller, however, was undeterred. He intercepted the report's author before he presented the results, and a few days later, McKinsey removed itself from the project rather than release its negative findings. As for the report, it found a safe, quiet home in the dusty filing cabinets of the Downtown-Lower Manhattan Association.

Without a stamp of approval or even enthusiasm, Rockefeller doubled down and appealed directly to the man in charge, the executive director of the Port Authority, Austin Tobin. Tobin also liked to think big—he had recently completed construction on the Lincoln Tunnel and ultimately ran the Port Authority for thirty years—and happened to be growing concerned about the decline in ocean-borne trade. Rockefeller's pitch to Tobin, therefore, fell on eager ears. Tobin immediately embraced the WTC idea and sold it to wary staff, officials, and the public as a virtual port for goods and money zipping around the globe. It would be a port, Tobin explained, that just didn't require water. With Tobin on board, Rockefeller hired the architecture firm Skidmore, Owings & Merrill, the same firm that designed his Chase headquarters (and the same firm that Larry Silverstein hired after 9/11 to design new skyscrapers) to begin drafting plans.

There were plenty of logistics to work out, of course. New Jersey, still half of the Port Authority, wanted to know what was in the World Trade Center deal for it. This is when David's brother, Governor Nelson Rockefeller, came in handy. Nelson drafted legislation that combined the Trade Center development with a plan to reinvest in the Hudson and Manhattan Railroad, a rotting commuter line that transported thirty million passengers from New Jersey to New York each year. The Trade Center, he proposed, would sit atop a brand-new transit hub. This deal made New Jersey happy. It also assisted with another prickly matter: how to clear sixteen city blocks on the west side of Lower Manhattan for the project. The Port Authority had its eye on a stretch of land filled with hundreds of mom-and-pop electronics businesses. It actually constituted the largest concentration of electronics shops in the world, dubbed "Radio Row." Roughly thirty thousand people worked there. Some of the shops were worn down, though, and the property they occupied was in the heart of the Financial District. The addition of a public transit hub (soon renamed the PATH station) greatly aided the Port Authority's efforts to tear these businesses down in the name of the "public good."

After claiming the land under eminent domain, the Port Authority gave each business $3,000 in compensation. Not surprisingly, many people were upset. Merchants on Radio Row sued to keep their businesses. The City of New York, long wary of the Port Authority's power, was angry too: it had suddenly lost sixteen blocks of revenue-generating properties. Critics raised alarms. "Who's afraid of the big, bad build-ings?" architecture critic Ada Louise Huxtable famously asked in 1966. "Everyone, because there are so many things about giantism that we just don't know.... The Trade Center towers could be the start of a new skyscraper age or the biggest tombstones in the world." (It's difficult to read her words this way now, but "tombstones" referred to the death of Radio Row.)

None of this resistance constituted a real threat to the Port Authority and Rockefeller, however. By 1962, the major components of their plan were set. And in 1971, at a cost of $1 billion, the World Trade Center, curiously owned and operated by the Port Authority of New York and New Jersey, opened for business. Without a tenant in sight.

IT TOOK TWENTY YEARS FOR THE PORT AUTHORITY to fill the buildings. A miscalculation by Port Authority executive director Austin Tobin was partly to blame. After Governor Nelson Rockefeller made the transit hub deal with New Jersey, Tobin revised David Rockefeller's original vision and doubled the amount of office space in the Trade Center from five to ten million square feet, making it the largest office com-plex in the country. Tobin made the change because he feared that the Port Authority would suffer great losses on the PATH station and he decided that the only way to offset such losses was to double the office space. Tobin was right about the PATH—it accrued huge debt—but he was wrong about the commercial space. Demand for the Trade Center was so weak that in 1972 Governor Nelson Rockefeller helped out one more time and leased the entire South Tower for state govern-ment offices, further enmeshing taxpayers in the project. In mock, but also somewhat loving, honor of such patronage, many New Yorkers referred to the buildings as David and Nelson.

Today, architects and planners look at the Twin Towers as text-book examples of how *not* to build; it was a project with little public oversight, considerable public costs, and no private market. But for the general public, the Twin Towers gradually became lovable buildings. In spite of their enormous size, there was always something human about them, and artists in particular took great poetic license. In 1974, tightrope walker Philippe Petit turned the towers into an artistic spectacle and achieved what seemed impossible—*he* overshadowed *them*. Barely visible from the ground at a quarter mile high in the air, the slight Frenchman spent twenty-six minutes walking back and forth between the towers on nothing more than a cable hastily fastened upon each roof. He sat for a few moments on the cable; he even lay down. Petit immediately became an international media sensation. The Twin Towers were already well known—designed by Minoru Yamasaki, they were the tallest buildings in the world at the time of their construction—but it was only after Petit that the mythologizing really began. In the 1976 remake of *King Kong*, the Twin Towers replaced the Empire State Building in the film's famous final scene, the modern world's match for the primitive beast.

A more sobering kind of public attention came to the World Trade Center in 1993, with the bombing of Tower One, the North Tower (or, eerily, "Nelson"). The attack was led by Ramzi Yousef, the nephew of Khalid Sheikh Mohammed, the self-proclaimed mastermind of the 9/11 attacks. He and three others crashed a truck with over one thousand pounds of explosives into the tower's underground parking garage, killing six people and injuring more than a thousand. The stated intent of the bombing was to knock the North Tower into the South Tower. This kind of attack had actually been foreseen by the FBI. A 1985 report prepared by the Port Authority's antiterrorism unit, the Office for Special Planning, discussed the possibility of a car bomb set to explode after it had been parked in the basement. "The Assistant Deputy Director for the FBI thinks this is a very likely scenario for the WTC and has described it graphically in conversations with OSP staff," the report stated.

All this history was quickly forgotten, though. Neither the 1993 bombing nor the decades of struggle to find tenants kept Larry Silverstein or the other interested buyers from vying to lease the Twin Towers, mostly because, after the 1993 attacks, the buildings had returned to profitability. It was only after 9/11 that this history came surging back to the fore, at a time when the financial calculus looked different too. Businesses were leaving downtown, a recession had begun, and few were clamoring to work at the top of rebuilt skyscrapers at Ground Zero.

Still, Governor Pataki, the Port Authority, and Larry Silverstein—three parties who would disagree repeatedly on the WTC site—wanted to rebuild the destroyed office space. Pataki wanted to bolster the city's economy and he also wanted to build a tower that signaled national resilience. The Port Authority, meanwhile, counted on Silverstein's monthly rent payments for its budget. And Silverstein had only just completed the deal for the buildings, the pinnacle of his long career. He wasn't going to walk away now. In addition, his insurance agreement stipulated that he would receive maximum payout if he rebuilt all the destroyed space. So Silverstein agreed to continue paying $120 million a year in rent to the Port Authority, even though his buildings no longer existed, to ensure his right to rebuild. Similarly, the Port Authority agreed to honor Silverstein's lease and prepare the land for him to construct commercial towers. Once again, the Port Authority and a businessman decided to build ten million square feet of office space despite there being little market for it.

Few outside the inner circle knew the details of this early decision making, in part because public attention was directed elsewhere. New York City was in chaos. President George W. Bush was readying the military for an invasion of Afghanistan and a broader War on Terror. Amid the deafening din of all the other news, even the public announcements, such as Silverstein's press conference, garnered only moderate attention.

In addition, many people hoped, however naively, that not just some but all of the important decisions about the site's future would be made in an open, public process. This was one of the reasons Silverstein's announcement about four buildings didn't upset more people; they just didn't quite believe it. Larry Silverstein was going to build four fifty-story buildings at the place where nearly three thousand people had been killed only a week earlier? Surely this wasn't the real plan. Rebuilding was going to be a grand, symbolic part of the national response to the attacks—it was going to be "Rebuilding" with a capital R—and everyone from victims' families to downtown residents to architects wanted a say.

CHAPTER 3

ARCHITECTS

IN DECEMBER, THREE MONTHS AFTER THE ATTACKS, MORE THAN ONE hundred architects, designers, and city planners filled rows of folding chairs, sat cross-legged on the floor, and peered in the main door from the outside hall. It was 8 a.m. at the Van Alen Institute, a design studio and exhibit space in Midtown, and no one looked like they had slept very much the night before. Designers and architects who usually looked scruffy in a hip, intentional sort of way now just looked tired. And few looked more exhausted than Rick Bell, executive director of the New York chapter of the American Institute of Architects, who stood in the middle, poised to bring the room to order. His friendly, bespectacled face sagged. His lips were parched.

It was a meeting for New York New Visions, one of the most prominent civic groups to emerge after the attacks, made up of design professionals dedicated to reimagining Lower Manhattan. Rick was one of the founders. He had been downtown on the morning of September 11, attending a conference at 55 Water Street, a short walk from the WTC. "I was looking out at this beautiful view of the harbor, and there was paper fluttering and you could see, as we were standing around drinking coffee, that there was some smoke coming out of the first tower," he said. "I assumed it was a package bomb or something. It didn't look very serious from the angle to the northeast. But then we saw the second plane coming—it looked like directly at us—and then it banked into the second tower." By the next morning, Rick had transformed his office in Midtown into a temporary emergency resource center, "a kind of information clearinghouse," he said, to tell people how those who had offices in the building or across the street were doing. Bell and his staff also created a database of available office space in the city for those who had been displaced and, with the New York Building Congress—a private coalition of real estate professionals—created a memorial fund to provide immediate financial assistance to the families of individuals in architectural and construction fields who died. Rick was busy.

And then Rick began to receive phone calls. An endless stream of queries came from colleagues who wanted to know what they could do, how they could put their design skills to use to help rebuild. No one knew what rebuilding meant at such an early date; weeks after the attacks, Governor Pataki and other officials were keeping any emerging details quiet. Architects were angling to be part of a romantic ideal more than a concrete project. Still, simply going about pre-9/11 projects—sitting down and returning to that six-month-old commission in Atlanta, Seattle, or Miami—seemed delusional. By October, Rick had collected the names of more than four hundred people willing, begging, to be involved in whatever the rebuilding effort turned out to be. To channel their energy, and hopefully carve out a spot in rebuilding for all of them, Rick and a few colleagues founded New York New Visions.

Architects and planners were motivated to volunteer and put in long hours partly because they despised the World Trade Center. Not the sentimental symbol it became after the attacks but the actual compound. Part of the disdain stemmed from the backroom wheeling and dealing between the Port Authority and David Rockefeller, but most of it came down to design. Back in the 1960s, it had been fashionable to build "superblocks," seamless four-by-four-block areas, like the WTC, that blanketed over existing streets to make space for mammoth complexes and skyscrapers. As decades passed, however, design professionals reversed their judgment. The superblocks were so large and alienating that they silenced the kind of bursting, bustling street life that Jane Jacobs celebrated in *The Death and Life of Great American Cities* and that eventually became the gold standard for successful urban design. Even the public plazas included in superblock projects often went unused. Their dominant mood was cold and impersonal.

Those turning out at Van Alen, then, saw an opportunity in the destruction of the Twin Towers to correct many of the planning mistakes of the 1960s and '70s. What better response to the trauma and loss, many architects thought, than to achieve something completely innovative and original at the site, to invent a new form of public space, to design a new version of the American skyscraper, to create a new vision of urban memorial art? Like everyone else in New York, they wanted to join their city's recovery, but their sense of purpose was amplified by a professional obligation to make downtown better. Rebuilding could be important not only for New York, they thought, but for all cities, everywhere.

The designers in attendance at Van Alen that morning were those most interested in a future memorial—they made up the Memorial Subcommittee of New York New Visions. (Other subcommittees were dedicated to public transportation, the street grid, mixed-use real estate, and environmental sustainability.) Their chief concern, in November 2001, was making sure that there would be a memorial. "We are all familiar with how real estate works in New York," Jill Lerner said knowingly, wearily, to the crowd after Rick Bell brought the meeting to order. What they all knew was that vast, open, commemorative spaces did not tend to neatly jibe with the primary concern of builders: making money. After some discussion, the group decided to publicize the fact that the memorial in Oklahoma City, commemorating the 1995 bombing, served as an economic catalyst for the area. They figured it would give politicians ammunition to protect some of the WTC land for noncommercial uses. "But we need to avoid language of 'opportunity,'" Ray Gastil, another leader, added. That word, in particular, looked insensitive. He suggested they emphasize that a large memorial or public space would not turn the area into "one big bummer."

Many downtown residents and small business owners worried about living and working in an area overwhelmed by death and destruction. They wanted to mark the loss but also wanted their neighborhood back, as quickly as possible. The designers, some of whom lived downtown, were well attuned to these concerns, as well as the broader challenge that rebuilding posed: creating a place that would meet the needs of so many different groups. New York New Visions was feverishly doing research for a report of rebuilding recommendations that it hoped would find an audience with the Governor and the Mayor, and as part of this research the memorial subcommittee held a series of focus groups with downtown residents, victims' families, rescue and recovery workers, small business owners—anyone that it believed should have a voice downtown.

Those interviewed by the designers agreed on many issues, including the idea that the site should include a significant memorial that felt moving and reverent. But there were conflicts too, particularly about the tone the whole site should strike. Residents and business owners wanted to make sure a rebuilt site captured a sense of ongoing life and recovery. Meanwhile, families and rescue workers were more likely to use the term *graveyard*. Debate over whether the land was, in fact, a graveyard became so contentious that the designers stopped using the word after a few focus-group sessions. Tina Chui, a city planner who helped organize the discussions, told me that the memorial team instead began asking if participants considered the land to be "spiritual" or "sacred."

These words were milder, more abstract. They did not, directly at least, evoke bones and body parts.

But for many who lived through the attacks or lost family, the only way to talk about Ground Zero was to talk about the violence. Monica Iken, whose husband Michael was killed at the Trade Center, started the civic group September's Mission to advocate for a prominent memorial, and she frequently described the WTC site in graphic terms. Of the nearly 3,000 people who were killed, roughly 1,100 of them were never found, she reminded me. Not even a fragment of bone remained. The WTC site was a place, she explained, where people disintegrated into the dirt. "Bones became infused with building parts," she said. "People seeped into walls."

Iken and I spoke a few months after 9/11 in the renovated SoHo loft where she shared office space with a handful of other nonprofits. She was tall, pretty, and quite thin. Thinner than usual, she said, thanks to the sleeping pills and antidepressants she was taking. As we sat at her desk surrounded by ringing phones and quiet conversations, she kept her eyes focused on the floor for the entirety of our interview. Despite talking about the loss of her husband and her newfound advocacy work in front of cameras, reporters, and crowds of all sizes, she still avoided direct eye contact. But she didn't mince words. She had effectively winnowed down to two short sentences the impetus for her nonprofit: "After the event, it dawned on me," she said. "They would build over dead people."

Thinking about Ground Zero as Iken described it, as a place where people were physically and not just symbolically located, was unsettling. Perhaps this is why many involved in the rebuilding didn't tend to talk about the bodies or, rather, the absence of them. It was too visceral. It also made it difficult to hold onto other understandings of the land. There wasn't room for visions of urban renewal when death dominated the scene.

But, to some degree, the designers at New York New Visions seemed to understand this difficulty. With their focus groups and research, they were trying to bring the full scope of understandings together, from the most intimate and individual to the most political and global. "How do you capture the ripple effect, the impact, in a design?" planner Tina Chui asked me after a meeting one evening. "The WTC site is the epicenter, like an earthquake, but it doesn't have boundaries," she said. "There is New York, the United States, the world. We want boundaries, but it doesn't have boundaries."

BIG, SWEEPING THINKING WAS ENDEMIC TO post-9/11 New York. The aftermath seemed to encourage everyone not simply to pursue their ideas but to stretch them to their most ambitious, impressive ends, and the architects at New York New Visions were no exceptions. As the designers were holding discussions about rebuilding with victims' families and local business owners, they were also trying to convene a focus group with the "international community." It was a bold idea, perhaps even an absurd one. Unlike the designers' other groups, there was no central office for the international community, no phone number. You couldn't call it up and invite it over. But pundits and politicians certainly talked as if you could, so perhaps it was only natural that the architects tried.

Their effort was sincere. One morning, they brainstormed approaches. Someone suggested contacting all the United Nations representatives of countries with victims. "But there's a problem," someone else chimed in. "The amount of red tape to get to people is enormous."

"How about contacting nations most affected?" another colleague offered.

"We can't play *that* game," a fourth responded curtly.

Including an international perspective was not a traditional American approach. Americans don't usually like to talk about America's role in the world, especially when it involves listening to others' opinions on the matter. But times were different; internationalism was in the air. Days after the attacks, the French newspaper *Le Monde* declared on its front page, "Nous sommes tous Américains"—we are all Americans. (A few years later, when Al Qaeda–linked terrorists bombed commuter trains in Madrid, the *New York Times* echoed the sentiment. "We are all Madrilenos," it wrote.) And many designers thought the scope of 9/11—the multiple nationalities of victims, the global response to the attacks, the international politics unfolding in the aftermath—was critical to understanding it. It was why 9/11 was different from, say, Oklahoma City, and why previous national reconstruction efforts did not provide a map for rebuilding the WTC site.

The architects assembled at Van Alen never did figure out how to convene a focus group with the international community, but their desire reflected the collective sense of the enormity of 9/11 as well as the politics of the times. For many in New York, and perhaps elsewhere, a truly representative rebuilding process meant including the world too.

Not all of the aftermath's ambitious architectural projects were this unachievable. While many architects dedicated themselves to securing space for a memorial or setting in place the contours of a public process, a smaller subset focused on more immediate problems. These architects wanted to discuss Ground Zero's present-day incarnation, replete with unstable, temporary walls, around-the-clock rescue operations, and thousands of visitors peering over fences and even climbing lampposts trying to understand what happened. They wanted to help stem the chaos.

Architect Kevin Kennon belonged to this school of thought. Kevin lived on Hudson Street, in Tribeca, about ten blocks from the destruction. Every night, the glow from recovery crews' floodlights illuminated his street. The rumbling of jackhammers provided twenty-four-hour-a-day white noise. In the midst of all this, Kevin thought it was too soon to be thinking about rebuilding, so one October afternoon he took a break from the whirl of design meetings and walked to Ground Zero. "It was chaotic, and it was extraordinary," Kevin said of the site. "There were an extraordinary number of people. People were climbing fences, it was unsafe." He paused and gave me a knowing look. "Something had to be done."

Kevin called his friend and colleague David Rockwell, another young, well-known architect disenchanted with the frenzied talk about the future. David happened to be grappling with his own project—a query from city officials to redesign a private viewing platform for victims' families. He was still deciding whether to take the job, and he was going to Ground Zero in a few days to learn more about it. Did Kevin want to join him?

Two days later, Kevin, David, and his collaborators, husband-and-wife team Elizabeth Diller and Ric Scofidio, walked to West Street, the quiet, western boundary of the site, rarely visited by tourists. They met with police, received special passes, and wound their way down a narrow blocked-off sidewalk, bordered by fencing on one side and a building on the other.

The private viewing platform was plain and small. It was made out of plywood, and layers of fresh and dried bouquets filled its corners. Multicolored handwritten notes were tied around railings or penned directly on the wood.

Even in its brief existence, the platform had acquired an interesting history. It was originally constructed days after 9/11 for President Bush to visit the site. While it quickly evolved into a private space for victims' families, the president continued to make occasional visits through the fall, often joined by foreign leaders. Russian president Vladimir Putin, Israeli prime minister Ariel Sharon, Swedish prime minister Goran Persson, and United Nations secretary-general Kofi Annan, among others, all accompanied the president to the private viewing platform. Hanging from the platform's sole wall was an enormous canvas panel that displayed the flags of the ninety nations that lost citizens in the attacks. Above eight columns of miniature flags, a title read, "In Memory of the International Victims of the World Trade Center; September 11, 2001." By the time Kevin and his colleagues visited, the panel contained the signatures of many of the world's most powerful men.

The platform was Ground Zero's very first official memorial. It was also Tina Chui's "ripple effect," all on one 120-square-foot plywood stage. Families wept and penned notes remembering sons and daughters, spouses and parents, in the very same spot that the president prepared for war with foreign dignitaries alongside a memorial to their citizens—one that suggested, quite simply, that their countries had been attacked too.

Kevin, David, Rick, and Liz looked at the platform and then at one another. Immediately, Kevin said, they knew what they would do. David declined the city's proffered upgrade job, and the four architects set to work on a public viewing platform. As Kevin put it, "We needed one for everyone."

THE FOUR ARCHITECTS BELIEVED THAT THE PROJECT'S success depended upon moving quickly, which they decided also meant moving quietly. The platform would be the WTC site's very first piece of public architecture, and if word spread, opposition would surely emerge. The designers feared that time-consuming deliberation could undermine the whole effort. So the civic-minded architects dedicated themselves to proceeding as secretly as possible.

The team knew of one precedent, a project in Berlin in the mid-1990s called "infobox." Architects had built a sleek viewing deck that hovered over the once-desolate land around the Berlin Wall. It featured digitized displays on rebuilding and enabled residents and tourists to peer out over the new plaza, Potsdamer Platz, as the city constructed stores, offices, and housing. The four New York architects began to imagine something similar for Ground Zero, but it wasn't a seamless fit. The WTC site was not a construction zone but a gash in the ground overflowing with wreckage; a viewing deck here would look out over destroyed skyscrapers, not burgeoning ones. Still, the architects thought the general concept of a viewing area would work. "It was simple," Kevin told me. "It needed to be accessible, and to provide height. So people could look down at the site, up from the hubbub. It needed to provide solemnity."

It would be humble, they decided. No adornment whatsoever. For the architects, this was civic design in its purest form. It would fulfill a vital public need now: to see and understand what happened.

The architects began by contacting the Office of Emergency Management, which oversaw cleanup operations. Unexpectedly, it immediately embraced the viewing-platform idea. Thousands of people were congregating around the WTC site each day, and they needed a central place to go. The OEM reached out to the next two essential groups: the mayor's office and victims' families. Rudy Giuliani's staff liked the idea, but the group of families was hesitant. They feared the platform would turn Ground Zero into a tourist attraction. They were particularly concerned about people taking pictures and mugging for cameras. Richard Sheirer, the commissioner of the Office of Emergency Management, assured them that the platform was being designed to honor what he considered "sacred ground." So the families said okay too.

As the planning progressed, so did the architects' amazing good fortune. The designers met with Mayor Giuliani in late November to receive the official go-ahead, and he signed off on all the major issues, including the plan to complete construction by late December. The one hitch for Giuliani was the platform's bare plywood walls. The architects had been inspired by victims' family members' inscriptions on the private viewing platform, and they wanted to encourage similar expressions on the public one. But Giuliani wasn't so sure this was a good idea; after all, cracking down on graffiti was a cornerstone of his anticrime initiatives. How could he, famous for ridding the streets of graffiti, now be seen as promoting it? After a bit of back-and-forth, the architects explained that this graffiti would be different, perhaps shouldn't even be thought of as graffiti. Finally, the mayor signed off on the bare walls too.

With Giuliani on board, city agencies rushed the paperwork through and secured the necessary permits. The architects e-mailed friends and colleagues at New York New Visions and the many other new post-9/11 civic groups to raise funds for construction. Money poured in. The television producer Norman Lear donated $175,000. Developer Larry Silverstein gave $100,000. The scaffolding company, Atlantic Heydt, lent building materials at no cost and labor at discount. Forest Electric Corporation did the same. And no news was leaking to the press, either. The goodwill was so stunning that the architects began to think bigger. After they completed the first, they would build another two or three platforms around the site by summer.

After working through Christmas Eve and Christmas Day, contractors completed the platform on December 27. The twenty-seventh happened to be an important date. That same afternoon, Rudolph Giuliani delivered his final address as mayor of New York. And he chose to deliver it at St. Paul's Chapel, which stood next door to the viewing platform, at the intersection of Fulton Street and Broadway.

The speech was a big event. Giuliani was the country's most popular politician. A few days earlier, *Time* magazine named him its "Person of the Year," dubbing him "The Mayor of the World." But the speech became most noteworthy because Giuliani unexpectedly weighed in on rebuilding and decided not to follow the official talking points. After remembering his eight years in office and reciting sections of Abraham Lincoln's Gettysburg Address, Giuliani told the crowd that it would be wrong to develop the land commercially. "I really believe that we shouldn't think about the site out there, right beyond us, as a site for economic development," he said. "You've got to think about it from the point of view of a soaring, beautiful memorial. If we do that part right, then the economic development will just happen. Millions of people will come here, and you'll have all the economic development you want."

It was a radical thought multiple times over. America's most admired leader was questioning the wisdom of commercially developing one of the country's most expensive pieces of real estate. And, by extension, he was questioning building "taller, bigger, stronger" too. Only Giuliani, in that moment, could have gotten away with it.

After he completed his address, Giuliani exited St. Paul's Chapel and walked around the corner to the public viewing platform. Two long, gradually sloped ramps flanked a large, rectangular stage, thirteen feet high. A wall lined the inside edge of each ramp and a railing lined the outside edge. Like the private platform after which it was modeled, it was constructed out of bare plywood and metal scaffolding, which supported the platform from below. With camera crews in tow, Giuliani walked up the ramp, crossed the stage, and tagged his signature on the front railing.

The viewing platform architects were thrilled. A few weeks after Giuliani's speech, David Rockwell was invited to give his own lecture on the platform for the swanky TED series ("Ideas Worth Spreading" and "Riveting Talks by Remarkable People" are the nonprofit's slogans). Rockwell told the crowd that Giuliani's comments opened up nothing less than a national dialogue about the meaning of life and property in American cities. "There is a real opportunity to engage in a discussion about, why do we live in cities, why do we live in places where such dissimilar people collide up against us each day?" Rockwell asked the group. "I don't think it has much to do with fifty or sixty or seventy or eighty thousand new office spaces." At another time, the comment may have raised eyebrows—people living in cities *not* because of office space and capitalism?—but in the idealistic aftermath of 9/11, the TED audience nodded approvingly. Rockwell added that he hoped the viewing platform would continue this conversation. "Regardless of what one's position is about how this sacred piece of land is to be used," he said, "having it come out of actually seeing it, in a real encounter, makes it a more powerful dialogue."

The viewing platform looked modest and simple, but the architects' hopes for it were enormous. After 9/11, the call for dialogue was like the quieter, geekier sibling to the cry for "bigger, taller, stronger." For the architects, the viewing platform wouldn't merely facilitate dialogue about what to rebuild; it would celebrate the country's dedication to its founding principles. Like so much else connected to Ground Zero, the plain, plywood platform would stand as a symbol of democracy.

CHAPTER 4

THE VIEWING PLATFORM

DAYS BEFORE HE GAVE HIS FINAL SPEECH AT ST. PAUL'S CHAPEL, in one of his final acts as Mayor, Rudolph Giuliani joined with Governor Pataki to create the Lower Manhattan Development Corporation, an independent body tasked with distributing $8 billion in federal funds for rebuilding and coordinating the site's multiple stakeholders and interest groups. Giuliani and Pataki each appointed six board members, dividing the corporation's loyalties between the city and the state. The idea was that an impartial body like the LMDC would provide the best forum for everyone to participate and to have a voice. "You had a choice between a Robert Moses," Pataki said, referring to the city's influential and controversial mid-century planner, "which couldn't work in this day and age and at a site that had so much public attention and awareness and interest, or you could have a process that allowed broad public participation."

That was *one* reason for the Lower Manhattan Development Corporation. The other reason was not quite as magnanimous. "We were frightened because in fact we believed that Mark Greene was going to become the next Mayor," Pataki said, "and we didn't have confidence that he and his team would understand the importance of doing this right." In the fall of 2001, Greene, a Democrat, was ahead in the polls to succeed Giuliani, and the governor and the mayor, both Republicans, wanted to make sure that Greene didn't end up controlling the money for rebuilding. So "the LMDC was created essentially to give me control," Pataki said. Greene didn't go on to win, of course; Michael Bloomberg became the next mayor, thus allaying this initial impetus for the LMDC. But the corporation was still helpful for the governor, because he could count on it to tilt his way. It was an independent, impartial corporation except for those moments when the governor needed it to be his corporation.

Pataki wanted to have it both ways—he wanted to empower the public and he wanted to empower himself—which at times muddled both his and the LMDC's effectiveness. But Pataki believed he needed to use the LMDC to strengthen his control, not only to protect against Mark Greene but also to secure his influence with downtown's other powerful players. Particularly early on, power remained fluid and a number of people, including Larry Silverstein and the Port Authority, were vying against Governor Pataki for the top position of the rebuilding hierarchy. One of the best illustrations of this fluidity was a PowerPoint slide from a talk by Marilyn Jordan Taylor, chairwoman of Silverstein's chosen architectural firm Skidmore, Owings & Merrill, and a founder of the civic group New York New Visions. I heard Jordan Taylor deliver a speech about the rebuilding not long after the LMDC was created, and one of her slides depicted what she called the power structure downtown. The tiptop of her hierarchy featured one name: Silverstein Properties. The bottom included multiple groups: "businesses, large and small; residents; widows and survivor groups, and other public interest groups." And the middle contained a mix of private and public organizations, including Marriott, which owned a hotel next to the WTC, and, of course, New York New Visions. The

Lower Manhattan Development Corporation did not appear *anywhere* on Jordan Taylor's slide. Clearly, it was a subjective reading of decision making, but that was also the point. Control was sufficiently undefined that practically everyone perceived, and sometimes tried to will into being via PowerPoint, a different power structure downtown.

Despite the early uncertainty and jockeying, though, and despite the governor's built-in pull, many in New York City wanted to be part of the LMDC. It was the newly appointed body overseeing the city's most pressing challenge, and it was charged with the not insignificant task of distributing billions of dollars in federal aid. The LMDC quickly convened a set of high-profile advisory councils to assist with decision making. Victims' families received a council, as did downtown residents. So too did real estate CEOs; financial firms, such as JP Morgan; and professional firms, such as McKinsey & Company. To some degree, the distribution of councils reflected a downtown reality: a lot of bankers and consultants work there. But Lower Manhattan is also home to the Lower East Side and Chinatown, two of Manhattan's poorer neighborhoods, and they received considerably less representation in the LMDC than financiers and executive directors. One resident of Chinatown and one resident of the Lower East Side were appointed to the residents' advisory group.

In addition to convening councils, the LMDC also began to tend to emerging problems at Ground Zero. And one of the first on its list was the new, public viewing platform. It had opened a few days after Giuliani's speech and impromptu visit and immediately became downtown's most popular attraction. While the LMDC was holding monthly meetings and soliciting public feedback, Ground Zero's largest, most unwieldy constituency simply showed up on the sidewalk.

ON THE PLATFORM'S OPENING DAY, THE first visitor arrived to begin the line at 5 a.m. By late morning the line wound eight blocks down Broadway, and by the middle of the week, the streets around the platform were more overcome with picture-snapping tourists than ever before. Crowds had been coming to the site through November and December, but now tourist websites were listing the viewing platform among its top destinations in New York City, and neither the architects nor City Hall seemed to have anticipated the extra onslaught. Sidewalks were impassible, cops were overwhelmed, and downtown residents and workers, already weary of crowds, were intolerant and frustrated. One resident of an apartment building three blocks from the WTC site recounted to me, with disbelief, the January morning that he stepped out of his building only to be smacked in the face by a camera swung carelessly by a visitor. He suggested, somewhat wryly, that tourists be restricted to the eastern boundary of Ground Zero, which bordered Century 21, a large department store. "No one lives around there," he said. "And they can go shopping."

To control the crowds, the LMDC set up a timed ticketing system for the viewing platform, which it modeled after the system at the Empire State Building. An existing box office at the South Street Seaport Pier, eight blocks to the east of the platform, became the ticket hub. Everyone went to the pier in the morning, received a free ticket stamped with an allotted time, and then arrived at the platform at half-hour intervals over the course of the day. The LMDC posted maps and signs around the platform to direct traffic to the pier, and set up a team of police officers to keep watch over lines and platform entrances.

I walked down to the pier at 8:30 a.m. on a Wednesday. A lone ticket booth sat in the middle of a large plaza, and a procession of bodies wrapped in puffy coats, scarves, and knit hats wound its way, back and forth, along a chain of wooden, waist-high railings, like an airport security line. Perhaps 150 people were waiting. (Officials were giving out six hundred tickets a day; each person could take one or two. But you had to arrive early. Most days, all the tickets were "spoken for" before the box office even opened at 10:30 a.m.) The mood was calm and friendly; conversations were breaking out among strangers. For once, the eeriness of being at, or near, a sixteen-acre swath of destruction in the middle of New York City was not overwhelming. Everyone was familiar with standing on line and waiting for a ticket. *This* was recognizable.

A portly, middle-aged man took the spot behind me. His name was Tom and he was a public relations executive from Sacramento, California, in the city on business. He was at the site, he said, because he had watched the Twin Towers collapse on television with his two children. Susan, from Rochester, New York, stood behind Tom. She was here to pay respects. Her son lived uptown, she told us, but refused to come with her. "He lived it, he knew people killed," she said. Neil, a twenty-year-old traveler from Brisbane, Australia, stood in front of me and joined the conversation too. Neil was the least equipped for the cold morning. He wore a black corduroy jacket and intermittently cupped his hands around his mouth to warm them. He had just spent two weeks traveling around the United States. This was his first trip to New York City.

I asked if anyone had thoughts about rebuilding, and Tom said he was torn. "One, I think they should rebuild the towers bigger, higher, to give the message that we will rebuild, that they can't do this to us. The other side of me thinks they should make a really somber, contemplative memorial."

"They should just build a memorial," Susan said. "But they will rebuild something." She paused. "I couldn't talk to my son until two weeks later about it. It's a day we will always remember where we were. It's like the day that Kennedy was shot—there will always be the question, where were you?"

"It's the day America changed," Tom said. Susan nodded, and Neil did too. Tom continued. "And this affected the world. It is meaningful for people throughout the world. It was an attack on the free world."

This time, both Susan and Neil stopped nodding and Neil raised an eyebrow at me, as if to disagree with Tom's assessment. An awkward silence followed, which I felt compelled to break.

I asked Neil if he had seen the attacks on TV. He nodded. "It was midnight in Australia, and all the channels went blank and then just showed the attacks for a few days. That's all that was on TV," he said. "People were talking about it, but it was seen as an attack on America."

"It was an attack on the *free world*," Tom said again, louder and more forcefully than before. There was another silence, and this one was longer. Eventually, Susan chimed in. "It's really been a mild winter, hasn't it?" she asked.

And that was it. We chatted lightly for a few more minutes, but the conversation never quite recovered from the tense exchange. There was a reason, it seemed, people opted for where-were-you stories and pat phrases about paying respects. Bigger questions about what the attacks meant or America's role in the world—even mere hints at these questions—were likely to end a conversation cold. When the ticket office opened, we all said good-bye and went our separate ways.

A few hours later, with my ticket in hand, I arrived at the viewing platform and joined another line, a medium-sized one, which began at the platform's entrance ramp and extended two-thirds of the way down the block. St. Paul's Chapel and its memorial-filled fence stretched down the right side of us. Banners, flags, and bouquets still arrived daily. But the intermittent yet visible hate commentary continued too. Hastily added to the top of two laminated photographs of victims were the handwritten words "murdered by Islam." Someone had covered over the incendiary words with wide strips of blue tape, but the tape wasn't thick enough, and the words were still visible underneath, now highlighted in blue.

In addition to the reading, there was an unmistakable sound track for our line too. Ever since the platform opened and the people arrived, vendors clustered as close to it as possible, and one of the products they hawked in January was a DVD of the footage recorded on 9/11. A few vendors located across the street from our line had set up laptops to play their discs. Mini-speakers pumped the voice of Peter Jennings overlaid with the melody of "God Bless America" and small screens displayed images of fiery Twin Towers and cascading clouds of debris. We had all seen these pictures before; photographs of the attacks were ubiquitous. But listening to and watching the broadcast while standing in line with a ticket at the precise location of the violence? This was something a bit different.

In hindsight, the experience seems cumbersome and crass, like "Sacred Ground, by Disney World." But it didn't feel this way at the time. In fact, I didn't notice or talk to anyone bothered by the scene. Ground Zero was something noteworthy and important that we all wanted to see, and the viewing platform was how we could see it. We simply waited for our turn.

Once at the front, the police officer took my ticket and I walked up the ramp. There was a large stage with a waist-high, plywood railing. Then, in front of that, there was Ground Zero. Large equipment, like bulldozers and cranes, sat in the immediate foreground. Farther away, a few small, shrinking piles of debris and some recovery personnel working on the rim came into sight. And beyond that you could just make out the edge of the hole. But you could not see inside it. A few days earlier, a woman descending from the viewing platform leaned in and whispered to me, as if sharing a secret, "You know, you can't really see anything." At the time, I hadn't known what she meant, but now I did. Cleanup crews had made incredible progress since September, and, for those of us on the platform, the last remnants of destruction remained out of sight. The most visible damage belonged to the Deutsche Bank building, on the site's southern border. Black netting draped over its open, unsteady facade.

Everyone gazed out upon the open expanse of land, and some took photographs. Five minutes later, the police officer stationed at the top of the platform announced that our time was up. We shuttled off as the next group of ten walked up. But the officer allowed us to linger on the down ramp, where a long, rectangular canvas displayed the names of the nearly 2,800 victims. It hung from the wall, affixed with duct tape. The combination of the slope of the ramp and the list of names looked a bit like the Vietnam Veterans Memorial. And on the uncovered wood around the canvas, thousands of people had signed their names and penned notes, just as Kevin Kennon, David Rockwell, Liz Diller, and Rick Scofidio had hoped. About a dozen people scattered along the ramp and stood nose to wall, reading.

"United We Stand—All through the world—God Please Bring Peace to the World."

"Lieve mensen, ik leef met jullie mee. de wereld sal dit nasit vergeten! Blyf sterk want de USA is ean geweldig land! Leifs Susanne from the Netherlands" (Dear people, I sympathize with you. The world will never forget this! Keep strong because the USA is a terrific country! Love Susanne from the Netherlands).

The platform was like a massive sign-in book, a real life version of the online message boards and comments sections that, in 2002, were only just beginning to proliferate.

"Mahal Kayo" [love all of you]. Ni Hesus, From the Philippines, we (heart) America."

"I (heart) NYC, Kate, from Philadelphia, PA."

"NY the world is with you! God Bless! Olya from Ukraine!"

As I walked off the down ramp, I passed one last police officer monitoring the exit area. He was a bit distracted. Clamoring to his left were about twenty people asking about the location of the box office or holding tickets for him to sign. He looked beleaguered and amused at the same time. "I'm signing autographs at three p.m.," he announced jokily.

The lines, the tickets, the cluster of vendors, the sound track, the cameras, the celebrity officers. The four architects did not design the viewing platform to be a tourist attraction, but they could not prevent it from becoming one, either.

THIS TRANSFORMATION UPSET MANY PEOPLE. "It's like Disneyland now," Monica Iken told me. "You have to shuffle through people, I don't like it."

Iken spent her days advocating for a significant memorial, but the craziness of Ground Zero had become a pet peeve. She told me that she wanted more freedom to visit "without viewers." Every two weeks or so, she flouted the rules on restricted access at the site and snuck up to the roof of the shuttered, burned-out firehouse on Liberty Street, which bordered the WTC. The firehouse, three stories high, belonged to Engine 10, and it was the closest she could get, she said, to where her husband died. The least the city could do was build a few more private spaces for victims' relatives, she said, adding, "It's bad enough we have to share it with the world."

By late January, a group of victims' family members had organized an anti–viewing platform letter writing campaign to the new mayor, Michael Bloomberg, who had just taken over from Giuliani. "Perhaps I will be lucky and my brother's corpse will be rescued, but if it is, it absolutely sickens me to think that it will be done in plain view of a frenzy of onlookers, who, as I bore witness to earlier, will be read-ied with all forms of technology to record the events," wrote a New York lawyer. His brother was one of the roughly 1,100 people, 40 percent of those killed in the towers, whose remains were not found. "I once wished that my brother's body be recovered," he wrote. "Now I wonder if I should pray that it remain entombed in Lower Manhattan forever." He and scores of other family members demanded that the platform be removed immediately.

"Survivors Call a Viewing Stand Ghoulish," read one *New York Times* headline a few days later. Then international media picked up the story, and the outcry grew so heated that some of the architects began to apologize. "If we'd known just how many people were going to use it," Liz Diller told the UK's *Guardian*, "I'm not sure that we would have done it."

It was a bit of an odd statement. Architects usually hope that many people will use what they build. And these four surely knew about the public's interest in seeing the site; this was why, after all, they conceived of a viewing platform. But perhaps it made some sense that the site's first real piece of architecture provoked mixed feelings, even from the people who built it. Ground Zero was a fraught piece of land, and ambivalence increasingly seemed to be downtown's dominant emotion.

Ultimately, Mayor Bloomberg decided not to intervene on families' behalf and remove the public platform. He also decided not to help the architects build more of them. One was enough. But demand remained strong. By April, police increased the number of people the viewing platform could hold, and the box office at the South Street Seaport Pier started giving out four thousand tickets a day.

IT WAS EASY TO FORGET AMID THE FRENZY of the crowds and the furor of families that the viewing platform did not actually do the one thing it was designed to do: provide a view. Unlike the private platform for victims' families, the public one did not provide a sightline of the destruction. But this was mostly beside the point, because the crowded viewing platform served as a potent symbol of the public's sense of ownership over the land. Like the memorials and the graffiti, the platform was one more way the public was claiming space and marking territory.

And so, as months passed, other groups began to assert their presence more forcefully too. A group of downtown residents started a letter-writing campaign calling upon the city to clear away all the memorials around the site. The outpouring at St. Paul's Chapel, they said, was particularly oppressive. After months of rain, cold, sun, and snow, the clusters of cloth banners and T-shirts had grayed and stretched and looked a bit raggedy. The residents described them as ugly, unsanitary, and, most alarmingly, frightening to young children.

"What had been a tapestry of love and support has now become an eye sore for our community," one resident wrote in a letter to St. Paul's. "In fact it has become an impediment to our recovery."

For months, as I walked down Broadway and approached St. Paul's Chapel, I often found myself holding my breath until its fence came into view, wondering if this was the morning that residents' calls would be heeded and it would be clean and bare, back to normal. I had gradually grown attached to the piles of stuff that transformed downtown into an outdoor, homemade art exhibit. This kind of public expression wasn't unfolding anywhere else—thousands of people chiming in with a few words or a signature, saying "I was here" and perhaps "This is what I think" as well.

But people kept bringing things, and for the time being the memorials stayed. One morning at St. Paul's, I came upon a two-foot-high, glass-encased diorama of smoking Twin Towers. Gray duct tape held together four glass panels. Inside, blackened cotton balls, pasted upon three-dimensional, cardboard Twin Towers, served as billowing, debris-filled smoke. It wasn't fine artistry. Frankly, the frozen-in-time quality was a little creepy. But it was astonishing that people were still making elaborate reconstructions and delivering them to the site. Nearly a year later, more people, not less, were coming. "It was an historic event," a father from Pennsylvania, accompanying his eighteen-year-old daughter on a visit that spring, said. "It seemed appropriate to come see it."

Still, vendors and police frequently told me that the memorials and platform would soon be gone. "They'll burn it, that's my guess," said one police officer about the viewing platform.

"Really?" I asked.

"It's time to reopen the streets," he said. "It's time to rebuild."

The officer was only partly right. The platform came down that summer, but it wasn't burned down. Instead, Craig Williams, a senior historian at the New York State Museum, in Albany, oversaw its dismantling. At 11 a.m., the flatbed truck next to Williams was empty, and by late afternoon it was piled high with a series of pen- and marker-covered boards. Williams numbered each piece of board before the platform was disassembled so that someday it could be reassembled as part of an exhibit. The viewing platform had become an official part of history. And a few weeks later, for the first time in ten months, Fulton Street reopened to traffic.

CHAPTER 5

THE FENCE

O REDEVELOP GROUND ZERO QUICKLY, AS WAS THEIR PLAN, THE Port Authority and Larry Silverstein needed to do a number of things efficiently, including hire architects, design buildings, prepare the sites, construct underground infrastructure, hire contractors, and find tenants. Before they could do any of this, however, they needed to do something even more difficult: transform Ground Zero into a construction zone. After eight months of towering wreckage, spontaneous memorials, crowds, vendors, and viewing platforms, Ground Zero had become a very distinctive place, and people were still arriving to remember and grieve. Change, therefore, was a delicate proposition.

Rebuilding officials first signaled change with a solemn ceremony in late May, when Governor Pataki declared the end of recovery operations. On a late weekday morning at Ground Zero, sorrowful bagpipes filled the air as a steady line of soldiers marched, two by two, out of the hole. Thousands of people filled the sidewalks and stood on tiptoes to photograph the procession, pausing to wipe away tears under sunglasses. Flashes of light popped from the camera-draped crowds on nearby rooftops. After the last soldiers emerged, a single, empty coffin draped in an American flag rolled up the ramp on the back of a flatbed truck.

The ceremony signaled that the recovery of human remains at Ground Zero was officially over. But *officially* was the operative word; recovery was not, in fact, complete. Workers continued to find pieces of body parts and microscopic traces of flesh at and around Ground Zero for years. Indeed, given the nature of the violence and ever-improving technologies, the discovery and identification of remains will likely continue for decades. But many human remains had been found, and, more pragmatically, construction couldn't begin in the midst of an active recovery operation. So the ceremony marked the recovery's relative end, and provided an opportunity for people to collectively express their grief and, perhaps, to begin to move on. The ceremony signaled that the time for thinking of Ground Zero first and foremost as a somber space of death and loss was coming to an end.

In addition to the ceremony, the Port Authority also planned to build a new structure around the WTC site, something to stand for five to ten years as it rebuilt. Officials first announced news of this structure in March, on the eve of the six-month anniversary of the attacks, when Governor Pataki and Mayor Bloomberg held a joint press conference to announce the fast pace of cleanup and recovery work. In the first weeks after the attacks, officials estimated that cleanup would take at least one year, likely longer. But firefighters and paramedics worked through holidays and the winter cold, laboring in the pit twenty-four hours a day, seven days a week, and made faster progress than anyone anticipated. After Pataki and Bloomberg celebrated the news of the rapid cleanup effort, another official announced a series of upcoming changes to the site. The tattered temporary, plywood walls that had gone up the prior September would come down, he said, and the Port Authority would soon build a solid, thirty- to forty-foot-high wall around the hole. The official took a moment to justify the choice of an opaque wall, explaining that it would "protect" those who lived and worked in the area from seeing "disconcerting views" as they walked through Lower Manhattan.

It seemed simple enough. There would be a wall to mark the edge of the hole. But the comments about protecting people suggested something more complicated and more carefully considered. This wasn't a regular wall, after all; it was a wall at Ground Zero, where nothing was simply what it appeared to be. Recall that the public viewing platform had triggered extended debate not because it helped people see the destruction but because it embodied the ambitious ideals and controversial consequences of the public's sense of ownership. At Ground Zero, even "seeing" was a metaphor for something else. And so a wall wasn't simply a wall, either.

Minutes after the press conference ended, city architects shot off two- and three-line e-mails across list serves to notify colleagues: Ground Zero was going to be walled off for the rest of the decade! "[The wall] was the stupidest thing I heard," architect Rick Bell told me. Bell and his colleagues at New York New Visions saw a solid, thirty-foot-tall wall as a direct affront to one of their most important goals: a democratic rebuilding process. Bell dismissed the notion that a wall would protect people. Downtown employees and residents lived and worked in tall buildings, he explained, looking out windows into and across the WTC site all the time. A wall would hardly prevent their sightlines. Rather, Bell believed the primary function of the wall was to restrict the public's view. "The viewing platform demonstrated that people were coming from all over the world to connect with this place," he said. By cutting off these views, he thought the Port Authority aimed to stem the public's access, and, by extension, their voice in what would happen to it. A wall was a symbol of exclusion and secrecy. And, not inconsequently, it would literally prevent anyone from wandering by and taking a look at what the Port Authority and Larry Silverstein were building.

New York New Visions appealed to the Lower Manhattan Development Corporation and Alex Garvin, an architecture professor at Yale who had recently been appointed as the organization's vice president of planning. Garvin agreed that the wall was foreboding and problematic, and encouraged New York New Visions to come up with an alternative design. In late March, twelve architects spent a weekend at the Van Alen Institute to revamp the Port Authority's proposal. If, as New York New Visions believed, the Port Authority's wall aimed to restrict public engagement, this new design was all about encouraging it.

In place of the opaque wall, they imagined a structure that emphasized "transparency" and "openness," said landscape architect Diana Balmori, who participated in the charrette. Their design featured a twelve-foot-tall fence—a height more to scale for visitors—made of stainless-steel mesh that welcomed people to view Ground Zero from multiple angles. It incorporated small ledges hanging from the fence so people could leave homemade memorials, as well as signs explaining that people's memorials would be collected and archived by state officials. In a later version, the fence also held white, erasable panels with markers for people to continue to leave their own comments, signatures, and drawings.

Victims' families had ideas about the wall/fence too. When Alex Garvin and the LMDC presented New York New Vision's design to its victims' families advisory group, the group said that any new structures at the site, particularly something that would stand for five or ten years, must include a memorial to the attacks' victims. This was the place, they reminded everyone, where nearly three thousand people were killed. Many families were already worried that the Port Authority was not invested in a significant memorial, and news of a bare wall only amplified their concerns. The advisory council requested a series of panels listing all victims' names.

The Port Authority said it was completely surprised by the negative reaction. It had imagined nothing more, and nothing less, than an opaque wall. The Port Authority's response to the LMDC's proposal, however, suggested that it understood something more was at stake.

After the architects revolted against the wall, the Port Authority agreed to build a fence instead, something that people could see through, but it refused to adopt a number of the LMDC's recommendations. "We didn't want anyone calling it a memorial—it was a construction fence," Mark Wagner, a consultant to the Port Authority who spent his summer dedicated to finding a solution to the wall/fence to-do, explained to me. The Port Authority's goal, he said, was to build a structure that no one missed when it came down years later to make way for office buildings, a permanent memorial, a train station, and more. An elaborate commemorative fence designed to encourage civic engagement and public expression was precisely the kind of thing the Port Authority wanted to avoid. The Port Authority feared that a fence full of memorials and handwritten notes could engender a sense of attachment. And this, in turn, could complicate its plans to redevelop the land. "We wanted to maintain the fact that it was temporary," Wagner said. "Giving people a place to leave a teddy bear, that would make it permanent."

"GOOD FENCES MAKE GOOD NEIGHBORS." For the past one hundred years or so, the most influential line on walls and fences has come not from architects or archaeologists but from a poet. In his poem "Mending Wall," Robert Frost and his neighbor are discussing a wall that divides their property when the neighbor utters the most memorable words. The funny thing, given the line's ubiquity, is that Frost wrote the poem to question his neighbor's thinking, not underscore it. "Before I built a wall I'd ask to know," the poem's narrator says, "What I was walling in or walling out, and to whom I was like to give offence." The line

Frost gave his neighbor was so catchy that it, not Frost's skepticism, became the conventional wisdom on the matter.

The Port Authority, like the neighbor, believed in a good, carefully designed fence. It spent the summer revising the design submitted by New York New Visions to make sure that its fence struck just the right tone. It took some time for consultants to get it right. One of the first ideas that consultant Mark Wagner and his team came up with was a fence that honored the international scope of the victims' nationalities. They conceived of a fence that lined Church Street and contained a series of flagpoles, each holding the flag of a nation that lost citizens in the towers. They sketched designs of the flagpoles and imagined round plaques adorning each pole engraved with the number of dead from each nation. But when the consultants presented this idea to the Port Authority, it told them they were going in the wrong direction. Not because the design celebrated internationalism or remembered the non-Americans who lost their lives, but because it was too commemorative in a general sense. "It was becoming a memorial plaza," Mark said of the flag-poled design, "and we wanted to get away from that."

Ultimately, the consultants decided to bar memorials from the fence entirely. Mark Wagner consulted with the National Park Service at the Vietnam Veterans Memorial in Washington, D.C., which allows people to leave objects and then archives them, before deciding that such a system would be too unwieldy at Ground Zero. They expected to receive thousands of objects and notes, far more than the Vietnam Memorial receives, and had no place for them. "People come and sign their name, and what do you do with them?" Mark asked. Even more importantly, though, such objects would undermine the temporary-ness of the fence. "If we started to establish areas as a memorial, and then removed [it]," Mark said, "people would be upset."

Even the fence's metal came under scrutiny. Stainless steel was the usual choice for a fence around a construction zone, Mark said. But because stainless steel "looks permanent" they opted for something else that "looked cheaper." Ironically, Mark noted, "it actually may have cost more in the end for these materials."

As I listened to Mark, I found myself both skeptical of and awed by the Port Authority's approach. Were people really likely to grow attached to a fence surrounding the site? To hold rallies to save the fence? Were these measures necessary? It was impossible to know. But the Port Authority wasn't taking any chances. And it showed considerable insight as it developed a design. The last thing it needed to do was to build something temporary that people ended up liking and wanting to stick around—or, even worse, that people decided should stay permanently. That could create all sorts of problems, from delaying construction to undermining its plans more broadly. The Port Authority knew (better than most, it seemed) that it was the small, everyday, even reflexive gestures—like the simple act of leaving a bouquet of flowers—that shaped people's thoughts about what kind of place the WTC site was. Was it a destruction zone or a construction zone? A site of memory or a site of redevelopment? The difference between these two visions could mean the difference between public support for the Port Authority's rebuilding plans, including building all of Larry Silverstein's destroyed office space, or public opposition to them.

For this reason, perhaps, the Port Authority wasn't shy about using the fence to direct how people should think. Instead of designing flagpoles or hanging erasable panels, the Port Authority decided to draft a complimentary history of Lower Manhattan as the centerpiece of its design. The Port Authority did honor families' requests and created an alcove at one end listing the victims' names, but it also worked with the design firm Pentagram to create a long stretch of photographic panels, thirty-four in all, that told a stirring, patriotic history of the economic development of Lower Manhattan over the past century. Each panel contained an old black-and-white photograph of the Lower Manhattan skyline as it evolved from 1915 through the 1970s, when construction on the Twin Towers was completed. The earliest panels showcased some of the world's early "tallest building" record holders: "A view of the Lower Manhattan skyline from the Hudson River around 1915 is dominated by the Woolworth Building, which at 792 feet was the tallest in the world from 1913 until the late 1920's. The second-tallest spire visible is an earlier record holder, the 612-foot Singer Tower, completed in 1908." The later panels celebrated the towers. One, dated 1973, displaying an aerial view of the Twin Towers just after they were completed, described them as "simple, slender, silver, and soaring," and compared the effort to build them to the "can-do competitive spirit that fueled the Space Race and moon shots." The final panel in the narrative displayed an aerial photograph of the wreckage caused by the towers' collapse.

It was the first official history, the first narrative of any sort, to appear at Ground Zero and frame the meaning of the attacks. And it told a big story, a story of American power and innovation. The history showed taller and taller skyscrapers filling in the open spaces of the Financial District until, finally, the Twin Towers rose. Then the narrative skipped over decades of skyscraper history and new tallest-building record holders (all of which, by this time, stood in Asia) to arrive at the destruction on 9/11. There was only one way to rebuild and recapture America's greatness, the panels suggested: rebuild big, tall office buildings.

Historian Carol Willis, head of the Skyscraper Museum in New York, consulted on the photographic series and said that it evolved out of a desire to inform visitors about the history of the WTC site. The goal was to provide "a sense of scale, of the proportions of the buildings, the plaza, a sense of the whole complex in the urban fabric," she said. The panels powerfully displayed the evolution of scale and proportion downtown. But, at the same time, it omitted many aspects of the Trade Center's history. There was no mention of Radio Row, for instance, the stretch of immigrant-owned electronics shops that occupied the land for decades, nor of the controversy surrounding the Port

Authority's decision to build the Trade Center in the first place. Still, Willis described the story told on the panels as a "neutral history." It was neutral, she said, because it informed people about downtown rather than memorialized 9/11.

The difference between the panels being a history or a memorial may seem academic, but it was important for the Port Authority at the time. It came back to the idea of perceived permanence. The Port Authority figured that people could become attached to a memorial but were less likely to grow fond of a history lesson, particularly one that advertised the virtue of building skyscrapers. Creating a history lesson instead of a memorial also dovetailed with the Port Authority's desire to transition Ground Zero from a place of death and violence into a construction zone.

"The trick is that it's not really a memorial to the events of September eleventh, it's a memorial to the site," Mark Wagner said of the history panels. "There is a panel that says this is what happened on September eleventh, but there are more panels that show pictures of the construction and the development of Lower Manhattan. I think that's an important thing for people to keep sight of. The site has to redevelop. There are groups out there, diehards, that don't want you to do anything on the site. You know, for months after the event everyone was saying, nothing's going to be built there. Of course something's going to be built there—it's a major transportation hub, you know, mechanical systems, substations, all kinds of things that have to go back into that site. It's not realistic to say that the whole site is just going to be, you know, that you'll fill in the hole and that it's gonna be green space. And so I think it's important to show people, on those graphic panels, the development of Lower Manhattan."

THE PORT AUTHORITY UNVEILED ITS FENCE at the end of the summer. Which meant it also unveiled Ground Zero. For the first time, someone standing at ground level could see into the vast, craterous pit. Instead of shimmying up streetlights or waiting in line for a viewing platform, people stood in long, straight rows against the fence's metal links, noses smushed, hands and feet splayed apart. They looked down and watched the engineers and steelworkers, dump trucks and cranes, as they began to piece together again transportation lines and building foundations. There were men in hard hats and work boots, stacks of construction materials, and a muddy floor marked with bulldozers' and trucks' criss-crossing tire tracks. It was surprisingly ordinary work.

One hot day, I watched a family of seven cluster around an edge of the new fence. They were from Scotland. As his kids and wife watched, the father, Paul, entwined a homemade memorial into a few of the fence's metal links. It consisted of a half-dozen small, white bouquets, tied with string; a handful of blue plaid ribbons tied into bows; and, in the middle, framed by the bows and flowers, a yellow banner emblazoned with a red lion. The banner was frequently used as an unofficial flag of Scotland, Paul told me. Paul and his family wore the typical summer tourist uniform—shorts, T-shirts, white socks, sneakers. The flag was the only sign of their international roots. Paul said that they made the memorial "to show sympathy, to tell that Scotland's behind you."

The memorial was intricate and the family large, but they stood out on the crowded sidewalk because Paul had chosen to hang the memorial directly under one of the Port Authority's new signs declaring, in bold red letters, that "All items will be removed at the end of the day." Of all the spots on the two-block-long fence, Paul picked this one. It was a curious image: Paul sweating profusely as he devoted time to each delicate piece underneath the impersonal sign telling him it would soon all be gone. But when I asked Paul what he thought about the fact that someone would be removing it shortly, he paused, looked at the sign, and shrugged. "It's so hot," he said, sweat beading down his forehead, "[the flowers] won't last that long anyway." After toting it across an ocean, Paul didn't care that the family's memorial would be removed. What Paul cared about was putting it up.

When he finished fastening the final flowers and ribbons into place, Paul and his family stepped back and admired their design. Paul took a number of photographs, some close up, some from a distance, some with the kids posing in front. Then they walked off down the sidewalk, long gone from Lower Manhattan by the time the Port Authority worker arrived a few hours later, removed each piece, and carried the bundle down the block and dropped it into the trash.

That summer and fall, the Port Authority worked diligently to keep Ground Zero clear of any new homemade memorials. At the same time, St. Paul's Chapel honored residents' requests and began to remove the items on its fence too. Over three months beginning that fall, chapel volunteers removed one section of banners, flags, and notes a week; it wanted to ease everyone into the new normal. Still, some tourists grew alarmed and frequently told the volunteers to stop. Some even tried to re-hang just-removed items lying in boxes on the ground. Eventually, the chapel posted signs to calm the public. "The memorial items on the fence are being removed periodically by St. Paul's Chapel personnel for permanent preservation."

It was poignant watching all the homemade, handwritten items being systematically cleared away, especially since people still wanted to express their loss and grief. Like the family from Scotland, many continued to hang bouquets and laminated cards and poems on the Port Authority's new fence. But the Port Authority always removed them, and gradually, as the months progressed, people stopped bringing and leaving so much stuff.

The Port Authority's diligence turned into a near obsession, however, when it came to the public's other activity at the WTC site: the writing. Writing on walls, writing on the new fence, and even writing on the photographic history panels. Mark Wagner told me that he and his team had anticipated this. They instructed the Port Authority to construct the photographic panels out of fiberglass and cover them in a synthetic so that writing on them would be difficult. But people continued to find ways. In the white parts of one photograph someone scribbled, "We will miss you twin towers," and another wrote, "9/11, forever in our hearts, forever in our memory." The pen and marker writing was faint, and it did not interfere with the readability of the other text, but it was there, legible. And it was not allowed. Eight months after the panels first appeared, the Port Authority removed the entire series, recovered them with clean photographs and text, and then re-hung them about six feet higher than before, above visitors' heads, so no one could write on them or, consequently, read them.

With the panels safe, the cat-and-mouse game moved over to Liberty Street, which bordered the site, and where a temporary wall lined one side of a semi-enclosed tunnel. It was the only open, non-policed space left, and as time progressed, people wrote more and more comments on the long stretch of wall.

"May God have mercy on the souls of these coward terrorists. Because America will not. Long live freedom. God Bless the USA. We support our President!"

"Blame Bush!"

"Who did the damage? Not Bush. Thank <u>God</u> for Bush!"

A few months later, the Port Authority painted over the tunnel and erased all the writing. But it used gray paint, and many of the comments, still reflecting the politics and policies of the day, could be made out underneath.

"Bin Laden you suck. Husane [*sic*] is next!"

Within days, the real-life, life-sized comment board again buzzed with messages. Entire families, including little kids just old enough to grip the marker, scribbled notes.

"America the Re-build-iful."

"We are from Czech Republic. We (heart) NY."

"Osama you will burn."

"War is Peace."

"God Bless Afghanistan."

But the Port Authority wanted to stop the writing once and for all. So a few months later, it repainted the wall again, this time using *black* paint. And this put a stop to it. No more writing. No more homemade memorials. No more public expression.

The upshot of all this clearing, cleaning, and painting was that Ground Zero soon displayed very little reference to 9/11. A history of commercial development in Lower Manhattan? Yes. Discussion of the event that was bringing everyone to Ground Zero? No. For this reason, victims' families soon pressed for the viewing fence to include more information about the attacks. And eventually, years later, the Port Authority revised its history to include a detailed timeline of events on the eleventh and a list of victims' names from the Pentagon and Shanksville, Pennsylvania. By this point, the commercial development of the site was long under way, and fears of an emotionally compelling memorial fence seemed to have subsided.

Of course, many people found emotional and historical meaning at Ground Zero regardless of what did, or did not, appear around the site. One morning when I was sitting, taking some notes, a man in a jacket and jeans, pushing a stroller, approached the fence. He leaned his whole body into it, and after a few seconds reached down and lifted his infant child into the air, facing the site too. They stood in an extended silhouette for almost a minute, the baby's arms and legs dangling freely over his father's head. He used to live three blocks away, he told me, on West Street. He knew five people who died here and was seeing Ground Zero for the first time. I asked him what he thought about being here, and he said he didn't know. He was still making sense of it. But he knew why he came. "This is the most important thing to happen to our country," he said. I asked him what he meant. "It's changed everything, everyday ideas," he said. "At airports, security at sport events, no backpacks anywhere." He glanced at his son, now back in the stroller. "I know he won't remember this. But I want him to see it. So I can say that I brought him here when he grows up."

CHAPTER 6

THE PEOPLE VERSUS THE PORT AUTHORITY

A T THE SAME TIME THE PORT AUTHORITY WAS DESIGNING ITS special viewing fence, the Lower Manhattan Development Corporation organized a series of town halls to collect public opinion. The first occurred in late May, and participants arrived at the auditorium—at Pace University, a few blocks from Ground Zero—hours in advance; eventually, the line wound its way down multiple blocks. Team Twin Towers, a group advocating for rebuilding the Twin Towers precisely as they were, worked the crowd most aggressively. A middle-aged bearded fellow collected signatures in support of the proposal while a few others handed out an assortment of paraphernalia: round pins with a sketch of the Twin Towers filling the skyline above the phrase "Standing Tall Together," and sticker nametags that said, brashly, "Yes! I'd work on the 110 floor." A few stuck the nametags on their chests but more tucked them in handbags

and briefcases. Many people stood with arms full of rolled-up drawings and full-length poster board displaying color printouts of homemade memorial designs.

This particular hearing was dubbed a "listening session." Chairman
John Whitehead and the eleven other board members of the Lower
Manhattan Development Corporation sat quietly on a stage while
people took turns and testified. After the auditorium filled to capacity, the LMDC hastily set up a satellite viewing room across the hall
for another three hundred people, and then the meeting began. Each
speaker had three minutes—a clock on a large screen counted down
the remaining time—and for four hours, it was testimony after testimony. One person spoke and everyone else listened.

"Green architecture is important and so is excellence in design,"
Battery Park City resident Josh Hubbard said. "I lived in Berlin for
a few years. They are rebuilding the area around the wall with bold
and exciting architecture. We need an international competition for
the best architecture. We can learn from other cities. I don't want to see
the boring architecture of Battery Park City extended east."

"My wife died on the ninety-seventh floor," Charles Wolf said
moments later. "If a memorial is around transportation, it will be a
mistake. History will judge us based on how we choose to remember
this event. The memorial must be the beginning of this process."

Residents from the Lower East Side and Chinatown, the more
working-class neighborhoods that border the Financial District,
turned out for the hearing in particularly large numbers. "I am a
refugee from the World Trade Center, a security worker, so a lower
echelon of beings there," Carleton Wong said. "We need to recognize workers and a memorial. There were many foreign workers
who kept the place spick-and-span, secure, and they lost their lives
there. I came out of fire and steel with God's help, a lot came out
with burns, a lot died. We think something should be made about
us, we think part of the memorial should be dedicated to us. Parents

overseas want to see where their kids died, something needs to be there for them."

Then, moments later, Sharon Green: "The treatment of the WTC site as an urban renewal opportunity is losing sight of the event. This is about terrorism," she said. "I would without a doubt get a job at the top of the rebuilt towers. On September twelfth, everyone said that we would rebuild better than ever, what happened? The answer is to rebuild the World Trade Center. If not, we will have a skyline imposed on us by Al Qaeda."

Each person seizing the microphone wanted something different, often radically so, from the person who had spoken just before. But something, a sense of shared purpose, perhaps, kept everyone from openly deriding and fracturing from their neighbors. People were nice to one another. No one spoke out of turn or responded to specific comments. No one cheered or jeered. Occasional applause for particularly heartfelt and shared sentiments was the only feedback the audience provided. Meanwhile, the LMDC board members remained silent the entire time, even as some criticized the group for a lack of transparency and disengagement from the community.

The civility continued through the summer, mostly. The May listening session was only the beginning of what officials promised would be an unprecedented, truly public rebuilding process, and multiple hearings throughout the five boroughs dotted summer and fall calendars. The most important public hearing was called Listening to the City, dedicated to the site's master plan. In July, the architecture firm Beyer Blinder Belle released six master-plan designs for the site, commissioned by the Port Authority and the LMDC. "What we create will be consistent with and testament to the principles which came under attack on September 11—democracy," Lou Tomson, the president of the LMDC, said when he unveiled the six master plans. The master plans mapped and divided the site's sixteen acres into different configurations of commercial, memorial, and transportation spaces, but there were a handful of features that every master plan shared, including the same amount of office space—Silverstein and the Port Authority's ten million square feet.

Listening to the city was different from the other public hearings, officials said, because people would make decisions. Instead of sitting quietly and listening to testimonies, officials promised that attendees would be given time to discuss the essential features of each plan and vote for their favorite. It was an appealing prospect; by mid-July, more than four thousand people had signed up to participate.

ON THE MORNING OF LISTENING TO THE CITY, a large banner hung over the entranceway to the Jacob Javits convention center reminding everyone of the day's task: "Remember and Rebuild." By 8 a.m., it was swarming with people picking up packets of architectural master plans and searching for their table in the vast, cavernous room. Many walking through the hall had pinned pictures of family members and friends who were killed onto their shirt pockets. Monica Iken, 9/11 widow and sudden television personality, stood against a wall surrounded by lights and television cameras; later in the morning, when Iken stood up from her table and walked to the bathroom, the cameras followed. Celebrity family members were rivaling the governor and the mayor for media attention.

I was assigned to table 453. It was located in the back of the convention center, but not in the way back. There were still rows of round tables behind ours, each outfitted with a laptop computer, a trained facilitator, and six to eight people, usually but not uniformly New Yorkers. Once everyone at our table arrived, we turned our attention to a podium far away in the center of the hall for some introductory remarks by Lower Manhattan Development Corporation chairman John Whitehead and Port Authority executive director Joseph Seymour. Since Silverstein Properties was not directly involved in the town hall, Larry Silverstein (who had been staying out of the public eye ever since his poorly received press conference) was not in attendance. Instead, the Port Authority was taking the lead. Seymour and Whitehead outlined our collective task, which was a little surreal. Somehow, we and four thousand other people, untrained in the arts of design, city planning, or architecture, were going to come together, select a master plan, and make astute decisions about how to rebuild.

But thousands of strangers coming together and settling upon anything sounded unlikely. Indeed, even the six people at my table were poised to disagree. Denise, our facilitator, was from Iowa and had watched the towers collapse on TV. Pat, sitting next to her, lived in Connecticut and was following news of cleanup operations. Freyda, a New Yorker, spent a few weeks volunteering at Ground Zero. "I consider it a burial ground," she told us. Susan, from New Jersey, explained that she was here because she did "not want real estate interests to dominate." Last around the table was Louis. Louis lived downtown and watched the towers collapse from the roof of his building. But his chest said more. Pinned to the center of his black T-shirt was a piece of white paper and the typed words: "2x110. A story less would be a memorial to DEFEAT."

Louis's sign gave a few around the table pause. People stared, but no one said a word about it. Instead, we pulled out the large, rectangular booklets of master plans.

The six plans, two-dimensional reprints on thick sheets of white paper, were color-coded to map different arrangements of commercial and commemorative spaces. Red squares marked commercial areas and blue squares marked memorial ones. Every plan displayed at least one blue square (and sometimes only one), often alongside a green patch demarcating a park. And every page had many red squares.

The simplicity and uniformity of the plans were the first signs that something was not right. Every plan included the word *memorial* in its title. There was "Memorial Garden" and "Memorial Plaza," followed by "Memorial Park" and "Memorial Square." Lest anyone think that all words meaning "stretch of land" had been exhausted, there were still two more. "Memorial Promenade" and "Memorial Triangle" rounded out the group. The need to underscore the presence of a memorial in every plan was puzzling. Why the constant reminder? And then there were the red squares. Before we started examining the plans, officials told us that each one accounted for ten million square feet of office space. The number sounded significant, but it was also abstract. It was difficult to imagine what ten million square feet of anything looked like, until, that is, we saw the color-coded blocks. A woman at the table behind ours summed it up loudly. "They shouldn't call these memorial gardens!" she said. "They're commercial gardens!"

This was the reason our table discussion on the six plans proceeded more smoothly than I anticipated. People wanted different things—Louis wanted to rebuild the Twin Towers, Freyda thought the site was a burial ground, and Susan didn't like developers—but it quickly became clear that we all hated the vast amount of commercial space. All of us disliked *all* six plans.

Part of our problem had more to do with the premise of a master plan than with office space per se. Master plans map the architectural "program" of a piece of land—the different amounts of space devoted to different functions, including commercial, retail, transit, memorial, cultural programming, and park spaces. By definition, there is no architecture involved in these discussions; it's about how to best divvy up land. But we were hungry for architecture and design. Everyone at our table (and everyone at all the other tables, we soon discovered), wanted to see images of soaring and innovative spaces that captured the intensity of feeling and the overwhelming sense of history that the attacks provoked. We didn't agree how this history should be represented or even what it was, but we did agree there should be something monumental and historic, and the problem was that there was no way a master plan of color-coded blocks could achieve this. It wasn't meant to. For the Port Authority, the LMDC, and everyone else involved, the master plans were an enormous public relations disaster.

But the other part of our problem had to do precisely with office space. Ten million square feet of it is a lot, and there are only so many ways one can rearrange it on a sixteen-acre parcel. Since all the master plans contained the exact same program, they conveyed, in very clear visual terms, the true limitations of the program, and the limitations of the public process too. Nearly five thousand people decided to spend their Saturday in a windowless hall staring at color-coded pages for one reason: to have a say in what should stand at Ground Zero. The plans communicated very clearly that, when it came to this fundamental question, the Port Authority had no intention of allowing the public to participate.

The trashing of the master plans was swift and merciless. The hearing was outfitted with a sophisticated technology system that linked each table to a mainframe computer via laptop. After everyone entered their preferences into the table laptop, the computer tallied the votes and displayed them on a large screen in the middle of the hall. When the results appeared, we all took a moment to register the dismal approval rates for all the master plans, and then applause and cheers erupted across the room. The plans were terrible! Over four thousand people from all walks of life, and with all sorts of ideas about what 9/11 meant, agreed. Many people entered comments into their laptops alongside their votes, and the screen displayed some of these too. "Start Over!" one wrote. "It looks like Albany," another table concluded. You could feel the contempt. The most significant complaints were that the plan to build ten million square feet of office space was too much and that too much power belonged to one particular man, Larry Silverstein. People called for an end to his lease.

The day after the hearing, an article in the *New York Times* noted that the results from Listening to the City were not very "New York."

"It seems hard to ignore the fact that greed has always been a driving force in the city—and not always for ill," it said, chronicling the history of the city's growth from the traders of old Amsterdam to some of its more successful public-private partnerships, like the building of the Brooklyn Bridge. "The images of other major cities are captured in emblems of church or state: the Eiffel Tower, Big Ben, the Kremlin, the Coliseum, the Washington Monument," it explained. "New York has office buildings."

Not everyone, it seemed, was ready for the city to take a respite from its love affair with greed. As the article pointed out, the relationship was deep and long-standing. But many people thought Ground Zero constituted a reasonable exception, cause for a temporary break. It may have been heretical, but office buildings were not good enough. This didn't mean, of course, that people didn't want to build something monumental. In addition to coming together around their rejection of the master plans, most people at Listening to the City favored building something tall and symbolic, "a significant symbol on the skyline," as one of the LMDC's town hall questioners had phrased it. Being anti-developer while being pro–"significant symbol" was a bit of a contradiction, since it was likely that the symbol would be a commercial skyscraper. But it didn't *have* to be a skyscraper, which is perhaps why the results didn't seem contradictory at the time. Instead, they indicated that, when it came to Ground Zero, people wanted something better than business and politics as usual.

WHEN THE PUBLIC REVOLTED AGAINST ALL THE WTC master plans, the Port Authority was shocked. It had spent months developing the six plans with the firm Beyer Blinder Belle (nicknamed "Blah, Blah, and Blah" by Herbert Muschamp, the incisive, cantankerous *New York Times* architecture critic), and it didn't know how to make the changes the public was clamoring for. Neither Larry Silverstein nor his ten million square feet of office space were going anywhere. The public was supposed to have accepted the plans' underlying principle, the previously and privately determined architectural program, and given it their blessing, too. When it didn't, the Port Authority was entirely unprepared.

The man responsible for finding a solution to the debacle was Governor George Pataki. He controlled most of the LMDC and, for the purposes of rebuilding, most of the Port Authority. And he, not the appointed executive director of the Port Authority or private businessman Larry Silverstein, was the most accountable to the public. Pataki was also running for reelection that fall, and he could not afford to ignore the town hall's verdict and go merrily on his rebuilding way. He had to offer people something new. Or something that seemed new.

As Pataki tells it, after Listening to the City he told the Port Authority that its original plan wasn't going to work. "The Port Authority was advised, forget about this," Pataki said. "We have to have a completely different concept of how we're going to redevelop the site." The original six plans were "a wonderful thing to put over a reformed landfill," he said, "but when you're looking at a site of such emotional and historical significance to the world, it was not appropriate."

But Pataki's new concept was not, in fact, "completely different." Under Pataki's guidance, the Lower Manhattan Development Corporation opened an international design competition, or Innovative Design Study, as the LMDC called it, to collect new master plans from the world's best architects. More than four hundred architects sent in applications, and an independent jury, from the nonprofit group New York New Visions, helped narrow the field down to seven teams, which included some of the world's most famous designers, including Richard Meier, Peter Eisenman, and Lord Norman Foster. But a few other "starchitects," such as Frank Gehry and Rem Koolhaas, declined to participate, which raised some eyebrows, and drew attention to the competition's confining architectural program. Even though Pataki threw out the first set of master plans, he retained their organizing principle: the program that required the WTC site to contain, among other things, ten million square feet of office space. Despite the public's rejection, Pataki believed that replacing all the destroyed office space was critical to maintaining Lower Manhattan's status as a global financial hub. "It was important that the financial center of world see that this ten million square feet of office space isn't leaving Lower Manhattan forever," Pataki said. Without making too big a deal of it, the LMDC had transferred the publicly rejected office space from the old plans into the new international design competition.

It was impossible to know why some major architects opted out of the world's highest profile design competition, but some critics and civic leaders speculated it was because of the old, rigid program. "It's like putting lipstick on a hog," civic planning leader Robert Yaro said of the competition at the time. But, by and large, the general public seemed to feel differently. Many people appeared willing to accept the old architectural program in exchange for the competition's stated promise: exciting, historic, emotional architecture.

After the jury selected the seven teams, they each received $40,000 (a paltry sum for designers) and ten weeks to bring their creative visions to life. And in early December, the LMDC, the governor, and the Port Authority tried again, unveiling an exhibit of the seven master plans in the bright, airy atrium of the World Financial Center, across the street from the WTC site. Floor-to-ceiling windows on the atrium's east side provided one of the clearest views around of Ground Zero, which meant it offered the perfect contrast to the exhibition. Outside, there was a fenced-off hole littered with construction teams working on transportation lines. Inside, soft spotlights framed miniature models of innovative skyscrapers and the latest in green technology. Outside was the present: muddy, cold, uncertain. Inside: the future. Seven visions to choose from, all of them bold and hopeful. Not a single one blah.

All seven plans featured the next tallest building in the world. There was an incredible crisscrossing structure from Richard Meier,

Peter Eisenman, Gwathmey Siegel, and Steven Holl's team. Five narrow vertical sections, rod straight, were intersected by four evenly spaced horizontal floors that cut through the towers and poked out a bit on each end. "Nearly touching at the northeast corner of the site, they resemble the interlaced fingers of protective hands," the team wrote in its introductory text. It looked less like a building and more like an angry geometric design overtaking Manhattan, but it was eye-catching. The submission from United Architects, which one critic described as a "Brobdingnagian megastructure," featured five angled buildings that entwined at the sixtieth floor to form a large, connecting skyway, or "City in the Sky," full of "gardens, educational centers, shopping, cafes, a sports center, a broadcast center and a conference center." Each plan's signature skyscrapers dominated the others nearby, which stood at mere forty- and fifty-story heights. The scale was immense, and the visual contrast of these designs—now in three dimensions, now showing actual buildings—to the original six master plans was immeasurable.

The difference in the public's response was equally profound. For the next few weeks, people packed the exhibition and briefly shut down the LMDC's website, interest was so great. There was no formal voting this time around (that lesson had been learned); instead, the LMDC sprinkled a series of comment boxes in the hall and invited the public to submit thoughts and select favorites. Lord Norman Foster's design, a pair of towers very much like the Twin Towers that gently leaned into each other and "kissed," was immediately the popular favorite. "Above all, we have a duty to symbolize the rebirth of New York on the skyline," Foster wrote. "To demonstrate to the world the resilience, the resolve, the strength and faith in the future of all those who are dedicated to liberty and freedom." Foster knew how to market his design with a good story too.

Nonetheless, Foster's plan didn't ultimately make it into the top two. The LMDC favored Daniel Libeskind's "Memory Foundations" and the "World Cultural Center" from Think, a team that included

Rafael Viñoly and Fred Schwartz. These two were the most themat-
ically developed of the group, as well as the most idealistic. Think
offered a less traditional design centered on two towers of scaffolding
rather than regular, solid skyscrapers. The latticework surrounded the
original footprints of the Twin Towers, re-creating their silhouette on
the skyline, and provided the infrastructure for a series of inhabitable
pockets of space, or pods, visible through the scaffolding, some seem-
ingly suspended in midair. The largest pod cut across and connected
the two lattice towers. It would be the "first truly Global Center,"
Think said in its introductory text, "a place where people can gather
to celebrate cultural diversity in peaceful and productive coexistence."
The towers would house educational, cultural, and civic institutions
while the site's commercial space would sit in less ornate buildings
nearby. Think was the only team to devote its signature "symbol on
the skyline" to noncommercial uses.

The centerpiece of Libeskind's "Memory Foundations" was a skyscraper that reached 1,776 feet into the air with a graceful, asymmetrical, twisting spire, designed to echo the raised arm of the nearby Statue
of Liberty. Libeskind's plan expanded beyond buildings, however,
and was the most overtly commemorative. His design sectioned off
a large swath of land for a memorial park, which he recessed seventy
feet into the ground, creating a permanent public space to mark the
tragedy. This space made visible and memorialized the slurry wall of
the "bathtub," the foundation of the Twin Towers that did not crack
when the buildings fell, keeping the Hudson Bay from flooding the site.
Libeskind likened this wall to the American constitution because they
both "assert the durability of Democracy and the value of individual
life."

The two plans presented almost wholly divergent visions of
America. Libeskind focused his attention inward and embraced
national strength and tradition, while Team Think looked outward
and celebrated a New York–centered global harmony. *Times* critic

Herbert Muschamp (who was friends with architect Rafael Viñoly of Think) wrote that the two plans offered nothing less than a choice between peace and war. "From mourning, we will build towers of learning," he wrote, in support of Think. As for Libeskind's plan, he declared that "unintentionally, the plan embodies the Orwellian condition America's detractors accuse us of embracing: perpetual war for perpetual peace." Many others, however, preferred Libeskind's plan. They liked its sincere emphasis on memory, in contrast to what many saw as the fraudulent memorial celebration of the earlier six plans. Some critics even claimed that because Libeskind infused the entire sixteen acres with a spirit of commemoration, his design made a separate memorial obsolete. Regardless of one's preference, both plans offered a point of view, a commentary on post-9/11 America. They gave critics something to write about.

In early February 2003, the LMDC selected these two designs as its finalists, and the architects earned a bit more time and money to tweak their plans. Meanwhile, the architects became the newest celebrities around town and photographs of Libeskind and Viñoly graced the city's tabloids and magazines. Libeskind and Viñoly making rounds at parties and galleries; Libeskind and Viñoly schmoozing with artsy types; Libeskind and Viñoly chatting up business types. With their olive complexions and salt-and-pepper hair, the two men looked similar, but you could always tell them apart by their glasses. Libeskind wore a signature pair, thick, square, and black, while Viñoly liked to mix it up with a few pairs he wore simultaneously, one on his face and another pair or two pushed back on his head. As the two designers competed for the title of master planner, they competed in the society pages for the most avant-garde approach to designer eyewear.

For a moment, then, many people were happy. Americans had their stirring, emotional visions. New Yorkers had their artists. And the governor had his problem solved. He had garnered the public's approval.

There was a catch, though. A significant one. None of the soaring skyscrapers and eye-popping designs on display in the atrium of the World Financial Center was ever going to be built, not even the winner's. It was a major, almost unbelievable, caveat, and it came down to the distinction between a master plan and architecture. A master plan is about mapping space and determining the different functions of the land, while architecture is about designing buildings. Because the competition was for a master planner and not an architect, the architecture depicted in the master plans was not part of the competition. It was something extra, something pretty to look at. It was a flourish; a façade.

Indeed, only one person had the power to hire architects, Larry Silverstein, and he had already hired his a few weeks after the attacks.

THE COMPETITION WASN'T A HOAX. The fine print always stated that the teams were competing for the title of master planner, which is why they imagined new sixteen-acre sites rather than simply a few new buildings. But it was certainly misleading and confusing. For a competition that wasn't about design, the would-be master planners were instructed to design buildings. There was no way this *couldn't* be confusing. And because it was confusing, the public's ability to weigh in as informed citizens was compromised.

There were a few reasons for the confusion. Some LMDC officials said they instructed the planners to design buildings, even though they knew the buildings would never be built, with the hope of influencing Silverstein's designers. They reasoned that the architecture on display could affect future work and therefore have indirect but lasting power. It was a far cry from the competition's implicit promise, but it seemed to be a sincere goal. Perhaps most of all, though, the intricate models and miniature buildings were good public relations. The failure of the original six had illustrated that a plain master plan wasn't going to secure public support for the Port Authority and Larry Silverstein's redevelopment plan.

Rather than change the plan and introduce a new architectural program, Governor Pataki and the Lower Manhattan Development Corporation used the competition to make the sell, to present the public with fantastic visions that would hopefully persuade it to embrace not just a master plan but one that mapped a heavily commercial program too.

As Janno Lieber, who oversees the WTC project for Larry Silverstein, put it, "Nobody loves office buildings." But, he added, "they are the essence of New York economically." There were a number of reasons that Governor Pataki, the Port Authority, and Larry Silverstein wanted to rebuild the ten million square feet of office space, including Silverstein's bottom line and the Port Authority's budget, but another reason, they argued, was New York's economy. Janno Lieber, who worked for the Department of Transportation under the Clinton administration before arriving at Silverstein Properties, made a case for office space that was similar to Governor Pataki's. "From a public policy standpoint, we need to build new, green office space because you have this rare opportunity to do it," Lieber said. "Like it or not, this is what we do in New York City. People come here who are smart and creative in a lot of different fields, and they make money sitting in swivel chairs with computers and pencils and their brains. That's why you need this kind of office space, because we're competing against Shanghai and Dubai and London, and you can't compete for those brain-power jobs with sixty-year-old office buildings."

It was a variation of "If you build it, they will come," which was particularly resonant after 9/11, when many were afraid that Lower Manhattan would never recover. Not everyone agreed with this argument, though. Many feared that a flood of new office space would further depress rents and possibly remain empty for some time. Some believed that downtown needed housing, for example, more than office space. And many others simply believed it wasn't right to prioritize commercial space on an historic piece of land where so many people had been killed.

But there was one other primary argument for office space. "He had a lease!" Alex Garvin, vice president at the Lower Manhattan Development Corporation, said, somewhat exasperated, when I asked him why the LMDC didn't decrease the site's office space after people rejected the plans at Listening to the City. "There was never the possibility that the Port Authority would not rebuild the bulk of the office space, because it was dependent on the revenue from Silverstein," he continued. "If you took away the bulk from Silverstein, you had to pay him." Contracts are contracts, even after cataclysmic events.

But even this argument had a counterargument. Under eminent domain, federal, state, and city governments can seize land in the name of the public good. It's always a messy process, and, not incidentally, reclaimed land tends to belong to small business owners and city residents, not powerful developers. But Pataki said his administration and the Port Authority thought a lot about it. "There was serious consideration given to using eminent domain to end the lease," Governor Pataki said. "There were a lot of pluses to considering that. The negatives were to tie the site up in years of litigation." He continued, "We wanted to move it forward as quickly as practicable. It was an important message to send to the city, the state, and the country that this wasn't going to be something where legal impediments could prevent a vision from happening." Pataki calculated that it was more important to make sure things moved forward quickly, without ugly lawsuits, than try to get rid of Silverstein and open up the site's architectural program.

Nonetheless, the possibility of eminent domain fueled some interesting proposals. During the international design competition, Mayor Michael Bloomberg's deputy, Dan Doctoroff, leaked the idea of a land swap between the city and the Port Authority: the sixteen-acre WTC site for the land underneath New York City's two airports. Under the swap, the Port Authority would no longer have paid rent to the city for the airport land, and Mayor Bloomberg and Doctoroff, who many believed supported a more open planning process, would have gained control of Ground Zero and an ability to renegotiate with Silverstein or, perhaps, to condemn the land and eliminate his lease altogether. It was one of the few ideas that seemed to put Silverstein's lease in play. But the idea never progressed very far. Governor Pataki had little incentive to explore a deal with the mayor, since it would have removed him from overseeing the rebuilding, and there was little pressure on officials to make it happen, because the public didn't know much about the swap and didn't understand what it may have opened up.

A close look at the WTC site, then, revealed many arguments for and against an array of rebuilding scenarios. But these arguments were complicated and messy, and rather than continue to hash them out in a public debate, rebuilding officials turned to a design competition, and artful, emotional renderings, to help them make a case for what they believed should stand at the site, including lots of commercial towers. And it worked. In February, Daniel Libeskind's design, "Memory Foundations," won the master-plan competition to general acclaim. The public relations campaign succeeded.

A bit of controversy accompanied Libeskind's win too. The competing team, Think, had many supporters on the Lower Manhattan Development Corporation, but Governor Pataki hated Think's concept—"It looked like two skeletons rising exactly where the Twin Towers stood," he said with disdain. "It looked like replacing life with death."—and loved Libeskind's signature 1,776-foot-tall, Statue of Liberty–esque skyscraper. So when Pataki learned one morning, from a Libeskind supporter alerting him to a leaked story in the *Times*, that the LMDC was poised to pick Think, he went downtown with Mayor Bloomberg and told key board members to change their vote. And they did. It was one of the first but not the last times that Pataki would intervene and override the LMDC. Later that afternoon, to a fair amount of surprise and confusion, given the previously leaked story, the LMDC announced that *Libeskind* had won.

Pataki's fondness for the skyscraper was crucial to Libeskind's success, but some commentators suggested that Libeskind's status as a city architectural outsider (his studio was based in Berlin at the time) also contributed to his win. The thinking was that he would be easier to manage than the designers of Think, all of whom were savvy in the ways of New York City real estate. It was a reasonable theory, but it proved to be a faulty one, for Libeskind was no pushover. Indeed, he was just as ambitious, optimistic, and certain in the superiority of his vision as every other leader downtown. So while the international competition was in many ways a boon for Pataki, the Port Authority, and Larry Silverstein, because it generated public support for a master plan of their chosen architectural program, it also made things more complicated for them. It ushered one more big personality into the mix—a spiky-haired, black-clad artist.

ACT II

DIVISIONS AND DELAYS
2003–2008

CHAPTER 7

LADY LIBERTY AND THE FREEDOM TOWER

D ANIEL LIBESKIND HAD NEVER DESIGNED A SKYSCRAPER. IN fact, for much of his career, Libeskind specialized in architectural theory, and spent his days teaching design at universities and sketching buildings that defied contemporary laws of engineering. At the time he won the WTC site competition, only one of his buildings had ever been built—the Jewish Museum Berlin.

The museum redefined his career. When he won that competition, in 1989, many dismissed his design as too idiosyncratic and metaphorical, and some said it shouldn't even be built. The museum's central feature was a series of empty, angular spaces scattered throughout the building that Libeskind called a "void." He said it represented everything that did *not* exist after a history of genocide and destruction. In addition, the museum's footprint was a wild, zigzagging shape inspired by an unraveling Star of David. And the floor of an outdoor garden was tilted to disorient visitors because, Libeskind said, "that is what perfect order feels like when you leave the history of Berlin." It was all a bit eccentric and puzzling. But Libeskind fought doggedly for his vision—and, on some points, compromised—and when the building finally opened ten years after the competition, it was an enormous success with critics and with the public. People were so fascinated with the architecture that museum officials kept it free of artifacts for two years to provide tours of the empty building.

The Jewish Museum was such a sensation because it signaled a new way of manipulating space to elicit emotion and mark history. This is precisely what Libeskind believed people wanted for Ground Zero. "I start with what it's really about," Libeskind told me, of the WTC site project. "And it's really about an irreversible fact of history that is so devastating and yet, in the long run, has to be used as leverage for something that is good, something that is inspiring, something that allows people to have a greater sense of freedom, a greater sense of participation."

Libeskind's greatest strengths are designing spaces to evoke loss and resilience and speaking passionately and persuasively about how he does it. This doesn't equal experience building skyscrapers, of course, but it was part of the reason why Libeskind believed that he was qualified, perhaps even entitled, to design his iconic tower slated to stand 1,776 feet tall, a height that, at the time of the competition, made it the tallest skyscraper in the world.

I met Libeskind several years after he won the master-plan competition, when the angriest battles had quieted down and he was feeling overwhelmingly conciliatory. He didn't want to revisit past conflicts. Instead, he wanted to talk about the thrill of being WTC master planner and the beauty of New York streets. "I mean, who gets credit for a good street, right?" he said while we discussed his WTC master plan. "The ingenuity of the plan of New York, for example, is streets. That's maybe where its greatest genius lies. It's doing those things which seem to become part of the oxygen we breathe, but are actually what makes our lives truly beautiful." Libeskind talks in a free-form, stream-of-conscious manner, casually referring to Baudelaire and Gautier while discussing, say, the history of the Eiffel Tower or the New York street grid. He wears exclusively black attire, from his cowboy boots to his square-framed glasses. One victim's family member, enamored with the architect, described him as "that magical little guy with the black pants, black shoes, black socks, black belt, black shirt and black glasses."

Libeskind runs his New York studio, a few blocks from Ground Zero, with his wife, Nina—she handles the books and media relations (and is known to be the more confrontational of the pair), while he oversees the design work. Libeskind said that the bitterness and the numerous changes gradually made to his master plan were all inevitable. "That's the evolution of architecture. You don't come up with a picture and say, 'This is going to be built.' It's about depth. It's about, how do you make this happen?"

Libeskind made it happen by evolving, it's true, but also by fighting. When I asked him what, in retrospect, he would have done differently in the rebuilding effort, he answered through his wife. "My wife, Nina, maybe she'd say, in retrospect, 'I wouldn't have gotten into any of the fights.' But then I told her, 'If you didn't get into any of the fights, then it wouldn't have been the same project.'"

It was a smart answer, and not only because he deflected onto his wife. Libeskind knew the fights were an essential part of rebuilding. It was how things got done. First the city needed idealistic visions and the grand celebrations of democracy. And then, the fights. Intense, personal, years-long fights.

In the spring of 2003, the biggest questions had been settled. The Port Authority and developer Larry Silverstein would rebuild all their office space in five skyscrapers, and there would be a memorial, cultural buildings, and a train station, all to be designed later. Now it was time for the men in charge (and it was almost exclusively men) to figure out how to make it happen. Daniel Libeskind's master plan was the first step in solving this puzzle. The master plan is "a structure, it's an organization, it's a three-dimensional thing," Libeskind said. "It's the bodies of buildings, vistas and views, and moments of perception. It's much more complicated than looking at a plan and rendering of a building." He shaped the "character" of the site, he said; he told a story.

Libeskind wanted to emphasize that his work as master planner transcended the fate of any particular building, because, for the competition, he did both—mapped the site *and* designed buildings, most notably his iconic Statue of Liberty–esque tower. Yet he had been hired only to map space. It was immediately perplexing, especially since the skyscraper was a big part of the reason Libeskind won. Governor Pataki, in particular, loved it. Shortly after the master-plan competition ended, Pataki named it Freedom Tower and made it the priority of the rebuilding effort, promising it would pierce the skyline by 2006, the five-year anniversary of the attacks. "You had the Empire State Building, you had the Twin Towers," Pataki said when I asked him about the building's name. "It was logical to have this tremendous, iconic structure soaring above the New York skyline be something. It shouldn't just be, you know, One WTC. It should have a name. And symbolizing 1776 *and* showing the world that we weren't going to be frightened in the face of these attacks...it all logically came together that the perfect name for this is the Freedom Tower."

Libeskind shared Pataki's devotion to a building that told a story. In his vision, the building was a symbol as much as it was a corporate skyscraper. He designed it to echo the skyline of the Statue of Liberty, his primary inspiration. As he wrote in the introductory text to his master plan, "I arrived by ship to New York as a teenager, an immigrant, and like millions of others before me, my first sight was the Statue of Liberty and the amazing skyline of Manhattan. I have never forgotten that sight or what it stands for. This is what this project is all about." The tower's asymmetrical spire, its precise height, its narrow footprint, and its location in the northwest corner of the site all combined to create this reference.

As we discussed the early years of rebuilding, Libeskind said he knew all along that being the master planner did not guarantee him the job of being the architect of Freedom Tower. "I never thought I would build this whole project," he said. "I mean, I would have to be an insane madman to think that I am building all of these buildings." But the tower remained the organizing core of the master plan, and he wasn't content ceding the design work to another.

So, when Libeskind and his wife met with Larry Silverstein in mid-February, a few days after the master-plan competition, Nina explained that her husband planned to design Freedom Tower. But to Silverstein, this was a preposterous proposal. The idea that a theoretical architect was going to design his premier commercial building—what promised to stand as the legacy of his long career—struck him as a bad joke. "He's never designed a high-rise in his life," Silverstein said. "I said, 'Tell me something. If you were needing neurosurgery, would you go to a general practitioner who has never done any kind of operating in his life?' "

Silverstein planned to work with David Childs, of the venerable architecture firm Skidmore, Owings & Merrill. Over the past fifty years, SOM had created some of the country's most famous skyscrapers, including the Sears Tower and the John Hancock Center in Chicago. Childs, sixty-one at the time, was the anti-Libeskind. He had designed multiple skyscrapers of his own, including the Time Warner Center at Columbus Circle in New York. He wore suits with ties, and was very tall (about a foot taller than the notably short Libeskind). Most of all, Childs knew how to please corporate clients and move in high-powered political and financial circles. Larry Silverstein hired Childs to begin designing new buildings for the WTC site a few weeks after 9/11, and by the time Libeskind won the master-planning competition, Childs had already developed his own design for an iconic skyscraper at the site. Neither he nor Silverstein planned to accommodate Libeskind's demands.

But Silverstein and Childs had a problem. And it wasn't merely that Libeskind wanted to design the building himself. As Libeskind liked to declare over the years, when threatened with changes to his plan, "I am the people's architect!" It was a bit dramatic, but it was true. He had won the competition (with some help from Governor Pataki), and more than anyone else, he represented the public's voice downtown. Libeskind, who liked to employ metaphors and symbols in his designs, had become a symbol in his own right. Indeed, the public and Libeskind were kindred spirits: they both had limited power to define the particulars of the rebuilding effort, but they needed to be kept happy, lest they erupt in protest and upend the whole thing.

Larry Silverstein knew this all too well. He wasn't going to hire Libeskind, but he couldn't dismiss him either. On the same day Governor Pataki crowned Libeskind the winner, Silverstein appeared on the *Charlie Rose* show. Rose and Silverstein discussed his decades-long desire to buy the Twin Towers and his frightful car accident a few months before he purchased them, but mostly they discussed the new master plan. Now that Libeskind had won, was Silverstein going to build his plan? Was he Silverstein's architect? Silverstein smiled and dodged. "Well, interestingly enough, he's our architect," Silverstein said. "He's *all* of our architect."

Not mine, but everyone's. It was a nice turn of phrase. And it perfectly captured the privilege and predicament of Libeskind's position. He couldn't be fired by Larry Silverstein or the Port Authority, but he also couldn't demand that Silverstein rebuild precisely his way. Silverstein had a lease and legal rights. And, as he artfully implied to Charlie Rose, the people didn't.

FOR ABOUT SIX MONTHS, LIBESKIND AND CHILDS each proceeded as if he and he alone were the architect of Freedom Tower. There was no collaboration to speak of. They were designing two different buildings for one plot of land.

Governor Pataki and the Lower Manhattan Development Corporation attempted multiple reconciliations. In mid-July, they convened the two architects at LMDC headquarters, right next door to Ground Zero. Each brought backup: Libeskind his lawyer, Edward Hayes, a friend of Governor Pataki's; and Childs, Janno Lieber, head of Silverstein's WTC development. But the architects refused to sit in the same room, and LMDC officials spent the afternoon ferrying messages back and forth from either side of the building, as if brokering a peace between two warring middle-school cliques. After many hours, as the clock approached midnight, officials finally persuaded the architects to speak in person, at which point they established some new terms. Childs and SOM would be the official architect for Freedom Tower, while Libeskind would "meaningfully collaborate" with them on the project.

It sounded like progress, at least in moving past the ego-driven stalemate: Libeskind conceded. Governor Pataki, who wanted Libeskind to be involved but also supported David Childs as lead designer, even held a press conference to celebrate the deal. But the relationship between the firms quickly deteriorated. Libeskind sent some of his architects to work at SOM to keep tabs on the design, which angered SOM, whose architects didn't like being watched. For a short time, Libeskind was even barred from the SOM offices unless David Childs was there too. Then, in early December, SOM reported a break-in. A deadline was nearing—Governor Pataki had requested that the two architects finish their collaboration before Christmas—and Libeskind disliked the latest design. He planned to appeal to the governor, his most powerful ally, with a presentation. But all the images and renderings of Freedom Tower were at SOM, so Libeskind sent some of his workers, in the middle of the night, to photograph the drawings, and used these images the next day in a presentation to a few of the governor's aides. The *New York Post* called it a "Watergate-style" burglary, though by virtue of his collaboration, the drawings belonged, at least partially, to Libeskind too.

It had been nearly a year since the competition, and, in addition to working (or not working) on Freedom Tower, Libeskind had spent these months tweaking his master plan to fit the constraints of the site and its many owners. He had raised the sunken memorial area, which, in addition to Freedom Tower, was the other defining feature of his plan. Initially recessed seventy feet below street level, he raised it to lie thirty feet below street level so the Port Authority could better construct underground transportation lines. He had softened the angles on the building's footprints and made them more symmetrical to better accommodate office space. He had also attached the grand spire of Freedom Tower to the main building—the spire was originally a separate, free-standing structure—and decided it would house a restaurant and transmission tower rather than "Gardens of the World." He had shrunk the size of his parks, called Park of Heroes and Wedge of Light. Altogether, these changes created a more conventional, business-friendly master plan; in fact, these changes created a plan that was starting to resemble the earlier plans so memorably trashed by thousands at Listening to the City. Few noticed the likeness, however. The people paying attention to rebuilding were focused on Freedom Tower now. (But for the cynics who *were* paying attention, forcing revisions to the new master plan until it became the old master plan was a pretty nifty trick.) After so many compromises, Libeskind was loath to concede the iconic skyscraper itself. During his presentation to Governor Pataki's aides, Libeskind reduced his demanded changes to two features: the building's 1,776-foot height, and its signature, Statue of Liberty–esque, asymmetrical spire. David Childs had increased the size of the building (partly to create more marketable office space) and shortened the spire. But Libeskind convinced Pataki that these features needed to be preserved to honor the master plan. A few days later, Pataki called Childs from Bermuda, where he was vacationing at Mayor Bloomberg's house, and implored him to make the necessary adjustments. Childs spent the rest of his weekend frantically revising the design so it would be finished in time for its public unveiling, scheduled for later that week.

The unveiling, held in the grand Federal Hall on Wall Street, went smoothly. Everyone smiled and said mostly nice things, but the toll of the forced collaboration was evident. "Working with Skidmore, Owings, and Merrill has not been easy," Libeskind said, "but a civic process is about people." Larry Silverstein acknowledged the tensions too. "Working with talented, brilliant architects is a challenge in itself," he said. The problem hadn't changed. There were two architects and only one building. But as the unveiling made clear, Freedom Tower had only one true architect now. The building clearly belonged to Larry Silverstein and David Childs. It consisted of three parts: nearly one hundred stories of office space; an open-air "superstructure" of cables on top of that, filled with wind-producing turbines; and, finally, Libeskind's off-center spire, which now looked tacked on to an entirely unrelated building. The sharp angles and asymmetries of the original design had been replaced by cleaner, more conventional lines; it no longer looked like Libeskind at all. But Childs did include one element that captured the spirit of the original: a gentle twist to the building that resembled Liberty's raised, torch-wielding arm. Libeskind's symbolic echo remained intact.

But the master planner was piqued. A few months after the unveiling, Libeskind sued Larry Silverstein for $800,000 of unpaid fees for his work on Freedom Tower. In the scheme of rebuilding, this was a small sum. (Freedom Tower would go on to cost over $3 billion.) But it was symbolic—and it required Silverstein to spend more time and money on litigation. Silverstein initially refused to pay, arguing that the

Lower Manhattan Development Corporation had paid Libeskind in full. A few months later, the two settled the matter for the diminished sum of $340,000.

LIKE THE SIXTEEN-ACRE WTC SITE ITSELF, Freedom Tower meant different things to different people. To Daniel Libeskind, it was a symbol of hope and resilience and, ultimately, of the limits of his influence downtown. Larry Silverstein considered the building both a public service and a private right, not to mention a quarter of his future office space. To David Childs, it was the highest-profile commission of his career and a hard-won, if ultimately compromised, urban design triumph. And to Governor Pataki, it was a symbol of freedom and the legacy of his governorship.

It was with this last meaning in mind that Pataki decided to coordinate the start of construction of Freedom Tower with the 2004 Republican Convention, in New York City. Pataki hoped to translate a swift, smooth rebuilding effort into a run for the presidency, and he believed the convention was the perfect venue to start telling his story.

This simple plan would soon take on epic meaning, and become one of the most-discussed components of the rebuilding effort. The problems began when news of Pataki's plans spread, and people accused him of politicizing the rebuilding. The outcry prompted Pataki to move the cornerstone ceremony up two months, to the Fourth of July—just enough in advance of the convention to shield him from accusations of politicization, but close enough to still receive credit at the convention for moving rebuilding forward. On a hot summer morning, amid cheering, sweating crowds, a crane lowered the twenty-ton Adirondack granite cornerstone into the ground.

But the ceremony proved hasty, for a few reasons. After Childs and Libeskind completed their design, an army of engineers, consultants, and architects began the long process of translating the concept into a workable construction plan, and, in early July, their work was not yet finished. This meant that construction could not begin, regardless of the cornerstone. After Pataki's grand ceremony, the cornerstone sat, and sat. Eventually, construction workers built a little blue shed around the granite to protect it from the elements.

Then the New York Police Department weighed in. (In fact, it had been weighing in for a little while.) After Pataki, Silverstein, Libeskind, and Childs unveiled their Freedom Tower design, the NYPD reviewed the building codes and determined that the skyscraper was not safe. Freedom Tower would be the third-tallest building in the world (after the master-plan competition, Dubai and Saudi Arabia began construction on taller skyscrapers), standing at the site of two previous terrorist attacks. "Due to the history of Al Qaeda strikes at this location and the symbolic nature of the Freedom Tower itself," the NYPD wrote to the Port Authority, "it seems clear that this building will become the prime terrorist target in New York City as soon as it is occupied." The NYPD believed the building required the most sophisticated, advanced security features.

The police communicated their concerns to Larry Silverstein and the Port Authority, but no one reacted. The Port Authority had designated the building as safe as a federal courthouse, and it believed this was sufficient. It also believed that the police department didn't like the idea of building tall at the WTC site and was using security as a pretense to impede progress. But the NYPD persisted, and increasingly specified what appeared to be real concerns. After Pataki laid the cornerstone, the police wrote another letter citing the tower's relatively close proximity to the street and its mostly glass base. Again, the Port Authority disagreed with the assessment and ignored the warnings.

As the months passed, questions of safety and security plagued other parts of the rebuilding. A traffic tunnel adjacent to Freedom Tower, designed to help contain damage from a car bomb, was scrapped when the investment firm Goldman Sachs argued the tunnel would create too much traffic near its entrance. Goldman said it wouldn't build its new headquarters across from Ground Zero if the tunnel construction went ahead. Since the Pataki administration desperately wanted Goldman Sachs to move to West Street, to signal confidence downtown, it removed the tunnel from the master plan and also gave Goldman $1.65 billion in Liberty Bonds—roughly 20 percent of the $8 billion in tax-free bonds the federal government had given New York to rebuild. "If Goldman Sachs sent the message that it was not a safe place to attract the best and brightest talent, everyone would have followed," John Cahill, Pataki's chief of staff, said. "The message would have been, we're not ready to invest in the city and the state. We're not sure about the future here." In exchange for the revised streetscape and more than a billion in bonds, Goldman decided to stay. *This* was the power Goldman Sachs clearly wielded.

In stark contrast was the lack of power of the NYPD. After being ignored for months, the NYPD upped the ante and publicly detailed Freedom Tower's failings. Two years after Libeskind won the master-plan competition, more than a year after he and David Childs unveiled their Freedom Tower design, and just as engineers and architects were completing their construction plans for the skyscraper, the NYPD declared that the building shouldn't go forward. It stated that the building needed to be moved farther from the street and constructed to the standards of an American embassy, which would require a completely new design. It was the first time the NYPD had specified the level of security it believed necessary, and it finally caught Governor Pataki's attention. Pataki announced that Freedom Tower would be redesigned again and moved farther from the street. "My feeling was, first of all, you don't want to just blatantly contradict a security warning from the police department," Pataki told me. "And on the other hand, I wasn't about to emasculate Libeskind's plan by taking down the Freedom Tower." The redesign couldn't be a simple touchup, however; it presented real challenges. As John Cahill explained it, "You're building a skyscraper in Lower Manhattan basically to the same standards as an embassy in Kabul." T. J. Gottesdiener, SOM's managing partner for the project, put it more bluntly. The challenge, he said, was "to build a great urban building that did not look like a concrete bunker."

Whether David Childs succeeded in that quest remains up for debate. To meet the increased security requirements, he designed a new base for the building, a two-hundred-foot concrete and steel pedestal designed to withstand a major bomb blast. Nicolai Ouroussoff, reviewing the redesign in the *Times*, wrote, "The new obelisk-shaped tower, which stands on an enormous 20-story concrete pedestal, evokes a gigantic glass paperweight with a toothpick stuck on top." And that was one of his kinder comments. Redesigning the base required Childs to rework other parts of the building too, including straightening the tower, removing the open-air superstructure and wind turbines, and shortening and centering the spire. Once again, the result was a completely new building.

All told, this second redesign cost $30 million. Over two years' worth of engineering and architectural work was scrapped. And Governor Pataki's ceremonial cornerstone, now sitting under a shed in the wrong place at the site, was quietly removed and sent back out to Long Island.

Larry Silverstein and Janno Lieber were furious about the late-in-the-game changes, but they worked with Childs and got behind the new design. "We thought we were just great Americans and team players and problem solvers and we redesigned the building on the double," Lieber said. Libeskind supported the new building too, which was important for public relations. Libeskind now had less to do with Freedom Tower than ever, but he knew it was important for the public to feel that his vision was being honored. Libeskind released a statement describing the new building as "even better than the tower we had before."

In our conversations years later, Libeskind refused to share any frustration or disillusionment he felt toward the redesigned Freedom

Tower, preferring to emphasize his general satisfaction with the project, but he must have been at least a little disappointed with the new revisions. While Freedom Tower still stood 1,776 feet tall, it had lost its elegant, Statue of Liberty–esque twist. Squaring and fortifying the base had required Childs to straighten the building. The most visible reference to Lady Liberty, Libeskind's inspiration for the master plan, was now gone.

It was impossible for critics and observers not to ruminate on the broader meaning of the redesign. From the beginning, debates about Ground Zero doubled as debates about American identity, and Freedom Tower in particular invited sustained analysis. "For better or worse, it will be seen by the world as a chilling expression of how we are reshaping our identity in a post-Sept. 11 context," Ouroussoff wrote in the *Times*. "It is exactly the kind of nightmare that government officials repeatedly asserted would never happen here: an impregnable tower braced against the outside world." Ouroussoff's critique was a bit alarmist, but looking at a model of the fortified base, you could see his point. It was windowless, intimidating, and cold. David Childs promised he would find a safe, glasslike material to cover the base so it didn't look so much like a bunker, but that only partially quieted critics' contempt. The facts themselves spoke almost too poetically. A building called Freedom Tower had been fortified. To make it safer, designers had erased its references to the Statue of Liberty.

CHAPTER 8

FAMILIES

FREEDOM TOWER ENSURED THAT THE RELATIONSHIP BETWEEN Daniel Libeskind and Larry Silverstein would always be chilly, but the artist had delivered a significant gift to the developer with his master plan. "A great thing about Libeskind, and one of the reasons I think our connection has grown over time," Janno Lieber at Silverstein Properties told me, "is that we credit Libeskind with showing people how it didn't need to be one or the other." Libeskind's plan eased the conflict many had originally seen between rebuilding vast amounts of office space and memorializing 9/11. He illustrated how the commercial and the commemorative could coexist.

Libeskind understood that while Ground Zero meant different things to different people, it was, most universally, a space of history and loss. And so rather than secularize the office space, and divide the land into separate commercial and memorial areas, Libeskind sanctified the entire sixteen-acre parcel. He made even commercial development symbolic. It was a paradox: by infusing the entire site with a spirit of commemoration and American history, Libeskind made it easier for people to embrace those pieces—even the big ones—that had little to do with commemoration and history. It was a paradox for Libeskind too: unsurprisingly, he told me he felt most strongly about the site's public spaces, not the commercial ones. (He also always believed a rebuilt site should contain housing.) But by making commercial development part of a broader emotional, even sacred, project, Libeskind helped people accept it. This sense of transcendence wouldn't last forever. The symbolism Libeskind attached to the buildings would create conflict and headaches down the road—at least for those with financial interests in the site—and the land would gradually be divvied up into distinct commercial and commemorative parcels. But these interconnected layers of meaning were important in the short term, particularly for Larry Silverstein and the Port Authority. Before Libeskind, people overwhelmingly rejected Silverstein's ten million square feet of office space, but after Libeskind, no one talked anymore about decreasing his square footage or voiding his lease. Instead, they debated the virtues of asymmetrical spires and fortified bases.

For Larry Silverstein and the Port Authority, this was a welcome development. And for much of the public, even those who didn't swoon for Libeskind, it worked. But for those most opposed to developing the land, notably victims' families, the Libeskind master plan was something of a bait and switch. Many victims' families believed that Ground Zero was a burial ground, and that the memorial was the most important piece of the project. It should be designed first, they argued, with any- and everything else designed around it. The widespread embrace of Libeskind's commemorative plan was, oddly enough, proof they had lost the argument. They agreed with Ada Louise Huxtable, architecture critic of the *Wall Street Journal*, who had described the masterplan competition this way: "The objective is still the reinstatement of real estate, not the revitalization of Lower Manhattan, with the memorial an afterthought to be plugged in later."

Many families didn't trust officials to build a significant, appropriate memorial, a skepticism that some officials, most notably Mayor Bloomberg, contributed to. "I would argue that sometimes less is more, and that we run the risk of making [the memorial] much too big," Bloomberg said at a news conference in the summer of 2002. "When people say 'Well, that's a cemetery,' that's not exactly what a rental agent wants to have out there. So we've got to find a balance like anything else."

The mayor—who had a knack for saying insensitive things about grief and loss, and upsetting victims' families—had little direct power over the rebuilding effort. The Port Authority, not the city, owned the land. But he was still the mayor, and his comments underscored many families' preexisting fears. By the time I met a group of 9/11 families in Philadelphia, a couple of years after 9/11, they felt alienated. "It's a *commercial* project," Bob Mcilvaine said, with disdain, when I asked him and the dozen or so others in the group if they were following the rebuilding effort. They had formed a support group in the months after the attacks, and while the ultimate destiny of the WTC site was important to everyone there, they didn't think the rebuilding included them, and so they barely followed news about it. A narrative was forming downtown—one of skyscrapers and resilience and American fortitude—and their stories didn't fit it.

THE PHILADELPHIA SUPPORT GROUP MET IN AN old church outside the city. Once a week, usually on Tuesdays, they arranged chairs in a circle and talked about their grief, their latest news, what it was like to be a "family member." Most who attended the group were, like Bob and his wife, Helen, parents who had lost children at the WTC, young adults in their mid-twenties to mid-thirties who were beginning careers in finance and trade. Susan Mathes, a psychologist who had volunteered for three weeks at the WTC site immediately after the attacks, led the discussions.

I met the group by posting a message about my research on a few 9/11 listservs and asking for anyone who was willing to contact me—the same way I met all the victims' families I spoke to. I didn't want to pester families for an interview, but I did want to make sure that I included as many voices as possible, particularly theirs, and this seemed like the least intrusive way. My first note reached about five thousand people, eighteen of whom e-mailed me back. One of them attended the Philadelphia group, and after we met, she mentioned my project to everyone else, and they invited me to join some of their meetings.

No one in the group knew one another before 9/11, but they all lived in Philadelphia—not New Jersey or Connecticut, where most of the non–New York families lived—and they quickly found one another and grew close. Indeed, non–New York-ness was one of the group's defining features. It wasn't that they didn't *like* New Yorkers, but they always felt their physical distance kept them out of the "in group" of victims' families—and they preferred it that way. Most of them weren't activists; they didn't go to public hearings or town halls to weigh in on rebuilding, and they hadn't mastered the art of talking to reporters. They usually regretted giving television interviews, they said, mostly because lengthy discussions were always edited down to that one moment of sobbing, turning them into hysterical clichés. They didn't need the hoopla that came with being a 9/11 family member, so they stayed away from it. They attended one another's charity events in honor of their kids, and every now and then they traveled to the city together to visit Ground Zero.

One Tuesday night, everyone arrived at the church with bags full of stuff: homemade posters, clothing, quilts, pictures, jewelry, books. They had decided to share their own private memorials with one another—memorials that, in some cases, no one else had ever seen; memorials that didn't belong to the Port Authority or Larry Silverstein, bureaucratic agencies like the LMDC or the masses of tourists at Ground Zero.

"Okay, we should start I think, because, you know, time is going to fly tonight," Susan said, as everyone chatted and found a seat. Susan wore a black V-neck sweater and round, wire-rimmed glasses. "There is so much to talk about."

Janet, whose son Christopher died, opened a cardboard box holding twenty bracelets, each one forming a sequined American flag. She was selling them as a fund-raiser for the memorial foundation she created in her son's memory. A few of the other attendees quickly handed over some bills. After Susan bought one, she crossed the floor to me. It was a gift from the group, she said. "You have to have your own memorial too."

Bob, who always wore a few pieces of his son's clothing to the meetings, was the first to share his items. Tonight, he wore a brown leather belt and a light blue cotton button-down that had belonged to his son. Bob held a square plastic case, and peeled back the tape holding it shut. Then he opened the next layer of wrapping, a thick plastic bag that read "Biohazard. Specimen Bag."

"It smells like Ground Zero smelled," he said as he gently held a worn, dusty, once-brown wallet between his thumb and forefinger. Many silently nodded in agreement as they took in the musty odor that filled the room. The wallet had belonged to his son and was found by police in the Financial District a few days after 9/11. In a quiet voice, Bob explained that the wallet made him more at ease with his son's death. Because the wallet was whole, he told everyone, he felt more certain that his son had not died jumping from a window but instead had most likely been hit on the street by falling, burning metal.

"This has a lot of meaning for me. I never found out exactly what happened. And it sort of gives you a clue, the fact that his wallet was found, the fact that the wallet's intact," he said. "You know, at first we weren't sure if he jumped, and you know, that was a horrible thought. And then the fact that he was burned over ninety-five percent of his body. So I figured, my thing is, that he was on his back when he went down because the wallet is so intact. So it just gives me a certain clue what happened. I won't leave it out, I'll just show you. It always gives me a reminder of the smell. Not that I bring it out a lot, but it really is the memory of that day."

Bob held the wallet out for a few more moments. Then he sat down and slid it back into its layers of casing. Bob and his wife were among the few in the group to receive a body from Ground Zero. (Most received nothing at all.) But it had been stripped of all possessions and clothing. Bob figured his son's personal effects had to be somewhere, and so he spent the next two years tracking the wallet down. He began with calls to the police department and then to the city's Office of Chief Medical Examiner. He finally claimed the wallet after befriending a New York City detective, who helped him navigate the city's maddening system of offices, bureaus, and request forms.

The pain that the wallet eased for Bob—the pain of not knowing how his son had died—came up frequently in the meetings. There were lots of unknowns for everyone in the group. Not knowing how their child or sibling or spouse had died; not knowing where they had died; not knowing where the bodies were now. Even Bob, who was lucky to have more knowledge than most, was plagued by the uncertainty of it all. The cold numbers were horrible to contemplate. The destruction of the Twin Towers left no measurable trace of more than one thousand people. Sophisticated heat maps, taken aerially as the towers burned and fell, show that in some sections of the buildings, the heat reached crematorium levels.

"You know, I don't know whether Kenny was able to jump out of a window, or run down steps, or if he was just simply smothered," Elsie said one night. Elsie was a single mother, and Kenny was her only son. Kenny's remains had never been located, and no objects found. "Is it more painful to find something than not know anything at all?" she asked.

Katie, whose brother Sean was killed, nodded. A year after 9/11, Katie's sister-in-law Holly received a knock on her door from two police officers who told her that rescue workers had found a fragment of Sean's shoulder. Holly picked it up at the police station—the piece of bone was sealed in a small plastic bag—and the family held a service to bury it. "We really thought that we would never find him, especially as time was going on," Katie said. They still don't know how Sean died, but the burial provided a new sense of certainty. "I know that when I go to the cemetery, I know that he's there," Katie said.

Burying the bone gave Katie a place to go to be with her brother. Elsie, like a few others in the group, didn't have that place. Instead, their place became Ground Zero. But even as these families described Ground Zero as a burial ground, they knew that the WTC site was different from a cemetery or gravesite. In the end, it was a euphemism. Technically speaking, no one was buried at Ground Zero. They couldn't be.

One evening, the group recalled visiting the WTC site for the first-anniversary ceremony, when they could walk on the bottom of the pit. "I felt like I was walking on the dust of people who died," Karen said. Karen's stepson Kevin was killed and never located. "I actually looked down at my feet where I walked," she continued. "I wondered if I'd see a bone or something."

Elsie remembered similar sensations. "The wind, it was swirling," she said. "It was amazing how the dirt just layered on your body. Not just on your shoes, but your face. I got back to the hotel, and washed my face and the entire washcloth was full of it, almost giving us a hug or a kiss and becoming a part of us. 'Cause we never found him." For Elsie and Karen, and others in the group, Ground Zero was more than the symbolic location of their loved ones. It was the place where the dirt was made of them.

THIS BELIEF, THAT THE DIRT AND LAND at the WTC site consisted of people, convinced many families, survivors, and rescue workers I spoke to that the site should not be redeveloped, regardless of the commemorative nature of the master plan or the large size of the space put aside for a memorial. They told similar stories. Gary Smiley, a paramedic and 9/11 first responder, remembered kicking up some dirt as he walked on the bottom of the pit during the first-year anniversary. He smelled a burnt odor, familiar to him from his months working on the pile. "It was just the smell that was very unique, and I'm like, to [my friend] Brian, 'It's that smell again.' And he's like, 'Yeah, dude, 'cause there's people here.' We were walking on people."

Gary thought the whole site should be turned into a park with lots of trees. "Who cares how much the land is worth?" he said. "You're building on a cemetery."

Gary was another of the eighteen who had responded to my message. Gary lived in Staten Island, and he spent his day off—the only one he had that week—traveling to a Midtown Starbucks to meet with me. He also participated in Columbia University's 9/11 Oral History Project, which collected thousands of histories from survivors and witnesses of the attack, and attended various support groups for people suffering from post-traumatic stress disorder. Gary wanted to be heard.

Gary's unit, part of the 31st Battalion of the New York City Fire Department, in Brooklyn, was one of the first to arrive at the WTC on the morning of the eleventh, with the understanding that a small plane had mistakenly hit the North Tower. They headed to Church Street, where Gary had helped run a triage unit during the 1993 WTC bombing, and began to assist employees coming out of the North Tower lobby. "I was carrying a woman across the street who had come out of the building, all cut up and stuff. She was actually tucked behind my shoulder, and then she started yelling, 'Plane, plane!'" Gary said. "I thought she was yelling about the plane that hit, but then she pushed my head up and at that point the second plane flew over us." Heavy debris began to fall from the explosion a hundred stories above. "That's when I started to realize that it wasn't an accident. You know, looking up, you knew it wasn't a small plane."

Three hundred and forty-three firefighters were killed that day, and Gary knew many of them. When we met, he was still struggling to make sense of the fact that he had survived. After the South Tower collapsed, a wave of rubble propelled him down the block, and he rolled under an ambulance for protection. He dug himself out and made his way to a field hospital. His leg was injured and he had some trouble breathing, but he stayed, working at the field hospital until 2 a.m. Wednesday morning. The next day, Gary went to the hospital and was treated for severe dehydration, kidney failure, and extensive burns. He was released on Friday and, after that weekend, worked a daily shift at the WTC site through mid-December.

Then Gary started to feel bad. He grew withdrawn—"indifferent," he said—and his supervisors recommended a few weeks' rest. When he returned to Ground Zero, he felt he couldn't stay. He began "canceling out" of work on the days he was assigned to the site, and soon decided to work solely in Brooklyn. He was eventually diagnosed with post-traumatic stress disorder, as were one out of every eight 9/11 rescue workers—three times the national average. Gary was suffering from a bad cough too, and taking multiple medications to manage his depression and nightmares.

Gary told me his history methodically, calmly. He had told it before, and was practiced in the art of describing gruesome scenes without growing too upset or sad. But he grew angry when he started to talk about the present. "Life sucks," he said. "And the majority of people don't give a shit anymore. People are forgetting." Gary was the epitome of the 9/11 hero, but it was a story that no longer represented his life. "You know, people say, 'America's stronger,'" Gary said. "Yeah, it is, but..." He paused. "I don't think people realize that there's no voice for the people that lived through it."

Gary's experience with PTSD support groups illustrates his struggle to tell his story and receive help. He never loved the groups—he thought most of them engaged too superficially with people's challenges—but he kept attending because they were better than no support at all. Then one of the city's mental health organizations sent Gary to a gay men's health crisis group, though Gary is not gay. "People start talking, and I'm like, 'This guy's got issues,'" Gary said, still incredulous months later. "I called [the organization] and the person said, 'Well, we thought you needed a group environment,' and I said, 'Well, didn't you think about the group I needed?'" Gary stopped attending PTSD support groups after that.

GARY'S SENSE OF DISEMPOWERMENT WAS PROFOUND, but it didn't completely define him. Before we said good-bye, he showed me the two bracelets he wore on his left wrist. One was in memory of his close friend Jimmy, who was killed at the Trade Center. The other read "in memory of New York's bravest," which Gary received from the Los Angeles County Fire Department. "I wear it every day," he said. "It does not leave my arm." Gary knew that some people were thinking of him, and this provided a measure of comfort. It was one of the paradoxes of losing family and friends in such a public, national event. While Gary fumed at his loss of power, at Ground Zero and everywhere, he cherished the things he received from strangers. He hated the costs of being part of 9/11, but he appreciated the gifts.

Bob, Karen, Elsie, and others in the Philadelphia support group also knew that their status as 9/11 families privileged them to receive more than most recovering from the loss of a family member. The memorials they shared on that Tuesday night included a quilt from a nearby elementary school, a handmade American flag from a neighbor, and personal letters from people around the country. A few brought in the certificate they received from the International Star Registry, which named a star after every victim of the attack. A few others brought in "Portraits of Grief," the compilation of *New York Times* sketches of victims. Had their sons and daughters died in a car accident or of cancer, the loss would have been no less personal, but much less public. Certainly it would not have been chronicled in the *Times*.

But the balance between private grief and public celebration was constantly evolving, and delicate. Karen visited the National Museum of American History at the Smithsonian when it held a first-anniversary exhibition on 9/11. (The museum also held a well-received special showing exclusively for family members of victims, but Karen was not part of that group.) "Here were all these people standing around, walking around, drinking their sodas or doing whatever, and just talking," she said. "And to me, it was such a personal thing. I didn't feel comfortable there, because there weren't people like me there.

"And you want to talk about it, and you can't," Karen continued. "I didn't know any of those people. I mean, it was my own private grief then. But I want everybody to know, I want everybody to remember. I want everybody to see that there's pain in me, and it touches more than just in the news. It's a real honest-to-God grieving person in pain from a death, this horrible death."

Others in the group recalled similarly upsetting stories: of walking into Philadelphia's 30th Street Station to catch a train and running into a traveling memorial that contained rocks and rubble from the WTC site; of visiting a 9/11 exhibit at a local museum and having to pay entrance fees; of watching a museum film of the towers collapsing as others laughed and chatted around them. In their stories, they were unprepared for the exhibits and upset that others around them were unaware of their feelings. But at the same time, they didn't necessarily want the memorials or exhibits to be removed, because, as Karen said, they wanted everyone to remember. They wanted everyone to know.

This was the problem at Ground Zero too. They felt as if it belonged to them. They hated the rebuilding decisions made by bureaucrats and businessmen. They hated being dismissed as unstable or "stuck on the past." But they were heartened by the public's interest in their loss and in the memorial, and they expected public funds to be dedicated to the project. "It's ours," Karen said. "Eventually that feeling will change; I mean, it should," she continued. "But right now, it's too personal a place." The members of the Philadelphia group had great insight into the messy push and pull of creating a public response to a trauma that they knew was both personal and national. I wondered if they could see the issues clearly because they had mostly removed themselves from the political process. They had decided to opt out.

At the end of the Tuesday night meeting, as everyone was returning their memorials to their bags and grabbing their coats, one of the group members asked if anyone wanted to sign a petition. The design for the memorial at Ground Zero had just been selected, and some victims' families were mobilizing against it. A few in the group stopped to read the petition, but most didn't seem that interested. It was a strange moment. For months in New York, officials had been running the competition for the official memorial, but here in Philadelphia, as the group talked about their own memorials and human remains and sacred ground, no one had even mentioned it until now.

CHAPTER 9

THE MEMORIAL

ANIEL LIBESKIND ALLOTTED NEARLY EIGHT ACRES OF THE land, half the WTC site, for what he called the "memorial quadrant." He recessed it thirty feet below street level because he wanted "people to be able to understand the story whole, the bedrock where people perished," he said. "To understand the site from the point of view that we have never really seen, which is the foundations exposed." Libeskind mapped this space very precisely; his master plan even included dimensions for the long ramp (13 feet by 314 feet) that would lead visitors down into the quadrant, which included a memorial, a museum, and a set of cultural buildings. As master planner, it wasn't Libeskind's job to design the memorial, but by plunging it into the earth, and imagining every inch of space around it, he came pretty close.

Five thousand, two hundred and one people submitted entries for the memorial, making it the largest design competition in history (the previous record holder, the Vietnam Veterans Memorial competition, drew 1,421 submissions), and most of them adhered to Libeskind's site boundaries. They honored the recessed space, the ramp, and his arrangement of buildings around the memorial. But for those who wanted to think a bit more broadly, there was, embedded amid the countless pages of maps, sketches, and photographs of Libeskind's plan, a rather counterintuitive bolded statement on page ten informing artists that they could, in fact, ignore those parameters completely. "Design Concepts that propose to exceed the illustrated memorial site boundaries may be considered by the jury if, in collaboration with the LMDC, they are deemed feasible and consistent with site plan objectives."

Architect Michael Arad chose the caveat over the existing measurements and boundaries. It was a risk, but Arad's design didn't neatly fit into Libeskind's master plan, and he preferred to preserve his vision rather than make awkward, compromising changes. "I entered the competition without any illusion that I was going to win," Arad said a few years after the competition. "In other words, I was free to suggest whatever I wanted to suggest." And so he did—and then he won.

Arad is tall and thin, and has dark, close-cropped hair. He's also a little brusque and guarded, and in the months after he won he frequently displayed a sharp temper when things didn't go his way. Which, of course, given the politics of Ground Zero, happened frequently. Because Arad wasn't part of a larger firm, he was asked to select an associate firm to help him further develop his design. But he didn't like the suggested firms, so he sabotaged the process by grading the prospects a "zero," ensuring that their average scores stayed low. After other jurors discovered his trick, he was thrown off the jury in charge of selecting the associate firm. Ultimately, Arad was paired with Davis Brody Bond, a well-known firm in New York, as well as landscape architect Peter Walker, and he fought, resisted, and undermined them all. Arad was young when he won—only thirty-four—and entirely unknown in the design world. Perhaps he believed he needed to be uncompromising to survive in the shadow of the Libeskinds, team Silverstein, and the Port Authority and Governor Pataki, which might have been true.

Before he won, Arad had worked briefly for the large architecture firm Kohn Pederson Fox, designing corporate skyscrapers, but had recently left that job for a more modest post in the design department of New York's Housing Authority. The Housing Authority won him over when it built a police station he liked in his Manhattan neighborhood. But he always had bigger ambitions. He entered the Pentagon's 9/11 memorial competition in 2002, and began working on his concept for a New York City memorial a few weeks after the attacks.

Arad archived the evolution of his idea, and developed a polished PowerPoint to share with interested journalists and lecture audiences. When we met, he delivered it to me too. "So let's start with this," Arad said, holding an iPad at an angle. "This was the sketch that I drew about a month after the attacks." (Arad clearly wanted to give his presentation without being interrupted. When I asked him if he was paying attention to the rebuilding debates that were emerging when he began thinking about a memorial, he answered briskly, "Well, yeah, a little bit, but this is kind of separate from all of that," and then turned back to the iPad.)

"I couldn't actually imagine building on that site. And so I was actually drawn to the Hudson River," he said. "I was drawn to this idea of the water being shorn open, forming two square voids, two sort of empty vessels the water would flow into; they would never fill up. It seemed like sort of an impossible idea—can you take water and cut it open and form an emptiness? And so I spent a year sort of trying to understand that idea, whether you could just do that. And this was long before there was a competition. This was really something that I did for myself."

The heart of Arad's design happened to also be one of the compulsory components of the memorial competition: the empty footprints of the Twin Towers. Every submission needed to do three things: recognize each victim of the attacks; create a separate, private space for victims' families; and make the square footprints of the Twin

Towers visible. The footprints are particularly special to victims' families because, while human remains are located all over the WTC site, particularly large concentrations were found in the footprints. In the summer of 2002, during the master-plan competition, when victims' families were growing increasingly worried that commercial space was being privileged over a memorial, Governor Pataki declared the footprints "sacred space" that would remain free of commercial development. Daniel Libeskind marked the footprints in his plan too.

So what distinguished Arad's design wasn't his memorialization of the footprints themselves, but the *way* he memorialized them, with water and waterfalls. Arad missed seeing the Twin Towers in the skyline and was taken by the idea of somehow giving material, liquid form to their absence. In the year following the attacks, Arad constructed a model of little fountains with slicks of water falling over the edges of two square pools. When the Ground Zero memorial competition was announced in the spring of 2003, he moved the two square voids he imagined in the Hudson to the actual footprints on the site. "And so you have this flat plain, that then carved to form those voids," he said, "like the voids in the Hudson." In the version he submitted to the jury, and which he showed on his PowerPoint, water fell over edges into pools thirty feet belowground, creating waterfalls that echoed the Twin Towers' form underground.

This was where Arad's plan deviated, quite significantly, from Libeskind's master plan. For Arad to have waterfalls that flowed into pools belowground, he had to have a plaza at street level for the voids, the empty square footprints. Arad's square pools erased Libeskind's recessed memorial area, one of the defining features of his master plan. Libeskind was in the midst of fighting (and losing) his battle with David Childs and Larry Silverstein to design Freedom Tower when Arad won, and upon learning the news, Libeskind yelled, "I will fight this!" adding once again, "I am the people's architect!" Unfortunately for Libeskind, he would lose this battle too.

Arad's street-level plaza wasn't simply a byproduct of his vision. He wanted to create an active, thriving public space, and to him, Libeskind's recessed area was the opposite of this. "It was cut off from the rest of the city," he said. Arad believed that only a plaza contiguous with the streets and sidewalks of the WTC would enable people to mix and move and make the public square part of the surrounding neighborhood. Arad's inspiration was the impulsive outpouring immediately following the attacks. He joined the teeming, candle-lighting crowds in Washington Square Park and was moved by the sense of togetherness he felt. "Public space embodies the values we hold dear and is one of the reasons why we were attacked that day," he said. "Public space really forms a society. It acts as a catalyst, as an agent that affirms it, that allows it to come into being, that forms a venue for it to exist." Arad wanted to create this space permanently at Ground Zero.

Libeskind didn't disagree on the importance of public space. He wanted a bustling memorial plaza too. Arad and Libeskind even agreed on one of the ways to achieve it: more streets. Libeskind's master plan reinstated the street grid that the Port Authority destroyed when it constructed the World Trade Center in the 1960s. To build the WTC superblock, planners had paved over a handful of streets, or, as designers say, they "de-mapped" them. (Arad: "It has a very Orwellian ring to it, doesn't it. De-mapped.") Arad and Libeskind agreed that streets should run through the site again to increase foot traffic and bring life to the area. They agreed they should, as Arad put it, "de-de-map" Greenwich and Fulton Streets. But they disagreed on whether the plaza could or should be recessed. And since Arad was the designer of the memorial, his preference prevailed.

THE GENERAL RESPONSE TO ARAD'S DESIGN WAS warm but muted—not the media frenzy or public excitement generated by Libeskind and the master-plan competition, but not a scorn fest either. The competition was run very differently from its predecessor. There was no public voting or immense town hall to debate the merits of the top plans. Instead, a jury of experts—artists, architects, memorial scholars, and one victim's family member—met privately for a few months, announced six finalists, and then selected the winner. Only *after* the competition were all five-thousand-plus entries scanned and uploaded to a public memorial website. It was a less transparent process, but it ran more smoothly and may have ultimately had more integrity. There were no competitors lobbying jurists or critics to garner support. There was no need for the independent jury to run a public relations campaign.

The privacy and independence was insisted upon by the jury's most famous and influential member, Maya Lin, who was also Arad's greatest advocate. Twenty years before, Lin was, like Arad, a young, unknown architect thrust into the political spotlight—but she was even younger and more unknown. It was 1981, and she was a twenty-one–year-old undergraduate at Yale when she suddenly won the competition to design the Vietnam Veterans Memorial, in Washington, D.C. In video footage from her first press conference, you can hardly see her; her long, straight black hair hangs over her face and obscures her eyes and mouth, as if she's hiding from the crush of photographers and reporters yelling questions at her from a few feet away.

Despite her diminutive appearance, Lin was a fierce defender of her radical concept. Instead of a soaring white monument, Lin designed a dark gash in the earth—a long, low wall of black granite that listed dead soldiers' names. When Lin's design was unveiled, politicians and many veterans attacked it as unpatriotic and dwelling in America's defeat. They attacked Lin too, questioning why an Asian-American was picked, and for months Lin was ridiculed in the press. But Lin fought, testified, and ultimately prevailed, and after "the Wall," as it came to be called, was unveiled, veterans and practically everyone else embraced it as an elegant, intimate representation of their experiences.

One of the memorial's most popular features was also its most controversial: the way Lin listed veterans' names. Rather than list them alphabetically, Lin ordered the names chronologically by year of death. The Wall grows taller as the war proceeds, and more die. For Lin, the chronological listing was nonnegotiable—instead of crucial battles and famous generals, the Wall tells a story of the immense loss of ordinary soldiers' lives. For many veterans' families, however, this element was, at first, new and confusing, and they fought it. How would anyone find their family member's name? Lin's solution—a book near the memorial that would provide the coordinates of each name—initially struck many families as cumbersome and burdensome. But after it was unveiled, many willingly, thoughtfully, performed the work. The act of finding a name—walking to the book, looking it up, walking back to the Wall, discovering and touching the carved letters with their finger-tips—became a defining part of the memorial process. Lin's memorial was experiential as well as architectural. Her concept worked.

Lin's unlikely success proves a well-worn lesson: what stands as time-honored is often despised at first. But few seemed able to hold this thought during the Ground Zero memorial competition. Everyone, of course, wanted the brilliance of Lin's design, but no one wanted to go through the pain of adjusting to something new. (Later, people would read a fictional account of such a battle in Amy Waldman's *The Submission*, which imagines an Islamic woman winning the memorial competition.) Tellingly, many victims' families simply wanted Lin to design the Ground Zero memorial. They wanted already established greatness, and perhaps even a design that looked something like her original. When Lin agreed to serve on the jury, people were pleased but also disappointed—her appointment meant that she wouldn't be submitting her own vision. It was an elegant way to let everyone know she had no desire to design the Ground Zero memorial.

One of the reasons Lin liked Arad was that she believed he had the stamina to persist in the face of endless controversies and challenges.

And the first controversy was already under way before Arad had even won—before the competition was even announced, in fact. It had to do with names.

The issue was status. Many families of rescue workers and fire-fighters believed that their loved ones were different from others killed in the towers, and they wanted the memorial to mark them differently. Because first responders ran into the buildings while others tried to get out, the families said, they were heroes. Perhaps rescue workers could be grouped separately from everyone else, they suggested, or a distinguishing symbol, like a shield, could appear by their name. These requests quickly upset civilian families, however, who complained that it would create a hierarchy of victims, and maybe even an inaccurate one. Certainly some civilians died helping others, they argued. Before the specter of names etched permanently in stone loomed, the dodge to the hero question had been simply to call everyone a hero. This was how the Port Authority did it on its fence a year after the attacks; "The Heroes of September 11," read the title of the alphabetical list of victims. But this was no longer good enough. After first responders' families made their requests, the non–service member families asked for identifying symbols or information next to *their* relatives' names, something that marked the company they worked for, perhaps, or the floor they worked on. Everyone wanted a distinguishing marker.

When Arad won, his plan for listing names only fanned the flames. Arad proposed listing victims' names in random rather than alpha-betical order, to reflect the randomness of who lived and who died on 9/11. This seemed crazy to almost all the victims' families. Though far from a homogenous group, if they agreed on anything, it was that they wanted *more* clarity and order surrounding their family mem-bers' deaths, not artsy, abstract "randomness." (Even a member of the battle-averse Philadelphia Families support group circulated a peti-tion against the randomness plan.) Listing names in such a way as to enshrine the chaos of 9/11 seemed to them a terrible idea.

The ordinary solution—an alphabetical listing of names—was problematic for Arad for the same reason it was problematic for Maya Lin: it was meaningless. "Two people share the same last name and they end up having their names side by side because of an alphabetical arrangement," Arad explained. "Two other people might have been married but didn't share the same last name, and wouldn't have their names side by side. There would be an inherent inadequacy in that solution."

Arad did have a backup idea, though. He called it "meaningful adjacencies." He imagined listing names in a way that captured the relationships people had formed at the World Trade Center, whether relationships of years or only a few hours. "The reasons could be whatever was important to the family member," Arad said. "If it was that people had been friends or coworkers or related to one another or had gone to college or these two widows might have met after the attack and wanted the names of their husbands there, even though [the husbands] never knew each other."

"We had two Michael Patrick Finches," Arad recalled. "There is no way to distinguish between them if the only information is their name … [but] if you went and saw his name next to a friend or relative, you would know which one that is. Even if you go to a cemetery and see two people that have the same name, their placement in different parts give them individuality."

Arad suggested this concept to the Lower Manhattan Development Corporation soon after he won the memorial competition, but the agency rejected the idea as too complex. For a group of twenty, a hundred, or five hundred people, perhaps it was possible to collect the necessary information and meaningfully adjoin their names. But a group of nearly three thousand? Not possible. The LMDC chose to stick with the randomness plan, and victims' families continued to fight it.

The random listing of names wasn't the only upsetting feature of Arad's plan for many families. In some ways, it only epitomized the larger problem: abstractness. The square voids, the waterfalls, the pools, and the plaza constituted a very minimalist design. It was about a concept—loss—more than it was about what actually happened on 9/11. There was nothing that dramatized the events of the day. And many families wanted people to understand 9/11 beyond a general feeling of loss, however beautifully represented. Arad's original design didn't include any of the artifacts collected from the site, the pieces of dramatically twisted steel and crushed vehicles, nor any sort of exhibit space for it. When Maya Lin and the jury suggested he add such a space, Arad sketched out the confines of an underground center to display select objects, but that was as far as he would go, and many families remained unsatisfied. To help Arad better understand what families wanted, Christy Ferer, the widow of the Port Authority director and a liaison to victims' families for the Mayor's Office, took Arad on a trip. They went to an airplane hangar at John F. Kennedy Airport, Hangar 17.

I WENT TO HANGAR 17 AT ROUGHLY the same time as Arad, in the spring of 2004. Three large American flags hung high on one wall, the only color in the vast space. In one corner was a makeshift conference room/office. But the majority of the hangar's eighty thousand square feet was dedicated to steel, sorted by size and type.

Around the hangar's periphery lay the "large objects." Tons of enormous steel beams and pillars were stacked on top of one another, to a standard height of about five to seven feet. Some pieces were covered with thick tarps to protect their deteriorating surfaces. Some were still rod straight, charred but uncompromised, while others formed immense curlicues and twists, as if shaped by a mysterious welder. A walkway marked by back tape ran alongside the steel, and separated it from a cluster of four softly humming, temperature-controlled rooms in the center. This is where they kept the "small objects." One contained shelves of distinctive items recovered from the shopping concourse that lay under the towers, including a dusty, charred, life-size Bugs Bunny from the Warner Brothers Studio Store (the only item that could reasonably be described as "small"). Another room was dedicated to the pounded, mangled automobiles found around the site: crushed police cars, half of a taxi cab, and fire trucks with doors and hoods smashed in.

The collection belonged to the Port Authority, which had appointed a three-person team (two architects and a city planner) to gather objects from Ground Zero a few weeks after the towers fell. The team's initial goal was to help engineers decipher a structural history of the towers' destruction—what fell first, why certain structures stood longer than others, and what fire destroyed. This mandate required them to collect objects that bore marks of particular kinds of destruction—from fire, from collapse, from explosion. But as the team navigated the heaping tons of burning rubble, and saw with their own eyes the extent of crushed building parts, they expanded their criteria to include items that would inform a broader understanding. "It could almost be broken down into three different chapters," Mark Wagner, the head of the Port Authority's collection team, said. "The Trade Center before September eleventh, the Trade Center on September eleventh, and the Trade Center after—the community [of rescue workers, and construction workers] that was developing." After a few months, Wagner and his team had identified 217 pieces that they felt best told this story, and began transferring them to Hangar 17, the only place they could find large enough to house it all.

That spring, Wagner and his team had wrapped up their extensive cataloguing efforts—photographing, classifying, and preserving each object—and were at work on the final step: publishing all this information in large books for city and museum officials. Wagner fashioned the hangar as a kind of meta-museum, an archive out of which collectors would select objects to shape the stories they hoped to tell. He imagined the material would go to a range of places—city, state, and national museums, as well as smaller groups, like firehouses or regional memorial centers that had been requesting pieces of WTC steel. But the most iconic pieces, he believed, would go to Ground Zero. Exactly how they would be used there, however, remained uncertain.

Touring the hangar was overwhelming. My most lasting impressions were of the hulking pieces of steel stacked in rows and the plain shelves displaying objects arranged by size, fragility, and type. It was neatly organized chaos. Simple and bare. There was no text or elaborately constructed case to distract you from the twisted steel beam or the mangled metal that only barely resembled a car. There was nothing else to look at but the pieces themselves and the power they conveyed. It was the kind of devastation that only the collapse of two 110-story buildings could create. It was a completely modern sort of violence.

Talk about the meaning of these objects made Mark Wagner nervous. Despite the accelerated efforts to collect objects, Wagner didn't think it was his job to determine what should be known and remembered about 9/11. "We really wanted to keep the options as open as possible, and didn't want to decide what was going to speak to you," he said. "It was really just to get a little bit of everything, get a good cross section, because, how do we explain this event, how do we explain the Trade Center prior to it, how do we explain this whole thing to, you know, your grandchildren?" Wagner minimized his role in the creation of history. But touring the rubble, it was clear that the hangar was already telling a story, it was already providing a raw and powerful museum experience. Indeed, one city official who received a tour that spring told Wagner she believed the hangar, as it stood, should become the future exhibit space at the WTC site. In her opinion, it was the most powerful way to represent the history of 9/11.

Much of this story was told in the final two rooms. One housed the most delicate and unique objects—a half-dozen jagged mounds of compressed concrete, steel, and office items created by the power of the towers' collapse and ensuing fire. The mounds stood in a row in the center of the room, each one resting on a specially made pedestal. Wagner estimated that each three-foot-high mound contained roughly four or five building stories, compressed together. Poking out from the mounds, one might find a sliver of paper or a corner of a file cabinet that for some reason had not been consumed during the collapse and fire.

The last room provided work space to a small crew of engineers busy stabilizing deteriorating steel beams. Some of the collection's most prized objects were in this room. Two engineers worked to preserve a piece of the façade of the North Tower, which formed the often-photographed "chip" rising out of the heaps of rubble in the fall of 2001. It had obtained a kind of mythic status among those collecting items from the site. "Everyone said, 'Make sure you get that piece,'" Wagner recalled. Wagner's team dismantled it at the site, numbering and coding each section so that it could someday be reassembled. Engineers were also working on the surface of the last steel beam—the symbolic piece rolled out of the site in a coffin to mark the end of the rescue and recovery missions. The beam had acquired layers of messages and signatures from those who had worked on the pile during the previous nine months, and was one of the few objects that represented all three chapters Wagner had described: the tower's creation, its destruction, and the work of those clearing wreckage. These objects signaled resilience and recovery alongside loss and trauma.

I didn't have a chance to ask Arad what he made of Hangar 17. One news article reported that he grew teary-eyed during his tour. But whatever his emotional reaction, the tour did not prompt him to alter his memorial design, as many victims' families wanted. Arad declined to add pieces of steel to aboveground walkways or to his plaza. Instead, Arad decided the artifacts would go solely in the underground interpretive center, which he had already added at the jury's request. This, he decided, was enough.

CHAPTER 10

THE FREEDOM CENTER

WHEN MICHAEL ARAD ADDED AN INTERPRETIVE MEMORIAL center to his design, he was actually creating the second Ground Zero museum. Plans were already in the works for a separate museum in one of the site's designated "cultural buildings," adjacent to the memorial. This was to be an independent institution, tasked not with remembering 9/11 or telling the history of the attacks, but with considering the broader context and implications of 9/11. It was going to take on the *big* story, the one that no one had yet touched. It was going to explore what 9/11 meant.

This museum was the brainchild of Tom Bernstein, a New York City developer who was in fact much more than that. Bernstein was a close friend and former business partner of President George W. Bush. They had owned the Texas Rangers baseball team together, along with another close friend of the president's, Roland Betts (who was one of the fifteen board members of the Lower Manhattan Development Corporation, the body overseeing the WTC rebuilding effort). But

Bernstein's friendship with the president wasn't the only interesting thing about him. His father, Robert Bernstein, was the founding chairman of Human Rights Watch, and Bernstein was board president of Human Rights First, a nonpartisan advocacy group that tended to lean left. In addition, Bernstein sat on the board of the U.S. Holocaust Memorial Museum, the Council on Foreign Relations, and Mayor Bloomberg's transition team. Bernstein's connections cut across partisan lines; they didn't make neat political sense.

Not long after 9/11, Bernstein imagined a museum at the WTC site dedicated to the concept of freedom. He spent the next two years signing up advisory board members and fleshing out his idea. Bernstein imagined a top-notch, cutting-edge institution with exhibits, lectures, and seminars curated and delivered by the country's best-known scholars, writers, and public intellectuals. Henry Louise Gates Jr., Fareed Zakaria, Anne-Marie Slaughter, and Bob Kerrey, the former governor and senator from Nebraska, all agreed to be involved. First they called it Freedom Center, then the International Freedom Center; its organizing principal was "humankind's enduring quest for freedom"—a mission at once ambitious and mind-bogglingly nebulous.

"We're a work in progress," Bernstein told the *New York Times* in the summer of 2004, when the LMDC officially chose it to be part of the site's cultural buildings. (The museum went through the required selection process, but Bernstein's vision was always a leading contender because of his contacts.) The paper headlined its story "Freedom Center Is Still a Somewhat Vague Notion."

The team assembling the Freedom Center was well aware that Bernstein's friendship with the president, as well as the institution's name and defining premise, risked creating a certain impression, particularly in New York City. "This, as you know, is not a terribly conservative town," said Richard Tofel, president and chief operating officer of the Freedom Center, as well as a friend and former neighbor of Bernstein's. "We always figured that one day there would be some sort of political attack on us from the left.... We were very much in line with some of the things that the President was saying, particularly back in early 2005."

Tofel outed himself as a Democrat when we spoke, but he cited President Bush's second inaugural address, in particular, as informing the mission and spirit of the Freedom Center. "We have seen our vulnerability—and we have seen its deepest source," the president said in January 2005. "For as long as whole regions of the world simmer in resentment and tyranny—prone to ideologies that feed hatred and excuse murder—violence will gather, and multiply in destructive power, and cross the most defended borders, and raise a mortal threat. There is only one force of history that can break the reign of hatred and resentment, and expose the pretensions of tyrants, and reward the hopes of the decent and tolerant, and that is the force of human freedom." Despite his liberal leanings, Tofel was sympathetic to the president's vision. "I do think...that what began on 9/11 is a global struggle between forces of freedom and forces of intolerance and unfreedom," he said.

Tofel had personal connections to 9/11 too. Before joining the Freedom Center's staff, Tofel was assistant publisher of the *Wall Street Journal*, located across the street from the World Trade Center. He was at work when the planes struck the Twin Towers. "I thought the Freedom Center could be my answer to the question, 'What did you do in the war [on terror]?'" Tofel said. "It seemed to me quite an unusual opportunity."

After Tofel joined the staff, his team spent the next year developing a business plan, raising money, designing the building, and defining the content of the museum. They had a large space—250,000 square feet—and decided to use it for a range of purposes, including documenting historical injustices, like the Russian gulags, and chronicling contemporary campaigns against human rights abuses around the world. They planned a space at the end of the museum called "Freedom's Future," devoted to signing visitors up for public service. Meanwhile, the Aspen Institute agreed to work with a consortium of universities to plan lectures, conferences, and seminars. Bernstein and Tofel made concerted efforts to be bipartisan in their advisory appointments. John Raisian, director of the Hoover Institution, was an advisor, but so was Anthony Romero of the ACLU. And they made sure that museum programming would document the full story of freedom here in the United States, including its chapters of oppression and inequality alongside the championing of rights. "You can't talk about freedom without talking about slavery," Tofel said. "It's intellectually dishonest." For the most part, the museum didn't have many explicit connections to 9/11, except in one of its first galleries, where it planned to display an artifact from each of the eighty-two countries that lost citizens that day.

The inevitable attack against the Freedom Center came when news of the museum's programming spread, but it wasn't from the left, as they had expected. The left wasn't thrilled with the Freedom Center, of course. Reviewing it in the *Times*, architecture critic Nicolai Ouroussoff wrote that the museum's design "implies a direct connection between the cataclysm of 9/11 and a global struggle for 'freedom'—a bit of simplistic propaganda," adding that "Freedom Center is bound to be viewed by much of the world as a jingoistic propaganda tool."

But that was as far as any left-leaning critique got before being drowned out by a much louder attack from the political right. Writing in the *Wall Street Journal*, under the headline "The Great Ground Zero Heist," Debra Burlingame attacked the Freedom Center as inappropriate and unpatriotic. "Rather than a respectful tribute to our individual and collective loss, they will get a slanted history lesson, a didactic lecture on the meaning of liberty in a post-9/11 world," she wrote. "They will be served up a heaping foreign policy discussion over the greater meaning of Abu Ghraib and what it portends for the country and the rest of the world."

Burlingame's brother was a pilot on the flight that crashed into the Pentagon, and she was a member of the board of the 9/11 Memorial Foundation. Early in her op-ed, the museum's non-9/11 content seemed to be Burlingame's primary concern. Burlingame writes that the museum treated "important subjects" but "for somewhere—anywhere—else." As the essay progresses, however, she shifts her attention to what she believes is the political agenda of the museum and its advisors, a list of people she calls a "Who's Who of the human rights, Guantanamo-obsessed world."

"What does it mean that the 'story of humankind's quest for freedom' doesn't include the kind which is fought for with the blood and tears of patriots?" she asks. "It means, I fear, that this is a freedom center which will not use the word 'patriot' the way our Founding Fathers did." Burlingame ends her essay with a populist appeal. "Ground Zero has been stolen, right from under our noses. How do we get it back?"

The op-ed caused a furor. The next day conservative pundit Michelle Malkin cribbed from Burlingame's essay and ratcheted up the rhetoric, in her own piece called "The Desecration of Ground Zero." "A Blame America Monument is not what we need or deserve," she wrote. "Do we really want Ground Zero to be the playground of anti-war financiers, moral equivalence peddlers, and Guantanamo Bay alarmists?" Soon, another conservative pundit, Robert Sherbet, based in California, registered the domain name takebackthememorial.org. He contacted Burlingame, and together they started a movement to defeat the Freedom Center.

It took three months.

Tom Bernstein, Richard Tofel, and their many supporters and backers tried to save it. Tofel quickly wrote his own op-ed in the *Wall Street Journal*. He quoted Bush's second inaugural speech and Abraham Lincoln's Gettysburg Address and made a call to rise above politics. "To be sure, the International Freedom Center will host debates and note points of view with which you—and I—will disagree. But this is the point, the proof of our society's enduring self-confidence and humanity," he wrote. "It will not exist to precisely define freedom or tell people what to think but to get them to think—and to act in the service of freedom as they see it. And it will always do so in a manner respectful of the victims of September 11." The Freedom Center had victims' families on its advisory board too.

But Tofel and Bernstein were caught completely off guard by the attack, and never really regained control of the public conversation. They had actually talked to Burlingame before she published her op-ed, but she played her cards close to her chest. "She came to see us a couple of weeks before that and, uh, we had a lovely chat," Tofel said, "during which she never told us that she had already written a piece attacking us."

"I didn't tell them," Burlingame said, "because I really felt that I was working with people who were much bigger than me, much more powerful than me, incredibly connected. I mean, look at them, look at the cast of characters. And I thought, why give them any advantage?"

TOM BERNSTEIN AND RICHARD TOFEL WERE NOT ON par with Larry Silverstein and George Pataki, of course. But Debra Burlingame saw them as part of the same group—a group of "cultural elites," as she called them. Powerful, wealthy, well-connected men who, as she understood it, had pretty much gotten to do what they wanted when it came to rebuilding. To her eyes, the Freedom Center was part of this exclusive process too. "I really felt, and I know now, they did a lot of this behind closed doors," she said. "It was really sneaky and I really resented that, because, who the hell are they to decide, not just for New York, but for the entire country, what 9/11 is going to be about?

"To appropriate that site, behind closed doors, for a project that was going to be, I mean they were going to be, at the very end of their museum journey, they were going to have a thing called 'public engagement' where they were going to literally be signing people up to be working for human rights organizations. Inside the museum. Tom Bernstein, at that point, was president of Human Rights First. This is an organization that goes down to Hugo Chavez country and pimps oil for Harlem. Give me a break."

The Freedom Center controversy was Burlingame's coming-out. She soon became something of a celebrity, frequently giving interviews and appearing on television to weigh in on the latest downtown kerfuffle. After spending some time with her, it was easy to see why. She's great fun to talk to, disarming, passionate, persuasive, charming.

"So you're prepared to meet a right-wing, uber-patriotic, George Bush girl?" she asked, moments after sitting down at our table in a café above Grand Central Station. I laughed and nodded. I appreciated her remark; it cleared the air.

Before 9/11, Burlingame worked as a flight attendant, then became a lawyer, and then worked as a producer for Court TV. She had also been a registered Democrat—"Gore girl, Clinton girl," she said. But then her brother was killed, and her politics gradually changed. "I wanted to know what happened in the cockpits of those four planes; I wanted to know every detail of what happened on that day. It became sort of a quest, to witness, for my brother, what happened," she said. "I wanted to know how an attack like 9/11 could have succeeded." Burlingame began to read political philosophy about national intelligence agencies, and found herself growing more critical of large, bureaucratic institutions. As her politics became more conservative, she founded a group called 9/11 Families for a Safe and Strong America, and began writing blogs and op-eds about national security and politics. Her big break came in 2004, when the *Wall Street Journal* published an op-ed she penned to take on a group of 9/11 families critical of President Bush. The president, running for reelection, had used footage from 9/11 in a campaign ad, and some victims' families objected. Burlingame thought their protests were ridiculous, so she wrote a piece that, as she put it, "just slammed these families in as nice a way as I could." Not long after, Burlingame was invited to serve on the board of the 9/11 Memorial Foundation. While no one ever told her why they picked her, Burlingame speculates it was because she had established herself as someone who dared to break with 9/11 families.

"I think they perceived me as someone who would give some push-back against some of the families that were maybe giving them trouble, who were not going along with the program," she said. Burlingame imagines they saw her as "somebody who we can enlist who's going to help us get done what we want to get done. And that always amuses me."

Burlingame learned, and grew concerned, about plans to build the Freedom Center while at a board meeting. No one could answer her questions about what the Freedom Center would be to her satisfaction, so she began investigating. She found its list of advisors, which included scholars who had been publicly critical of the Bush administration. And then she heard someone describe the center as a "public square on sacred ground." "When you say 'a public square on sacred ground,' to me, I'm picturing the Speakers' Corner in Hyde Park," she said. "I'm picturing controversy and contention where all these people died."

After Burlingame published her piece in the *Journal* and started the website with Robert Sherbet, they steadily built a grassroots movement. They reached out to potential allies, hosted rallies, circulated petitions, held press conferences, and wrote press releases. They made sure the forward momentum never slowed. "When there wasn't news happening," Burlingame said, "we'd make news." They held more press conferences, wrote more press releases. "We always wanted to create the impression that we were funded, organized, backed by people with money, that we had a PR firm, maybe two, that was doing all this for us," Burlingame said. "None of that was true."

To appeal to conservative media, and to encourage them to link to the organization's website, Burlingame highlighted the liberal politics of select advisory members and the Freedom Center's desire to "talk about America's warts," as she put it, "to teach children it's been a bumpy road to freedom." But to reach victims' families, including those who didn't share her politics, Burlingame took a different tack. She highlighted the Freedom Center's dedication to events beyond 9/11. Moreover, she emphasized that the institution would turn Ground Zero into a political place, which many victims' families, tired of politics, didn't want. What most victims' families wanted, after all, was a memorial. And with half of Ground Zero's acreage already devoted to commerce and retail, it appeared the memorial was already being crowded out. Many victims' families groups felt they had already been accommodating enough. They didn't think they should be asked to give up more land for another project they believed was unconnected to memorialization.

Burlingame didn't necessarily plan in advance to appeal to these two disparate constituencies (as she confessed, very little was planned in advance), but Take Back the Memorial was most potent when it managed to speak to both the conservative blogosphere and 9/11 families. "9/11 Not 'World History,'" read one of the signs they hoisted during a rally at Ground Zero. Another read, "America, they are hijacking your memorial."

As the summer progressed, the movement gained steam. By August, its online petition had collected over thirty-eight thousand signatures, about two thousand of whom self-identified as victims' family members. (9/11 family members were some of the most vocal protestors, but the vast majority of the organizations' supporters were always interested citizens.) "An international freedom center should express varied and conflicting points of view," penned a letter writer to the *Times*. "The place for this is not on the graves of those who were murdered by terrorists." Until this point, Governor Pataki had backed the Freedom Center, but then he began to equivocate. He held a press conference demanding a guarantee from it and the other organizations in the cultural complex that they never offend 9/11 families or memorial visitors, a request exactly as unreasonable as it sounds. "I view that memorial site as sacred ground, akin to the beaches of Normandy or Pearl Harbor, and we will not tolerate anything on that site that denigrates America, denigrates New York or freedom, or denigrates the sacrifice or courage that the heroes showed on September 11," Pataki said at the time.

After Pataki's statement, the *New York Times* editorial page chimed in. "By attempting to appease one small, vocal group of protestors who are unlikely to be appeased anyway, [Pataki] is abrogating the rights of everyone else," the editorial read, under the headline "Keeping Ground Zero Free." "And he runs the risk of turning ground zero into a place where we bury the freedoms that define this nation." Now that the right's opposition to the Freedom Center was in full swing, the left's defense—or, more accurately, its attack of the opposition—could begin. But it hardly mattered; the unraveling of the Freedom Center was already in motion. After Pataki's decree, scholars began to remove themselves from its advisory board. To keep up the pressure, Burlingame and company soon called for a boycott of all memorial fundraising. "I was actually worried that I was going to get kicked off the board," Burlingame said, who was required, as a board member, to raise funds for the memorial. "But one of the things I felt we needed to do here was make this so controversial that no one would give it any money." Fund-raising began to stall. And then came the movement's coup de grace.

It was the fourth anniversary of 9/11, and New York senator (and soon-to-be presidential candidate) Hillary Clinton was attending memorial services in the bottom of the pit. One of the principal organizers of Take Back the Memorial, a victim's family member named Anthony Gardner, was standing behind her. He yelled over— "Senator Clinton!"—and told her that the firefighters' union was about to announce its opposition to the Freedom Center. "Are you going to stand with the union and stand with us?" he asked. "Are you against the Freedom Center?" "Yeah, I'm against that too," Clinton said. There had been no meeting, no formal conversation—just a few seconds of spontaneous exchange with Senator Clinton during the memorial ceremony. But it was enough for a press release, which Burlingame's team posted a few hours later, announcing Clinton's opposition to the Freedom Center. The *New York Post* quickly picked it up. Soon, former mayor Rudolph Giuliani and Governor Pataki noticed, as did Senator Clinton herself. A few days later, Clinton issued a formal statement opposing the center. Then Giuliani, also preparing a campaign for president, came out against it, and a few days later, Governor Pataki officially barred the Freedom Center from Ground Zero.

"SHE CAME OUT US AGAINST US, AND THAT WAS the end," Richard Tofel said. "Because then Giuliani, who we had worked very hard to keep on the fence, sent word that the families were a key political constituency of his, and he could not let her get out ahead of him politically with the families. So if Hillary was against us, he had to be against us. And then the governor said, 'I can't, I won't, fight Hillary and Rudy on the same side on this.' The whole thing was as deeply cynical as anything I've seen in politics."

Not surprisingly, Governor Pataki saw it differently. "We gave the public the chance to react, so they didn't just wake up one day and see this there, and ultimately it was clear that this was not the right thing to have at the site," he said. "So we decided it wouldn't be there." To Pataki, it was evidence of an "open process." When Pataki barred the Freedom Center and superseded, yet again, the authority of the Lower Manhattan Development Corporation, which the governor had tasked with determining the museum's fate, LMDC board members were furious, particularly the ones who were friends with Tom Bernstein and Dick Tofel.

Tofel remains considerably bitter about the defeat of the Freedom Center. He now works as general manager of ProPublica, a nonprofit, investigative journalism organization in downtown New York—a few blocks from the WTC site, in fact. But the whole ordeal has left him angry, particularly at the victims' families. "Mothers Against Drunk Driving have had a great effect on stopping people from being allowed to drive drunk. No one has ever suggested that they should be in charge of planning interstate highway systems," he said. "9/11 families don't know anything about museums, they don't know anything about the design of public spaces, they don't know anything about urban planning, they don't know anything about history. They suffered a tragic loss."

As Tofel saw it, he and Tom Bernstein lost a political battle that deftly tapped into the politics of 9/11 and the culture wars, the idea "that anyone on the left is unpatriotic and is trying to destroy America," he said. But he also believed that the failure could be chalked up to timing. Victims' families commanded power over the city and state's ambitious politicians because 9/11 was still emotionally raw. But it wouldn't always be, Tofel said. He repeatedly noted the significance of the decade's other great urban tragedy, Hurricane Katrina; he thought it played an important role in all this—or, rather, was important precisely because it failed to play a role. Katrina struck just before Pataki barred the Freedom Center, and Tofel reasoned that had the hurricane struck earlier—or had news of the Freedom Center emerged later—the controversy never would have happened. "9/11 victims lost their special status when it became clear that they were not the only victims in this country, and in fact that there were other people who in many ways had it worse," Tofel said. "I mean, would you rather be a 9/11 family member or would you rather have spent Hurricane Katrina in the Superdome?"

It was a dark, dismal question, and though provocative, it was mostly a distraction. Tofel's main point was that 9/11 families—or, really, a select group of politically active 9/11 families—had more power than they deserved. This might have been true. (One of the contradictions of rebuilding is that while the vast majority of victims' families were relatively powerless, every now and then a small group of families dictated major turns in the course of action.) But, of course, it was also true that, in the end, team Freedom Center lost. The well-connected, ideologically nimble friends of President George W. Bush lost a political battle to people with far fewer connections and a lot less money. As Debra Burlingame put it, practically bursting with glee, "this handful of very powerful people got snookered by a bunch of nobodies. Complete nobodies. And it drove them insane."

With the Freedom Center gone, the WTC site added a new problem to its growing list: Ground Zero was now museum-less, save for the interpretive memorial center that Michael Arad added, in part to display some artifacts from Hangar 17. No one knew what story the interpretive center would tell, but after the Freedom Center uproar, it was not likely to tell a story that Debra Burlingame, in particular, found too disagreeable. After all, she had won, and, as she reminded me, "the victors write the history, right?"

THE TAKE BACK THE MEMORIAL MOVEMENT predated the Tea Party by about four years, and seemed to me to presage its tactics and messaging. Both were grassroots efforts powered by passionate, frustrated people. And both were driven by a desire to confront the country's elites, to take something—the memorial, the country—back from the powerful interests that they felt controlled it. Debra Burlingame didn't see it this way. Their goals and stakes were very different, she said. One focused on a museum, the other on the government's role in public life. The Tea Party was a political operation, she said, while Take Back the Memorial was dedicated to removing politics from Ground Zero. "This really was not political," Burlingame said. "It was very important to us that we were all on the same page. One of our signs said, 'No Politics at Ground Zero.' That was a big slogan of ours."

To Burlingame, it was the other side, the Freedom Center side, which was political. Of course, to an outsider, there would likely be little difference. After all, cornering Hillary Clinton at a memorial service was about as political as you could get in New York. But I knew what Burlingame was getting at. It was the long-standing idea that Ground Zero wasn't a place for business and politics as usual. It was the idea that Ground Zero was sacred, perhaps in multiple ways, and that it should be a place where people aspired to something unifying.

The Take Back the Memorial slogan "No Politics at Ground Zero" was tricky, though, because it evoked two different meanings of the word *politics*. One was a question of tactics, of trying to win a battle in the public sphere; Take Back the Memorial was certainly political in this sense. But the other was a question of philosophy, of believing in the value and maybe even nobility of contention and debate. This was the ethos of the Freedom Center; it aimed to foster discussion about America and its role in the world. And some people just didn't want that at the WTC site.

I appreciated the spirit of the slogan, and even shared it myself at times. But the truth was, Freedom Center or no Freedom Center, Ground Zero was going to be political for a while. People thought Ground Zero should transcend politics for many reasons, one of them being that it brought so many groups together. But this was also the very reason it never *could* transcend politics. This was the reason it was the most political place imaginable. Ground Zero brought people together who wanted different things. It brought people together who never otherwise would have been in the same place, like Richard Tofel and Debra Burlingame.

In November 2001, the wreckage was most visible at the intersection of Fulton and Broadway Streets.

Memorials filled the fence around St. Paul's Chapel, one block from the World Trade Center site, in December 2002.

During the first year after the attacks, graffiti covered practically every surface on the streets around Ground Zero; "America the Re-Build-iful" was one of the common refrains.

Some people engaged in heated exchanges. One wrote: "Our grief is not a cry of war, . . ."

Another large shrine decorated the intersection of Greenwich and Park Streets.

In September 2002, the Port Authority cleared the areas immediately around the WTC site of homemade memorials and barred future ones on its new fence. In the sixteen acre pit, construction workers repaired the foundation.

While no one was supposed to write on the new fence, a few continued to leave their mark.

A man who used to live near the World Trade Center visited the site for the first time in 2003 and held his infant son so that he could see into the site too.

Between 2006 and 2008, controversies and conflict threatened to upend the rebuilding effort. During the seventh anniversary, in September 2008, a woman asked the question no one knew the answer to: "Where is Osama Bin Laden?"

In September 2010, rebuilding began to move forward and the memorial pools began to take shape. The eastern bathtub, along the bottom of the photograph, was excavated.

On the ninth anniversary of 9/11, this family from Florida joined thousands of others on the streets around the WTC site to protest an Islamic Center and mosque on Park Street, two blocks from Ground Zero.

One block from the WTC site, a polar bear offered "free hugs" during the protests against the Islamic Center and mosque. The bear said he was "agnostic" on the question of the mosque.

In the fall of 2011, a protestor in Zuccotti Park, catty-corner to Ground Zero, told people to "Wake Up" as part of Occupy Wall Street.

In October 2011, construction on the Freedom Tower had reached the 82nd floor.

The North Tower memorial pool sits just to the south of the Freedom Tower, the base of which is visible in the upper left of the photograph.

Red carnations on the parapet of names around the South Tower memorial pool, October 2011.

CHAPTER 11

THINGS FALL BEHIND

B Y LATE FALL 2005, POLITICS HAD BROUGHT PRACTICALLY everything at Ground Zero to a standstill. It wasn't clear what sort of museum would stand at the site. Victims' families continued to fight with architects, with the Lower Manhattan Development Corporation, and among themselves over the memorial design. And after the police inquiry and second redesign, construction was stalled on the newly fortified Freedom Tower.

Mayor Michael Bloomberg was one of the many people watching the unraveling. But he occupied a novel position in relation to Ground Zero. On the one hand, he lacked any sort of official role in the project—the land belonged to the Port Authority, making Governor Pataki the de facto leader—and this meant he couldn't be blamed for the chaos and incompetence. On the other hand, he was the mayor of New York City, which meant he had considerable interest in the site's future, as well as a significant bully pulpit at his disposal. That fall, Bloomberg asked some staff at the city's Economic Development Corporation to draft a report on the rebuilding effort. The EDC was

the wing of city government that handled big building and reconstruction projects, and it had been keeping tabs on the WTC site for a few
years. "Everyone knew there was something wrong at the WTC site,"
Seth Pinsky, who wrote the report, told me. "But nobody knew what
it was. We believed we had figured it out." In the midst of all the
problems plaguing Ground Zero, Pinsky's team identified another one:
insolvency.

Pinsky investigated how much money developer Larry Silverstein had
on hand (mostly from his insurance payout, which awarded Silverstein
nearly $5 billion), how much it would cost to construct Freedom Tower
and the site's four additional skyscrapers, and how Silverstein would
finance the buildings. The report found that Freedom Tower, which
accounted for a quarter of the site's commercial space, was going to cost
over $2 billion, and the commercial half of the project was likely to cost
over $7 billion. Because of the site's underground infrastructure and the
towers' upgraded security features, building at Ground Zero was more
expensive than building anywhere else in the city. Meanwhile, Pinsky's
analysis showed that the market for commercial space downtown was
struggling. "Given the rents they were likely to get at the WTC site,
the buildings themselves had negative value," Pinsky said. "The value
implied by revenues was less than the cost of construction." The report's
conclusion, therefore, was grim. "What we realized," Pinsky said, "was
that unless someone came from heaven with a big bag of cash, there was
no way financially to rebuild the entire site."

The report spelled out particularly worrisome consequences for
the Port Authority. It argued that Silverstein would run out of money,
and said that once he did, he could default on his lease and abandon
his obligation to rebuild, leaving the Port Authority with a half-built
site and a substantial gap in its annual revenue. The report concluded
that, under the current ownership structure—meaning, as long as Larry
Silverstein owned all the commercial space—rebuilding was, as Pinsky
put it, "a financial impossibility."

The team at Silverstein Properties ardently refuted the report's conclusions. They had both the funds and the wherewithal to rebuild all the site's buildings, they said. "It was inaccurate," Janno Lieber said of the EDC's report. "But it was sort of a self-fulfilling prophecy, which was, if Silverstein can only get this little rent—as the EDC report projected—then he can't afford to build buildings." Pinsky's analysis assumed that rents would continue to hover where they were at the time, roughly $35 per square foot. Silverstein, however, claimed he would be able to collect higher rates. It was impossible to know who was right at the time. Years later, however, Silverstein would be at least partially vindicated: he would secure rents of $70 and $80 a square foot, more than double the original estimates. "To this day we all joke back and forth about who was right about that," Pinsky said of his estimate, not quite conceding the point. But not all of Pinsky's numbers depended upon predicting the future. Silverstein had received $4.3 billion in insurance proceeds, but because he was paying $120 million a year in rent to the Port Authority, there was only $2.9 billion left. Regardless of what he received per square foot in rent, Silverstein's cash on hand was quite a bit short of the $7 billion it was going to cost to build the site's five skyscrapers.

In the fall of 2005, armed with Pinsky's provocative report, Mayor Bloomberg started to speak out. He wondered aloud if the project wouldn't be better off without Larry Silverstein. Barring Silverstein's departure (which wasn't likely), Bloomberg called for a major "restructuring" at the site, with Silverstein relinquishing control of some of his buildings.

Bloomberg's timing wasn't solely dependent upon the report. Governor Pataki was about to leave office, creating a hole in the decision-making structure downtown. In addition, Larry Silverstein had just asked the city to sign off on billions of dollars in Liberty Bonds. After 9/11, Congress granted $8 billion in tax-exempt bonds to the city and state of New York, and now Silverstein was calling for the city's half of the allocation to help finance rebuilding. Silverstein, in other words, was giving the city what it never had before: leverage.

As the fall progressed, the Port Authority and Governor Pataki joined Bloomberg's quest to pressure Larry Silverstein to renegotiate the terms of his lease. They had their own interests to tend to. The Port Authority was worried about Silverstein's possible default on his lease, as imagined by the report, and Pataki wanted rebuilding to turn a corner in the final days of his gubernatorial term. They told Silverstein that if he wanted the city's billions of dollars in Liberty Bonds, he was going to have to cede some of his property. Giving up some of his ten million square feet of office space to the Port Authority would make rebuilding more efficient, they argued, because the Port Authority and Silverstein could build at the same time.

For the next four months, Silverstein, the Port Authority, Governor Pataki, and Mayor Bloomberg engaged in a series of brutal negotiations. "It was one of the most complicated things I've ever worked on," Seth Pinsky said. Pinsky would go on to become president of the city's Economic Development Corporation and oversee the city's response to the 2008 economic crash. For Janno Lieber at Silverstein Properties, the negotiations were "the lowest moment that we can remember," he said.

One of the primary sticking points was Freedom Tower. Over the past two years, the signature building had become the white elephant of rebuilding. Once the object of everyone's desire—Silverstein engaged in months of ugly fights and a lawsuit simply to ensure that his architect designed it rather than master planner Daniel Libeskind—it was now the bane of rebuilding. It was the most expensive to build because it was the tallest and most symbolic and therefore mandated an exceptionally high level of security. All sides imagined it would be the most difficult to rent for the same reasons: its height and symbolism could make it a terrorism target. The irony was impossible to ignore: the same features that made Freedom Tower a symbol of resilience and

American power also made it vulnerable to attack. The popular icon of the rebuilding effort was now the least commercially viable skyscraper at the site.

Silverstein had his own problems with Freedom Tower. He never liked the building's symbolism, its aspiration to echo the Statue of Liberty or to stand at precisely 1,776 feet tall. He built commercial skyscrapers, not symbols. And he hated the tower's location. Silverstein wanted Freedom Tower to stand on the southeast corner of the site, where it would be as close as possible to Wall Street and a new transit hub. But Daniel Libeskind placed Freedom Tower in the northwest corner of the site, where it would best create the echo of the Statue of Liberty. Governor Pataki backed Libeskind on that battle, and the skyscraper stayed put. Which irritated Silverstein for years.

Early in the negotiations, Bloomberg and the Port Authority suggested that Silverstein give up three buildings and keep the Freedom Tower and a second skyscraper. But Silverstein wouldn't have it. He didn't want to lose any of his property, but if he had to give something up to get the Liberty Bonds, he told them, then rest assured, Freedom Tower would be part of the exchange. Governor Pataki, who wanted a (second) groundbreaking for Freedom Tower in April, asked all sides in the negotiations to come to an agreement in mid-March. But it wasn't to be. On the eve of the deadline, when many parties thought a deal was close, Silverstein made a new offer. He would give up Freedom Tower, he said, and nothing more.

The Port Authority walked out of the negotiations, and then it spoke out. "He clearly demonstrated that greed is his main motivation," vice chairman of the Port Authority Charles Gargano said of Silverstein. "We will walk away rather than make a bad deal for the Port Authority, the city and the nation."

Neither Silverstein nor Janno Lieber would forget being called greedy. "It was an ugly moment," Lieber said.

But it wasn't ugly enough to derail a business deal. Within days, everyone was back at the negotiating table, and a month later they signed a deal. Silverstein agreed to give up two properties, one of which was Freedom Tower, in exchange for the city's $3.35 billion in Liberty Bonds, a reduction in his annual rent, and a promise from the city and the Port Authority to lease 1.2 million square feet of office space at market rates. Given the complexity of the deal, it was difficult to parse its winners and losers. Because Silverstein always argued he had the money to rebuild the entire site, giving up two properties was probably something of a concession that there wasn't enough to rebuild. Of course, Silverstein's people disagree; they say they were forced to give up the properties because the city was withholding the Liberty Bonds. But this scenario still suggests a money problem for Silverstein, city officials say: he still needed someone, in this case the city of New York, to give him more. And city officials are probably right. Without the bonds, Silverstein's numbers didn't appear to add up.

But it was only partly a capitulation for Silverstein, because he still retained the site's most commercially-viable skyscrapers, the three buildings planned for the eastern boundary, and handed off the struggling Freedom Tower. At first glance, it wasn't clear why the Port Authority agreed to take Freedom Tower. The Port Authority was never a great commercial developer; it had taken the agency over twenty years to make the original WTC profitable. Indeed, the whole point of the Port Authority's sale of the Twin Towers five years earlier had been to get out of the real estate business. And now it was back in it with the site's least desirable building. But there was logic behind the transfer. "Even if One WTC [Freedom Tower] was a money loser, you had to compare that with an unfinished site," Seth Pinsky said. "It was the cost of One WTC versus the cost of permanently incomplete site."

More important, though, was the Freedom Tower's symbolism and meaning to the governor. Pataki felt very protective of the building, particularly in the face of Silverstein's known dissatisfaction over its location. Pataki and his team feared that if Freedom Tower remained in Silverstein's control, he could postpone construction on it or even "pull the plug on the concept," as Pataki put it. "We were very concerned that Silverstein didn't want it," Pataki said. Silverstein and company disputed this characterization, pointing out that Freedom Tower was the only skyscraper at the site actually in the process of being built. "We designed that building twice," Janno Lieber said, reminding me of its value to Silverstein Properties. "We'd finally gotten it off the ground. We'd bought the job, you know, procured it with all the trade contracts. It was a huge undertaking," he said. "We wanted to build it." But now, instead, the Port Authority would.

And just to make sure no one came along and disrupted construction on Freedom Tower, the Port Authority rushed to lay the steel for the tower's foundation before Pataki left office. "This wasn't a site for a Robert Moses to dictate everything and ram it through, because there was too much appropriate public interest in what was happening, but on the other hand I read [Robert] Caro's book on Robert Moses and how he got things done," Pataki told me, complimenting the way that Moses would complete a project halfway to ensure that the next office holder had to finish it. This was why Pataki wasn't worried when the new governor, Eliot Spitzer, ordered a review of the rebuilding project early in his term. "I knew we were so far along with the Freedom Tower," Pataki said, "there was no way as a practical matter they could pull the plug."

THE COMPLICATED RESTRUCTURING OF GROUND ZERO achieved a few important things downtown. It created a schedule to rebuild the office towers by 2012, setting a series of deadlines and fees if those dates were missed. It transferred the Freedom Tower to the Port Authority. And it established Mayor Bloomberg as a major player in the process (without committing the city to much, except the Liberty

Bonds). What it didn't do was speed up rebuilding or ease tensions or fix the politics downtown. In these respects, the worst was still to come.

In early May, days after Silverstein and the Port Authority signed their deal, bad news hit about the other half of the rebuilding effort, the memorial quadrant. A new report issued by the 9/11 Memorial Foundation, which oversaw the memorial, estimated it would cost close to $1 billion to construct the memorial-museum complex, almost double earlier estimates, and could cost nearly $60 million annually to operate it. As a means of comparison, the Vietnam Veterans Memorial cost $7 million to build, in 1982. The National World War II Memorial, which opened in 2004, cost $182 million. According to the report, the exorbitant price tag stemmed from expensive infrastructure and insurance costs, as well as rising rates for concrete and steel. The report also said that the World Trade Center Memorial Foundation's efforts to fund-raise for the memorial were lagging grossly behind, in part because a number of problems remained unresolved, including how to list victims' names.

The fallout was swift. Mayor Bloomberg declared the costs untenable and many victims' families, once again, were livid. John Whitehead, chairman of both the Lower Manhattan Development Corporation and the 9/11 Memorial Foundation, announced that he would step down, and a few weeks after that, the president and chief executive of the foundation also resigned. Many began to wonder if there would be a memorial at all.

Then the deal between Silverstein and the Port Authority started to unravel. The deal had stipulated a set of ambitious construction deadlines, particularly for Silverstein Properties, but Silverstein's construction timeline depended upon the Port Authority, and this complicated everything. Before Silverstein could start construction on his skyscrapers, the Port Authority needed to build its transit infrastructure, which ran through Silverstein's sites. This meant that when the Port Authority

missed deadlines—which it did repeatedly between 2006 and 2008—
Silverstein missed deadlines too. Everyone saw this coming; the deal
arranged for the Port Authority to pay Silverstein for any delays. But
then, in the fall of 2008, the economy crashed. And history changed
course once again.

After the crash, Silverstein demanded a new deal. Silverstein argued
that if it weren't for the Port Authority's tardiness, he could have built
and financed his buildings in 2006 and 2007, when he believed he could
have signed much higher rents. Instead, he was working in a "post-
Lehman economy," in the worst market since the Great Depression,
and he called upon the Port Authority to increase its payments to him
and help finance his buildings. Not surprisingly, the Port Authority
refused. They had a deal, the Port Authority said, and everyone, not
just Silverstein, was working in a poor economy now. Once again, the
two partners were at a standstill.

As Silverstein and the Port Authority argued, the atmosphere downtown grew bleak. People had been fighting at and over Ground Zero for
seven years, but they had almost always been fighting *for* something.
For a moving memorial, for towering skyscrapers, for reinstating the
street grid, for a Freedom Tower that, in some way or another, echoed
the Statue of Liberty. Even the Port Authority and Larry Silverstein,
plowing forward, arm in arm, to commercially develop the land, had
been fighting for their office space. But now Silverstein and the Port
Authority were simply picking fights with one another, and it was
depressing. For the first time, it seemed entirely plausible that Ground
Zero might remain a hole in the ground for decades. It seemed that
all the fights might have been for nothing. The intransigence between
Silverstein and the Port Authority, coupled with the memorial's freefall,
crushed any remaining sense of anticipation or possibility downtown.
As each side talked to their lawyers and prepared for another round
of litigation, Ground Zero stopped being stormy and impassioned and
instead became quiet. It became a little weird.

ON SEPTEMBER 11, 2008, I WENT TO Ground Zero to check in on the general mood downtown. By this point, anniversaries were the only time of year when lots of people went to the WTC site, so I always headed down then too. Even though the most recent battles weren't unfolding at the site, I wondered if they could be felt here nonetheless. I wondered how the conflicts between Silverstein and the Port Authority translated onto the street.

My first stop was Vesey Street, which bordered the site and was always crowded. Whatever was going on at Vesey was a pretty good indicator of the status of things more generally—the state of rebuilding, the public's feelings about 9/11, even the greater national disposition. In the first weeks after the attacks, people filled its intersection with Broadway to see the wreckage. Months later it overflowed with spontaneous memorials. Vendors selling Ground Zero hats and T-shirts arrived next, soon joined by a crush of tourists wielding maps and cameras. A few years later, the official "memorial preview site" opened, and visitors flooded the storefront to see intricate models and videos of rebuilding. If Ground Zero was America's public square, Vesey Street was its central artery.

On the morning of the seventh anniversary, Vesey was only half filled with people, the most visible of whom were two dozen scruffy-haired men in T-shirts and jeans. Some sat on the curb, some chatted, or tried to chat, with passersby, and some distributed bumper stickers. "9–11 WAS AN INSIDE JOB," one read. "Learn the truth at infowars. com, prisonplanet.com, jonesreport.com." Conspiracy theorists had taken over Vesey Street.

I had met many people over the years who subscribed to a conspiracy theory or two. Spending time at Ground Zero ensured it. There was Phil, whom I called "American Phil." He had long white hair and always wore an American flag shirt. Nearly every day, Phil could be found sitting cross-legged on the sidewalk, playing lovely, patriotic anthems on his flute, and wearing a sign around his neck that alerted everyone to the coming apocalypse. People noticed Phil—occasionally, a guy or girl would crouch next to him and smile for the camera, as if he was Mickey Mouse and we were all at Disney World. But because there were always lots of people around Phil, he didn't define the character of the place. Ground Zero was many things over the years— chaotic, sad, uplifting, touristy, sentimental, infuriating—but it was never fringe. Until, that is, people stopped coming.

On the morning of the seventh anniversary, I met Luke, who was sitting on the curb. Luke had long, dirty blond dreadlocks pulled back into a half ponytail, and an unkempt beard and mustache. He wore a white T-shirt that said, "no masters, no slaves," in English as well as Latin, and he played with a lighter in his right hand. "I was raised up in a constitutionalist, patriot-type family," Luke told me. "My father raised me to love the United States, to love the Bill of Rights, to love the Constitution and our liberties. At the same time, he always said that the people that are in control, they don't believe in that same stuff, they want to take those liberties away."

Luke and I talked for a while. He spoke confidently and thoughtfully, in a way that seemed just a bit practiced, as if he had said it all before. Luke had been a member of many groups over the years. As a teenager, he joined what he called the "greater patriot movement," an antigovernment group, but he was at the WTC site as a member of We Are Change, an independent media organization that, as its website explains, seeks "to expose the lies of governments and the corporate elite who constantly trash our humanity." Luke was just north of New York City, in Yonkers, on 9/11, and he said he immediately had questions about the attacks. Most suspicious to him was that the hijacked planes weren't shot down by the U.S. missile defense system NORAD. "Why weren't F-16s scrambled?" he asked me. "That's standard military protocol. A plane is hijacked, they scramble F-16s to shoot it down."

Luke believed that our leaders had lied about 9/11 to wage war, and he wanted to expose those lies. "Finding out about who done it, and who made out from it, the same people who made out, those are the people who lied. They're the ones lying about why we need to go into foreign nations because of this," he said, tilting his head toward the site. "These foreign wars aren't about terrorism," he said. "The war on terrorism is a farce. How can you have a war on a tactic? It doesn't make sense. I mean, are you going to have a war on kicking? Isn't *all* war terrorism?" Luke paused and made a dramatic lift of his left eyebrow to underscore his point. "You know, so where do we draw the line? I'm not telling you, I'm asking you. Where do we draw the line?"

It was easy to sit and listen to Luke. My problem was the one I had with nearly all the conspiracy theorists I had met: what to do when it was no longer clear what we were talking about. (What line?) I usually took it as a sign that it was time to say good-bye or maybe even head home for the day, but Luke was the first person I had spoken to. It was only 8:30 in the morning. I couldn't leave yet.

From Vesey Street, I walked a couple of blocks to the plaza designated for the public's viewing of the anniversary ceremony. For the first few anniversaries, rebuilding officials had held the ceremony in the pit and allowed the public to fill the surrounding streets, but, after a few years, when there was too much construction equipment inside the pit, officials moved the ceremony to a small square catty-corner to the WTC site called Zuccotti Park. It was a typical urban park, with benches, walkways, and a few scattered flower beds and trees; for anniversaries, officials closed it to the public and filled it with chairs for victims' families and politicians. Meanwhile, they sent everyone else to a plaza across the street, where they could peer in on Zuccotti Park and listen to the reading of the names, broadcast over an extensive speaker system.

That morning, the public plaza was, like Vesey Street, about half filled with people. In one corner, a small crowd crouched over memorial canvases. In another corner a large, youth Mennonite choir sang hymns. Meanwhile, the middle of the square was mostly empty except for two people: a man sitting in a chair with a handwritten sign explaining that he had stopped a second 9/11, and a woman standing and holding a sign that asked, "Where is Osama Bin Laden?" Passersby eyed the two of them suspiciously and, as if honoring an invisible force field, kept a distance as they crossed the plaza.

At the memorial canvases, I met Jan, a tall, blond, twenty-year-old from the Netherlands who seemed at first like so many people I had spoken to before. He had timed his visit to New York to coincide with the anniversary, he said, because 9/11 was important to him and his country. The more he shared, however, the odder his story became. Jan didn't know anyone killed or anyone who lived in New York. In fact, he didn't even remember 9/11, he said. Rather, a few years after 9/11 he fell in love with the U.S. men's soccer team, and his love for the team quickly expanded into a love for America and then for the foreign policies of George W. Bush.

"I have a tattoo," he told me. "Of the Twin Towers."

"Really?" I asked. "Where?"

Jan rolled up his sleeve to reveal a large, black-and-white sketch of the towers on his biceps. The words "Never Forget" ran across the top of the tattoo and the date "9–11-01" across the bottom.

I was stunned. 9/11 tattooing was a common phenomenon among rescue workers and firefighters as well as victims' family members, but I had never seen a tattoo on someone with no connection to the attacks. But maybe, I thought to myself, this wasn't as weird as it seemed. "Are other people back home doing this too?" I asked.

"No," Jan said. "Everyone in my village thinks I'm crazy."

I wished Jan well and moved on. Part of my surprise at the general sense of emptiness downtown and the prevalence of people like Luke and Jan and the two with the handwritten signs was that 2008 was an election year, a big election year, and Barack Obama and John McCain were scheduled to make a stop at Ground Zero. I had figured lots of people would turn out to see them, but this wasn't the case. Instead, the joint appearance had acquired an aura of weirdness too. Before the ceremony started, a few people in the public plaza told me the same rumor: that Obama had already been at the site early in the morning, without McCain, and that he simply jumped out of his black SUV, waved, and sped off. The rumor turned out to be false. Obama and McCain arrived later in the afternoon and walked into the pit together to lay some wreaths before heading uptown for another, increasingly attack-filled, campaign event. But at the time, the rumor seemed plausible enough, and this was telling. The two men running for president didn't seem to care much about 9/11. Even the candidates' appearance together suggested a de-emphasis, an obligatory pause in a campaign about other things. The wars and policies that stemmed from 9/11 *were* part of public debate—Obama opposed the war in Iraq and promised to engage more forcefully in Afghanistan—but the event at the center of it all was receding from attention.

Their appearance also suggested that Ground Zero was a special place, the only place in the country, perhaps, where people were supposed to stop debating and come together to grieve. This couldn't have been further from the truth, of course. Ground Zero was America's most battle-filled stretch of land, partly because, in fact, everyone believed it should be neutral and apolitical, which prompted fierce disagreement over what counted as political. Nonetheless, there was a prevailing sense amid all the battles that Ground Zero should be different, that it should be better, that it should bring out the best in people even if it often brought out the worst.

Obama and McCain weren't the only politicians that fall to advance this particular understanding. A few weeks after their visit, vice presidential candidate Sarah Palin visited Ground Zero, where she held her first-ever live press conference. Palin had recently been selected to be McCain's running mate, and she was in New York City to visit the United Nations and meet diplomats. It wasn't unusual for someone in her position to head to Ground Zero; politicians had been touring the site for years. But her visit became unusual when she decided to use it to talk to the press, a group she had been evading for weeks. Palin answered three questions, including what she thought about the site. "Every American student needs to come through this area so that, especially this younger generation of Americans, is to be in a position of never forgetting what happened here and never repeating, never allowing a repeat of what happened here," she said. Ground Zero provided Palin with some cover. It was a place that promised to temper even the most assertive reporter. But the decision to hold her first press conference at the WTC site was still puzzling. After all, it was a site of historic death and destruction mired by years of political infighting. It wasn't an auspicious locale.

Back on the seventh anniversary, I walked up Broadway, past the WTC site, one last time at the end of the day. The only people still hanging around were the conspiracy theorists. I didn't see Luke, but a number of the men stood in a loose circle, surrounding two people who were arguing. "Tower Seven!" one yelled. A pair of arms flailed above people's head. "Explain that!" World Trade Tower 7 collapsed about six hours after the Twin Towers, and it figures prominently in many conspiracy theories because some believe its later-afternoon collapse is evidence of planted explosives, of the U.S. government's involvement in the attacks.

I stood by the circle and listened to the debate. It looked like a rap battle, except no one provided a beat or rhymed or displayed much rhetorical skill. The mood was sort of sad, which seemed about right. Seven years had passed and Ground Zero remained a hole in the ground. And the battles continued.

ACT III

DEALMAKERS
2008–2011

CHAPTER 12

ANTI-
MONUMENTALISM

IN THE SPRING OF 2008, CHRISTOPHER O. WARD BECAME THE PORT Authority's new executive director, and he immediately set an ambitious deadline: in thirty days he would review the rebuilding of the WTC site, identify the Port Authority's mistakes and failures, and issue a new blueprint for how to move forward. A month later, Ward released a report—his first as head of the Port Authority—but it wasn't the blueprint. Instead, the report explained why the blueprint wasn't ready, and detailed a series of problems Ward needed to further investigate. It wasn't exactly a bureaucratic triumph, a report on the delay of another report. But it did signal change. It signaled that the Port Authority understood just how disastrous the rebuilding effort had become. Ward acknowledged as much when we spoke a few years later. "It was a difficult political thing to acknowledge that it was so complicated and so behind schedule and that there were so many fundamental disconnects that you couldn't just quickly fix the problems in thirty days," Ward said.

Ward was familiar with the Port Authority. He was a senior executive at the agency in the late 1990s and early 2000s, overseeing major projects and then helping it recover from 9/11. He left the Port Authority in 2002 to run the city's Department of Environmental Protection, and then became managing director of the General Contractors Association of New York, a trade group, where he received frequent updates from construction workers about the problems at the WTC site. "They would just say, 'Look, this project is really in trouble,'" Ward said. Which, of course, wasn't exactly a secret.

As Ward reviewed the project in the summer and fall of 2008, he developed an overarching theory to explain the failures of the rebuilding effort. As Ward saw it, Ground Zero had become the repository for the city's hopes and dreams and could no longer absorb the weight. Everyone wanted Ground Zero to answer big questions, he said, like "'Is America strong?' or 'Are we affirming our core values?'" The WTC site immediately became a symbol of the country's response to 9/11, Ward said—"Bush with the bullhorn," as he described the iconic image of the president speaking to recovery workers at the site—and it never stopped acquiring meaning. Ward believed the layers of meaning had been disrupting progress by imbuing each decision with too much make-or-break symbolism.

Then, Ward continued, there were the outsized components of the sixteen-acre parcel itself: the office space, a memorial park ("second in size to Central Park," he noted), a memorial museum, a transportation center, a vehicle security center, a new street grid. "It's a city in and of itself," Ward said. Consequently, the rebuilding had become "monumentally unmanageable because it had to answer all of those questions at one time," Ward said. "And you could never answer all of those questions and set priorities, manage expectations, and deliver a project. So the way that we approached it was to break through that paradigm of monumentalism." Any decision that Ward believed stemmed not from honest assessment but from an ethic of monumentalism, a belief in the New York's and America's greatness, was going to be revisited and revised. Stamped out.

One of the first stops on Ward's crusade against monumentalism was Freedom Tower. Everything about the building reflected a belief in bigness. Tallest building in the Western Hemisphere; a symbolic height of 1,776 feet; fortified like the world's most battle-tested embassy. Most of these features were immutable by the time Ward arrived—the building had already been redesigned twice—but he did have the power to change one component: its name. "I didn't find the name offensive, just unnecessary," Ward said. "We were free before 9/11 and we were free after 9/11. And freedom isn't found in naming a building."

The Port Authority was struggling to find tenants for the signature skyscraper, and Ward believed the name was too political, scaring off potential renters. Much better, the Port Authority decided, was a simple address: 1 WTC. It was cleaner, more marketable, less "freighted" with charged history, Ward said. "Saying, 'I'm in One WTC' is a lot easier than saying, 'I'm in the Freedom Tower,' 'cause then you're like, 'Oh, really? Why is that the Freedom Tower?'" Plus, Ward pointed out, the other buildings at the site were to be identified by their addresses too; there was going to be a 2 WTC, a 3 WTC, a 4 WTC, and so on. It made sense to him to start it all off with a 1 WTC.

The change got a bit of play in the news. Governor Pataki, who had coined the original moniker, expressed his concerns. "It's a little troubling to me that again there is a One World Trade Center, because a lot of great people and a lot of true heroes died in One World Trade Center," Pataki said. "I think that name should be reserved for those who did die on that horrible day." The *Times* posted a blog post on the change, and it collected the usual potpourri of reader comments, most of them bemoaning the state of the rebuilding effort. And then, a year later, in the spring of 2009, the change made news again, and uproar ensued.

The New York *Daily News* reported a new twist. It said the name change occurred after the Port Authority signed a lease with its first and only commercial tenant, Vantone Industrial Corporation, a Chinese real estate company with close ties to its government. Vantone leased just under 200,000 square feet of 1 WTC/Freedom Tower for a "China Center" that would facilitate business ties between the United States and China, and the *Daily News* suggested the Port Authority renamed the building to make its new tenants and therefore the Chinese government happy. The Port Authority denied that Vantone had anything to do with the change. And this appears to be true; it had been using "1 WTC" in memos ever since 2006. But it wasn't quite that simple. The deal appears to have ushered in a subtle grammatical change, which both the *Daily News* and the *Times* noticed. Instead of placing "Freedom Tower" after a comma, the Port Authority now placed the name in parentheses. It went from "1 WTC, Freedom Tower" in Port Authority documents to "1 WTC (Freedom Tower)."

Did the Port Authority adopt parentheses to appease the Chinese government? Perhaps, but it's more likely that the grammatical shift constituted one more step in the gradual fading out of "Freedom Tower" from official documents. In any case, it didn't really matter, because when CNN and FOX News picked up the story, they focused on the name change itself, not the question of Chinese interference, and it amplified from there. Conservative pundits and editorial pages accused the Port Authority of being anti-American, while liberal commentators celebrated the move. On the *Times* website, several hundred people wrote in. Some cheered: "This faux-patriotic Orwellian GOP BS won't cut it in NYC. Good work Port Authority!" Others rolled their eyes: "I love how a post like this can get a ton of Liberals to complain—literally!—that 'freedom' is a concept from the 'Bush years.' So tell me, what's the new ideal?" Some sighed: "If less time was spent focus-grouping the name and more time was spent building an actual memorial, I think we would all be happy with whatever the building ended up being called." And others snipped: "Why don't they just call it what everyone else is already calling it? Ugly."

Many people saw the Port Authority's move through a political lens, but the Port Authority wasn't really making a statement about freedom. It was making a business calculation. As Ward put it, "It was a better way to market the building." (Indeed, if the name "Freedom Tower" had helped it sell office space, the Port Authority might not have changed a thing.)

This is where the more potent critique lay. "The Freedom Tower is not simply another piece of real estate," Governor Pataki said when the change made bigger news. "And not just a name for marketing purposes." He continued, "Where One and Two World Trade Center once stood, there will be a memorial with two voids to honor the heroes we lost—and in my view, those addresses should never be used again." Pataki was making a point about the virtue of the name "Freedom Tower," but he was also making a point about the virtue of remembering history. Before 9/11, there were the Twin Towers, and then there was Freedom Tower; the change in name signaled that something happened. So when the Port Authority changed the building's name to 1 WTC, it erased a little bit of history. Not all history, of course—the planned memorial was far more integral to commemorating 9/11 than a skyscraper's name. But "Freedom Tower" told a story nonetheless, a story of the attacks as well as of the charged politics of the aftermath, when Pataki christened the building. When the Port Authority got rid of the old name, it chose a new name that was inherently less commemorative and political. Which is why it was a better name for the Port Authority. The building's future commercial tenants were going to sign leases *despite* 9/11, not because of it.

The person most dismissive of the Port Authority's renaming, as well as its anti-monumentalism agenda, was, not surprisingly, master planner Daniel Libeskind. "The symbol is there. People will see it. It doesn't matter what the Port Authority says," Libeskind said curtly when I asked him about the skyscraper's new name. "Call it what you want," he continued. "The tower has inevitable symbolic character no matter what voices from the Port Authority might say." The original name complemented Libeskind's symbol-laden master plan, as well as his view that memory, not commerce, should be Ground Zero's defining force. The Port Authority's renaming was one more change to his vision, one more recalibration of the delicate balance he had struck.

Chris Ward wasn't immune to the powers of symbolism and meaning, though. On occasion, it served his purposes too. In the middle of his first summer as executive director, Ward gave a speech at the Downtown Alliance to explain why his blueprint was late, and he ended his speech with an emotional, symbolic call to rebuild. He began his closing comments with a little Henry James. "James once said, 'The New York City skyline is swept clean every twenty-five years.' A Europeanist, James was decrying the rapid change that New York was going through as market forces swept away old economies for new ones, brownstones for skyscrapers," Ward told the crowd. "The loss of our skyline on September 11th was not this New York energy James described. Rather, it was the very opposite—an anti-modern view which sought to stop our future," he said. "But New York has rebuilt itself time and time again. And it will do so here again in Lower Manhattan. But unlike any other time or project in our history, we are rebuilding on a site fundamentally taken from us by those completely at odds with our town. And that remains our challenge. And it will take time, as it has. But rebuild we will. With the stakeholders in this room, the real estate market behind us, all of the efforts to date, and a roadmap going forward, a new downtown will be rebuilt."

WARD WAS AN UNLIKELY PERSON TO BE running the Port Authority. After
he graduated from Macalester College and worked on an oil rig in the
Gulf of Mexico in the late 1970s, Ward had gone to Harvard Divinity
School and studied the progressive social gospel movement, led by pas-
tor and theologian Walter Rauschenbusch. He received his Master of
Theological Studies, but then decided the academy wasn't for him and
went to New York City instead, where he started working his way up
the ranks in city and state government. He never looked back.

Despite his years in government, Ward's appointment as executive
director of the Port Authority was sudden and unexpected, because it
was a direct consequence of the state's biggest scandal in decades, New
York governor Eliot Spitzer's admission that he regularly patronized
the services of a high-end escort. After Spitzer stepped down, his lieu-
tenant governor, David Paterson, became governor, and he appointed
Ward. "I've never met David Paterson in my life, and I've never given
him any money," Ward said, explaining his surprise. But Ward, who
had been considered for the top post by Spitzer, didn't miss a beat
when Paterson offered him the job. He immediately said yes. Ward
told me he aspired to the top post at the Port Authority ever since
his first stint there in the 1990s, when he learned how the institution
worked and came to respect its breadth and capacity. "It's the best job
in government," he said.

Many of the officials and architects I spoke to credited Ward with
helping turn things around at Ground Zero. "This was the first time
when the executive director of the Port Authority came in and said,
'I'm going to make this work,'" said Josh Wallack, chief operating
officer of the city's Economic Development Corporation, which oversaw the WTC site project for the Mayor's Office. "You started seeing
the bureaucracy of the Port Authority come in and let contracts and
put their foot on the gas." Since City Hall didn't tend to hit it off with
the Port Authority, even muted praise from city officials was noteworthy. Memorial designer Michael Arad was even more complimentary.

"It wasn't until Chris Ward took control that we started to see things changing," he said. Of course, not everyone agreed that Ward played a transformative role. A few told me they thought the project had already turned a corner when Ward arrived, and that he merely capitalized on already-existing momentum. But regardless of his colleagues' and competitors' assessments, Ward did seem to appreciate the public's appetite for a new guiding ethic downtown. While many people wanted something grand and majestic to stand at Ground Zero, they were starting to realize that perhaps they wanted something else more: a finished site. By 2008, people wanted to get it done, and Ward understood this.

As part of his effort to break the paradigm of monumentalism, Ward aimed to simplify and neaten the site's boundaries. The WTC site consisted of many disparate parts, including a memorial and museum, real estate, public space, and a transit hub, and while Daniel Libeskind recognized these parts in his master plan, he also blurred the boundaries between them when he made everything symbolic. Ward tried to scale back the symbolism and boldface the master plan's lines. He aimed to untangle the land's different functions. A skyscraper should just be a skyscraper, he reasoned. The train station, a train station.

Sometimes, however, moving the project forward required a holistic approach. For example, the new subway tunnels ran through the entire site, and the only way to build them was all at once, across the site's distinctive parts. Meanwhile, the roof of the transit hub's mezzanine doubled as the floor of the memorial plaza. And the transit hub's ventilation systems, as well as parts of the vehicle screening center, needed to be housed under Silverstein's towers. All these construction schedules had to be coordinated. While Ground Zero was a collection of parcels, it was also, irrevocably, one piece of land. Boundaries made sense, except when they didn't.

Two problems, in particular, required Ward to employ a more integrated method. The first was the Port Authority's construction delays.

Back in 2006, the Port Authority and Silverstein agreed on 2012 as the completion date for everything—the five commercial buildings, the train station, the memorial, and the museum. All these pieces were significantly behind when Ward arrived, in large part because of Port Authority delays, but the Port Authority was still standing by the deadlines. So Ward revised the entire schedule in his much-anticipated blueprint (which arrived three months later than planned). The blueprint identified fifteen interconnected problems that had delayed construction, on everything from the transit hub to the memorial plaza to 1 WTC, and detailed the Port Authority's solutions to them. The highlights: Ward promised that 1 WTC/Freedom Tower would be completed by the end of 2013, the train station in 2014, and the infrastructure for the rest of the office towers in the subsequent five years. In sum, Ward promised construction at the WTC site for another decade, which didn't sound good, but didn't sound like a pipe dream, either. The most important promise, though, regarded the memorial: Ward vowed to finish it by the fall of 2011, in time for the ten-year anniversary of 9/11.

Unveiling the memorial plaza on the anniversary made sentimental sense, but it was also pragmatic. The stakeholders agreed they had to finish *something* by the ten-year anniversary, if only to stave off public humiliation and ridicule, and the memorial was actually the best candidate. Freedom Tower, which until now was always slated to be finished first, was too far behind schedule, as was the soaring train station by Santiago Calatrava. Meanwhile, over the past two years, officials had been slowly resolving the memorial's conflicts. Prioritizing the memorial met a political and emotional need, and it also created a new organizing principle for construction. "The memorial becomes the most important thing to make progress on," Ward said, "because it allowed you to tell everybody why you were doing what you're doing."

Of course, there was one other reason to prioritize the memorial over everything else. As of September 2008, right before Ward published his blueprint, the economy was in total disarray. The Great Recession had landed. There was no rush to complete brand-new, expensive office towers because, alas, there was no one to rent them. Which brought Chris Ward to his second problem.

Because the Port Authority had missed multiple construction deadlines on the eve of the recession, Larry Silverstein argued that the agreed-upon penalties were no longer adequate and that he deserved more money from the Port Authority. The agency was paying Silverstein $300,000 for each day its work extended past the deadline—by the summer of 2009, Silverstein had received roughly $100 million in fees—but Silverstein argued that he deserved more because the delays essentially forced him to miss the market. More specifically, Silverstein asked the Port Authority to finance two of his three buildings, at a cost upward of $3 billion dollars. (1 WTC/ Freedom Tower was a separate expenditure for the Port Authority, also costing just over $3 billion.)

I spoke to many people who conceded that Larry Silverstein had a point, including Chris Ward. "From a distanced perspective, there was validity to his argument," Ward said. "He did miss the market." But Ward believed that it wasn't the Port Authority's fault Silverstein couldn't secure private financing, and that Silverstein was asking the Port Authority, and by extension the public, to assume far too much risk. So Ward played hardball. For six months, Larry Silverstein, Janno Lieber, and Chris Ward tried to negotiate a new deal, to no avail. They described the meetings to me as "very frustrating" and, alternatively, "not getting anywhere." In May 2009, Mayor Bloomberg gathered the men, along with Governor Paterson and New Jersey governor Jon Corzine at Gracie Mansion for a high-profile "summit," where the mayor told everyone that another stalemate was not acceptable.

The city encouraged the two sides to find a compromise because it feared that a lengthy arbitration process could delay rebuilding for *another* few years. These fears led the city to apply more pressure to Ward. "The city's position is 'Okay, Port Authority, Silverstein, we understand both arguments,'" Josh Wallack, of the city's Economic Development Corporation, told me. "'But it really doesn't matter who we agree with, because, Port Authority, if you don't reach a deal with Silverstein, he will take you to court, which he has every right to do, and he will tie this site up for years. You'll lose more than you'll gain in this fight. The entire site gets locked up if you go to arbitration.'" Of course, no one knew what would happen during arbitration, but the threat of sustained delays was real. The mayor's hour-long summit was closed to staff members, but Wallack and a handful of others stood outside the door, watching as the distinguished guests soberly exited the room. "The implied threat was that the mayor would blame them publicly for the failure of Ground Zero, and no one wanted that hanging around their necks," Wallack said. "The mood was tense."

But being scolded by the mayor didn't exactly generate a new sense of camaraderie. It also didn't generate a deal. After the summit, the two sides stuck to their positions. "We were never going to settle, ever," Chris Ward said. "The Port Authority was not going to make the mistake of building the original WTC and losing so much public money." So Silverstein Properties did what everyone feared it would do. "We didn't have any choice," Janno Lieber said. "What were we going to do? Just keep paying them the money and not getting any rent?" As dictated by their original contract, Silverstein was paying the Port Authority tens of millions of dollars a year for nonexistent office space. So Silverstein took the dispute to arbitration.

The question before the arbitration panel was relatively narrow: did the Port Authority owe Silverstein additional penalties? But answering it meant investigating a bigger series of questions about the state of the market, the interconnectedness of construction, and the two sides' abilities to meet deadlines and build. For two months in the fall of 2009, the three-person panel heard twenty-seven witness testimonies, examined hundreds of "exhibits," reviewed scores of memos, and listened to lengthy closing arguments. Typically, arbitration panels issue a ruling five days after the closing arguments, but the case was so complex that the panel asked for an extension and spent another six weeks drafting its decision.

At first glance, it seemed Silverstein had the stronger case. In addition to the Port Authority's many missed deadlines, Silverstein could point to his success rebuilding WTC 7. Before it was destroyed on 9/11, Tower 7 stood just outside the boundaries of the sixteen-acre World Trade Center, a location that enabled Silverstein to rebuild this particular tower independently from the larger rebuilding effort. He completed construction on it in 2006, just as the rest of the rebuilding was falling apart, and moved the headquarters of Silverstein Properties into its upper floors. At first, Silverstein struggled to find additional tenants, but by the time of the arbitration he had leased nearly all the building's fifty-two stories, as well as won a "Merit Award for Architecture" from the New York chapter of the American Institute of Architects, and received praise for an art installation in the building's lobby: conceptual artist Jenny Holzer had selected poetry and prose about New York City and then projected this scrolling text on the wall behind the reception desk. The quick construction, as well as the tenancies and awards, spoke to Silverstein's competence as a developer. The Port Authority, meanwhile, did not seem to have comparable markers. It could point to the risks of investing public funds in speculative office space, and to the nascent improvements ushered in by Chris Ward.

When the panel issued its decision in late January 2010, Chris Ward was at home nursing a cold. "The phone rings, and it's our general counsel saying we have the decision," Ward recounts. "And I say, 'Just read me the last sentence.' And of course the last sentence is completely bureaucratic, it doesn't tell you anything." So Ward jumped into his car and headed across town to join his frantically reading employees. One sentence on page 16 caught everyone's attention: "Since Mr. Ward took over the directorship, however, much has changed, contracts have been let, and the infrastructure work is moving ahead." This was the key sentence. Silverstein had argued that the Port Authority acted in bad faith, but the arbitration panel disagreed. "It was clear we won," Ward said. "And the great thing about the decision is that Larry felt he won too."

Well, sort of. "It didn't really resolve anything," Janno Lieber said of the decision, exhibiting far less enthusiasm than Chris Ward as he chronicled the episode. "The arbitrators basically said, 'Back to the negotiating table.'"

The decision was mostly a win for the Port Authority because the arbitrators decided that it didn't owe Silverstein additional fees. Even though the Port Authority had missed multiple construction deadlines—the decision listed fourteen separate delays, though the Port Authority wasn't responsible for all of them—the panel ruled that Silverstein had failed to prove that these delays prevented it from building its towers. "There has been no proof that delay in these infrastructure projects have so far impacted construction of the Towers," the decision read. But the panel also ruled that Chris Ward's new schedule was not detailed enough to ensure construction of the site's requisite parts, so it gave the parties "one final chance" to resolve the outstanding scheduling and funding problems.

Two months later—and sixteen months after the conflict between Silverstein and the Port Authority first erupted—the two partners reached a new agreement. It was a compromise. The Port Authority agreed to finance one building, Tower 4 (the one that, in 2006, the Port Authority agreed to move into), to be completed in 2013. Silverstein agreed to finance one building, Tower 2, to be completed when he could raise the money. And they agreed to split the difference on Tower 3. The Port Authority would help finance it, but only if Silverstein passed a market test, which included raising $300 million from investors and securing tenants for 400,000 square feet of office space. If and when he passed these tests and everyone felt confident the building would turn a profit, the Port Authority would give Silverstein roughly $400 million to complete the project. So while Silverstein received some financial assistance, it wasn't as much as he wanted, and while the Port Authority "took a hit" on Tower 4, as Ward put it, it didn't give in on Tower 3, which would have cost it close to $2 billion.

"It was the key deal," Ward said of the new agreement, "because it meant you knew how every piece of the project on the entire site was going to get built. Until you had that Silverstein deal, you were still stuck with a site that was fundamentally flawed." The deal made commercial sense too. No need to quickly build office space (with public funds, no less) when there was no market for it.

But this was a substantial revising of the rebuilding effort, in multiple ways. Perhaps most notably, there would be less office space on the site, at least for a while. The Port Authority would complete its infrastructure work underneath the buildings and bring the land to grade so the site wasn't pocked with giant holes, but Towers 2 and 3 would go up only when the market improved, which was likely to take some time. At least six or seven years, maybe longer. The agreement also revised, again, the commercial distribution between Silverstein and the Port Authority. The Port Authority was now building or helping finance three (and a half) of the site's five commercial buildings. Indeed, only one of Silverstein's skyscrapers, Tower 4, was guaranteed to be built.

And so, when you put all the changes together, a curious picture emerged. Few noticed it at the time, but the rebuilding effort was starting to look a lot like the vision laid out back in 2002 by a feisty, unsatisfied public at Listening to the City. At that public hearing, people had demanded that leaders prioritize the memorial, reduce Ground Zero's office space, and renegotiate Silverstein's lease. Now, officials were building the memorial first, delaying construction of some office space until there was a market for it, and renegotiating Silverstein's lease—for the second time, in fact, counting the earlier "restructuring" of 2006. Nine years, scores of battles and billions of dollars later, officials were actually building something resembling the public's plan.

CHAPTER 13

THE MEMORIAL
AND THE MAYOR

C HRIS WARD'S SIGNATURE DECISION AS EXECUTIVE DIRECTOR of the Port Authority was his vow to complete the memorial by the tenth anniversary of 9/11, but Ward actually made the decision reluctantly. In the summer of 2008, he approached the memorial the same way he approached everything at the WTC site, with an eye to pragmatism and a desire to dismantle "the paradigm of monumentalism," as he put it. This meant that when city officials and executives at the 9/11 Memorial Foundation originally raised with him the possibility of completing the memorial on the tenth anniversary, he said it couldn't be done. Construction on the plaza was behind, he said, and rebuilding in general was a mess. And, he reminded everyone, the tenth anniversary was just a date. Why get stuck on an unlikely and symbolic deadline and risk breaking another promise and further upending the rebuilding effort?

City officials, as well as leaders of the 9/11 Memorial Foundation, strongly disagreed. "The eyes of the world are going to be on New York City on the tenth anniversary," Josh Wallack, chief operating officer of the city's Economic Development Corporation, told me. "Will it be just a construction site? Or will there be something there that families and the world can remember this by?" Ward may have been opposed to any sort of "grand idea" at Ground Zero, but a lot of other people were willing to embrace the land's symbolism, at least when it was politically prudent. Mayor Bloomberg, the foundation, and the staffers at the Economic Development Corporation believed that the media, victims' families, and many New Yorkers and Americans would skewer everyone associated with rebuilding if the memorial was still under construction ten years later. To city and foundation officials, the anniversary was a symbolic deadline that doubled as a political necessity. Mayor Bloomberg implored Ward to reconsider and commit to an anniversary opening for the memorial. And, over the course of a few months, Ward did. He concluded that the deadline would be difficult but not impossible to meet. And maybe the anniversary could add a sense of urgency and ambition to the otherwise ossified process. So when Ward issued his "Roadmap Forward" in October 2008, an anniversary deadline for the memorial was set.

Ward's change of heart was evidence of the progress that rebuilding officials had made over the past two years on the memorial's trenchant problems. The only reason Ward could set a 2011 deadline was because design and fund-raising problems no longer plagued the project—thanks in large part to the work of a most unlikely advocate, Mayor Michael Bloomberg.

The memorial's turnaround began in 2006. At the time, it had seemed that the mayor still wanted to build anything and everything *except* a large memorial at the site. While former mayor Rudolph Giuliani had advocated for devoting the entire sixteen acres to commemoration, Bloomberg had long advocated for building schools and housing on the land, and had wondered aloud about the negative effect a memorial could have on Ground Zero's real estate prices. He repeatedly told the press that when it came to remembrance, he believed "less is more." And, in the fall of 2006, during the fifth anniversary of 9/11, the *Times* published the mayor's most outlandish comments yet. The comments were not current—Bloomberg had made them to the Memorial Competition Jury a couple of years earlier—but the *Times* had only just received access to the transcript. Bloomberg told the jury that he was "a believer in the future, not the past. I can't do anything about the past," Bloomberg said. A few moments later, Bloomberg recounted the phone calls he had made to four hundred families of rescue workers on the eve of the first anniversary, and said that while many were moving on, "there were 15-odd families where the spouse, I think it was probably all women, they just kept crying and crying," Bloomberg said. "It's not my business to say that to a woman, 'Suck it up and get going,' but that is the way I feel. You've got to look to the future."

Bloomberg's meeting with the jury was private, but the Lower Manhattan Development Corporation had filmed it (for a documentary it eventually decided not to make) and a few years later the video recording made its way to the *Times*. Presumably, the mayor would not have spoken as frankly if had he known the comments would be made public. They certainly didn't help him win over victims' families (or women). Nor did they suggest a commitment to the memorial. According to the *Times*, Bloomberg concluded his comments with an appeal for the jury to remember that the world was plagued by famine and war, and to consider this broader context when choosing a memorial design.

But these and other statements turned out to be deceiving, or only part of the story. Bloomberg was growing increasingly concerned about the memorial over the spring and summer of 2006, when memorial fund-raising was stalling and its budget skyrocketing. The memorial's overarching problem was the same one plaguing rebuilding more generally: with so many committees and corporations, everyone believed the inevitable crises belonged to someone else. The memorial and museum were overseen not by the Port Authority or the Lower Manhattan Development Corporation but by the 9/11 Memorial Foundation (formally known as the National September 11 Memorial & Museum Foundation), a nonprofit started in 2003 to own and oversee the memorial quadrant. Despite this mandate, the foundation's mission was unclear; no one knew if it was supposed to oversee a redesign of the memorial to appease families and help rein in costs or if it was simply supposed to raise money. That spring, it was doing everything poorly. Many victims' families remained unsatisfied with Michael Arad's design, and the foundation, which estimated close to a $1 billion price tag for the memorial, had raised only $130 million. In May, both the foundation's chairman and its president stepped down.

Which meant it needed a new leader. Enter Mayor Bloomberg. In the fall of 2006, the foundation's executive committee appointed Bloomberg as its chairman of the board, with the hope that he could spearhead a new fund-raising initiative. (The committee also appointed Governor Pataki as "honorary lifetime chairman," securing Pataki an official role in the rebuilding even after his term ended.) Suddenly, Bloomberg had gained a considerable amount of power downtown. Before this appointment, Bloomberg's influence had been limited to his bully pulpit and to whatever he could persuade Silverstein and the Port Authority to do. Now, however, as chairman of the board, Bloomberg would oversee construction of both the memorial and the museum. Technically speaking, he was in charge of half the site.

When news of the mayor's chairmanship spread, many saw it as a power grab. "These appointments shamefully state the obvious," a former staff member of the 9/11 Memorial Foundation wrote in a letter to the editor published in the *Times*. "Building the memorial is not the public or private partnership that was envisioned, but a process completely driven by politics, ambition and greed. It is an egregious insult to the memory of the thousands killed on 9/11 and the impact that this tragedy continues to have on all of our lives." Many victims' families were also upset, and claimed that the appointment would only further disrupt fund-raising and construction.

But there were a few facts that suggested an alternative outcome. The mayor was indeed a good fund-raiser. And, before his appointment as chairman, he had donated $10 million of his own money to the foundation. A bit later he donated another $5 million, putting him among the memorial's top four donors. (David Rockefeller and Deutsche Bank also donated $15 million, while the Starr Foundation donated $25 million.) It was all a bit mystifying, and constituted one of the odder twists in the endlessly twisting rebuilding saga. Mayor Bloomberg, who disparaged the memorial with remarkably frequency, was now spending time and even his own money to construct it.

NOT LONG AFTER HE ASSUMED THE CHAIRMANSHIP, Mayor Bloomberg began work to resolve specific memorial design problems, the thorniest of which was the conflict over how to list victims' names. Ever since Michael Arad won the competition to design the memorial, victims' families hated the decision to list the names on the memorial in random order. Over time, Arad came to dislike it too. The families of firefighters had been the first to protest, calling for the memorial to recognize the difference between those whose job it was to rush into the towers and those who worked in the buildings; they fought for years, holding protests, circulating petitions, and issuing press releases. Arad said that while he came to believe that first responders should be recognized, for a long time he didn't know how to do it without alienating or minimizing others. "You're creating two classes of people," Arad said. "There's heroes and there's victims." But, he continued, "do you dishonor [first responders] by not adding an insignia?"

As the months passed, Arad kept returning to his idea of "meaningful adjacencies," which wouldn't include insignias, but would instead arrange all names according to the relationships people had formed. Arad believed this method would fulfill the desire of rescue workers' families to recognize their loved ones separately, and would tend to all families' wish for equal treatment. Arad had proposed the idea to the Lower Manhattan Development Corporation, but the agency rejected it as too complex. By the time Bloomberg became chairman of the 9/11 Memorial Foundation, the names problem had festered for two years, thwarting memorial fund-raising in the process.

Bloomberg decided the conflict needed to be resolved, and he was attuned to families' insistence that a random listing of names was inadequate and that first responders should indeed be recognized. So, soon after his appointment, Bloomberg met with Arad, who told the mayor he believed that his concept of meaningful adjacencies was the only way to arrange the names that didn't blur distinctions between individuals or privilege some over others. Bloomberg agreed, and he set out to convince everyone else of Arad's idea.

Bloomberg made a presentation on meaningful adjacencies to the executive committee of the 9/11 Memorial Foundation, and committee members quickly embraced Arad's concept. Likewise, families of rescue workers promptly signed off on the plan because it meant their family members would be grouped separately. Some victims' families remained unhappy. Edie Lutnick, whose brother Howard is chairman of Cantor Fitzgerald, the financial services firm that suffered the greatest loss of life on 9/11—over 650 of its employees died, including Edie and Howard's brother Gary—spearheaded a movement against meaningful adjacencies. She wanted the memorial to display more specific information about each person, like their ages or the company they worked for, to further humanize those who were killed. But many other families approved of the plan, and eventually, even those opposed came around. In 2008, Cantor Fitzgerald donated $10 million to the foundation for the memorial.

The system Arad and Bloomberg agreed upon combined meaningful adjacencies with a broader geographic layout. People were grouped in a way that reflected where they were that day: the four flights, the two towers, the Pentagon, the 1993 WTC bombing victims, and the first responders, which were arranged by firehouse. Then, within and across these groupings, Arad implemented meaningful adjacencies. For example, over one thousand people died in the North Tower, but rather than simply list these names alphabetically (or randomly) under a "North Tower" heading, Arad and his team solicited requests from families for the names of other people they'd like near or next to their family member. By the end, they received 1,200 requests.

A few requests linked people across the groups as well as within them. Arad recounted the story of one woman whose father was killed on Flight 11, which flew into the North Tower, and whose best friend from college was killed in the World Trade Center. To represent and connect these two deaths, Arad's team set the Flight 11 group directly before the World Trade Center group, and placed her father's name at the end of the Flight 11 list and her friend's name at the beginning of the WTC list. "These stories, they are very personal and human," Arad said. "You can relate to them on a personal level. When you see close to three thousand names, it's almost impossible to find a way to relate to them on a personal level. It's overwhelming. But when you hear one story like this, when you hear about someone losing their best friend and their father in an attack like this, meaning is embedded in the memorial."

While the arrangement inscribed emotion in the memorial, it did so in an incredibly subtle, almost invisible, way. To most people, after all, the names would appear to be listed randomly; only a victim's family and friends would recognize the immediately surrounding name or names and see the adjacency. The beauty of the arrangement was that it achieved a privacy and intimacy on an otherwise public memorial. "They would appear to be randomly arranged," Arad said, "when in fact they are very carefully arranged." This was also the disadvantage of the composition, though: only a select few were privy to the memorial's encoded meaning. To tend to this problem, Arad said he hoped that the memorial would include a way for people to learn about some of the stories behind the adjacencies, either through a brochure or an app or a video recording.

Arad and his team spent roughly a year arranging and rearranging names to fulfill every request. (In instances without a request, Arad said they tried to honor the person's history at the World Trade Center by placing their name near those with whom they had worked.) The team arranged the vast majority by hand in their office "with little cards," Arad said, before developing a computer program to assist with the final quarter. "It was incredibly laborious and emotional," Arad said. "If you move that name it triggers five other changes and so on." There were technical challenges too, like how to space names of varying lengths to create an even composition; every change meant a slightly new visual effect. "It had to look seamless," Arad said, "and it had to give every name its own place, a physical, geographical specificity."

Executing meaningful adjacencies wasn't simple, nor did it make everyone happy. But it did present a workable solution, one that depended, in large part, upon the involvement of Mayor Bloomberg. Years later, after the names' conflict had quieted down, after Bloomberg had helped raise over $250 million for the foundation, and after the memorial had opened, as promised, on the tenth anniversary of 9/11, Arad was unequivocal about the critical role Bloomberg played in the memorial's fate. "It wouldn't have happened without him," Arad said. He acknowledged the vital role of others too, like Chris Ward, but Arad repeatedly returned to the mayor. If not for Bloomberg, he said, "We'd still be talking about what kind of memorial we should have."

The mayor's work on the memorial remains one of the more inexplicable aspects of the rebuilding. What prompted his apparent about-face? Bloomberg has thus far avoided the topic with reporters and writers. Did he decide that he had made a mistake, that he had judged a large memorial incorrectly? Or did he decide that the memorial was crucial to the city's success, and that he should aid its construction even if it wasn't his preference for the site? Or did he decide that working on the memorial was a wise political move and would bolster his approval ratings? Perhaps it was a combination of motives. Maybe he liked Michael Arad and wanted to help him build his design.

Arad was certainly a fan of the mayor's. Still, Arad remained conflicted on the meaning of his patronage, on the essentialness of someone as powerful, wealthy, and unorthodox as Mayor Bloomberg. "If he wasn't there, then I don't know what would have happened," Arad said. "So to look at the system overall, if you ignore, for a second, the particularities of Ground Zero and of the terrorist attacks and the patriotic response of this country and the wars and everything else, and if you just focus on the mechanics of the city making decisions, does that mean we need a billionaire who doesn't care about politics-as-usual for this system to work? If that's the conclusion, then it's a really depressing one."

It was so depressing that Arad quickly pivoted, before pivoting again. "I don't think that's the conclusion to take," he added. "But that's certainly one way of reading what happened here."

What was the conclusion to take? Arad tends to oscillate between a more cynical and a more generous view of the rebuilding. "Did every person in New York get a say in what's happening here?" he asked. "No. Does that mean it's not fair? I don't think so." Arad said that he believed everyone had an opportunity to influence the rebuilding process, but that some people, as to be expected, had more power. "I don't think that anybody can be surprised that Larry Silverstein has more of a say than Larry Cohen, you know? It's just..." Arad paused and shrugged, as if to say, "It's just how things work." The thought didn't seem to sit well with him, however, because he kept talking. "But it's not that this was a process where only Larry Silverstein got to have a say, either. I think there was a balance here between all of these various forces that most projects don't have."

As Arad tells it, the rebuilding was dysfunctional and political and infuriating, but parts of it were participatory too. "Yes, there were plenty of decisions made behind closed doors," he said, "but there was also a lot of tension in the media and in the public that forced the people making decisions behind closed doors to consider certain things which otherwise they might not have."

As I listened to Arad wind his way to a reasoned, pragmatic, moderately positive view of the rebuilding, I thought that he sounded strikingly Libeskind-esque, touting the virtues of flexibility and compromise (after the battles had been won or lost, of course). Arad was less theatrical and more solemn than Libeskind, but they seemed to share similar understandings of the give-and-take of the artistic process. "There is that moment of creation, but then there is that moment of evolution that follows, where things sort of mutate and change," Arad said. "Design is a process constantly buffeted by constraints, and the process of creativity with which you respond to these constraints is what you end up with at the end of the day." It was an interesting idea: art and innovation not as one pure vision, like Steve Jobs's creation of the iPod, but as a series of creative adjustments, compromises, and revisions. Art as politics.

EVEN THOUGH ARAD SECURED HIS VISION for the names arrangement, quite a few of the decisions made behind closed doors did not go Arad's way. The most significant of these concerned a central component of his design, a system of underground galleries directly under his two square pools of water that marked the Twin Towers' footprints. Arad described the galleries to me as a "secular but spiritual place, a place of refuge, of quietness. Of encountering the nature of the dead." Arad wanted to list victims' names here, under the bustling plaza and away from the street's honking cars and the sidewalk's intrusive cell phone conversations. But problems emerged—problems that Arad helped make worse.

The galleries generated conflict from the beginning. Daniel Libeskind didn't like them because they required him to raise his recessed memorial plaza up to street level, which he did, reluctantly. Then, many victims' families balked because they didn't want to have to descend underground to see the names. But Arad insisted on the importance of the galleries to his design. The most heated battle erupted in 2005 when the architecture firm that Arad grudgingly collaborated with, Davis Brody Bond, redesigned an element of the galleries without Arad's consent; they decreased the number of ramps that led into the galleries from four to two. The firm argued that two ramps would cost less and be more structurally sound, but Arad countered that two ramps fundamentally altered his vision. Fewer ramps would create a more crowded path into the galleries, he said, and undermine their quiet, protected mood. And Arad couldn't believe that his associate firm went behind his back and made such an important decision without consulting him.

So Arad organized a campaign to fight the two-ramp solution. He appealed to friends and colleagues in influential positions of power, and then he and Davis Brody Bond made competing presentations to the Lower Manhattan Development Corporation. Arad's was less convincing, though, and the LMDC officially selected two ramps. According to *New York* magazine, then–Disney chief Michael Eisner, a 9/11 Memorial Foundation board member, told Arad, "If I were you, at this stage of my life, I would get behind this thing and claim victory at the end. Let things move the way they need to move, and don't obstruct things."

That could have been the end of it, but Arad continued to fight. A few months later, he appealed to Governor Pataki, who also told Arad to move on. By this time, debate and discussion over four versus two ramps had delayed construction on the memorial by six months, and Arad was beginning to truly alienate himself. Then officials at the Lower Manhattan Development Corporation met with Arad one final time and told him that there really wouldn't be four ramps. In fact, there wouldn't even be two ramps, they said. There would be no ramps, because there would be no galleries. After the lobbying and the debating and the presentations, the LMDC decided to eradicate the galleries entirely to decrease the memorial's cost.

It was the kind of conflict that typified the rebuilding: a protracted battle rendered meaningless by a committee's vote, or, in this case, a new report. In 2006, the LMDC issued the Sciame Report, by longtime city builder Frank Sciame, hired to analyze the memorial and museum and reduce their nearly $1 billion price tag; altogether, the report's recommendations, including elimination of the galleries, reduced costs by more than $250 million. Arad didn't fight officials this time around. While he voiced his regret to reporters over the loss of the galleries, he dutifully reworked his design and, by the time we spoke, seemed at peace with it. "In some ways, I think it's actually stronger," Arad said of the revised design. "All along I was saying how important it is to have both of these things side by side—life and death. And here I was forced to find a way to do that." Arad redesigned the square pools and waterfalls that marked the Twin Towers' footprints so the names could be listed around them, at street level, rather than underground. As Arad himself might have put it, he responded creatively to constraints.

And so, by 2008, every piece of the memorial's design was set. The names would be arranged according to Arad's concept of meaningful adjacencies; the memorial would be entirely at grade; and angled granite parapets, chest high and chiseled with names, would surround the edges of the large, square voids and waterfalls that filled pools thirty feet below. So once Chris Ward and the Port Authority committed to a September 2011 deadline, construction on the memorial plaza could blast ahead. And it did. For three years, thousands of engineers and construction workers labored around the clock to meet the ambitious deadline. It was contrary to Chris Ward's entire WTC site ethic, but striving to finish the memorial by the anniversary seemed to be just the sort of unifying, emotional, symbolic goal the rebuilding needed.

Of course, this kind of rallying tended to be the exception downtown. Much of the time, the land's symbolism did not unite people—as evidenced by the uproar over something called Park51, alternatively referred to as an "Islamic Center" or the "Ground Zero Mosque."

CHAPTER 14

THE ISLAMIC CENTER

I MAM FEISAL ABDUL RAUF NEEDED MORE SPACE. HE HAD BEEN LEADING Friday prayers at a mosque in Tribeca, the neighborhood next to the Financial District, for more than twenty-five years and had built a loyal and increasingly large following; indeed, his services were packed. The imam was popular in part because he had founded an interfaith group, the Cordoba Initiative, and was a leader in the city's religious community. So, in the summer of 2009, Imam Feisal teamed up with a real estate investment firm and helped purchase an empty five-story building on Park Street, twelve blocks from his mosque and two blocks from Ground Zero. Eight years earlier, the building had housed a Burlington Coat Factory outlet, but on 9/11 a piece of one of the planes fell through its roof and the store closed. For years, no one wanted to buy the building. Imam Feisal and Soho Properties, the real estate firm, paid just under $5 million for it (before the recession, the asking price was as high as $18 million), and then the imam secured a temporary permit for his Friday services.

Imam Feisal had more expansive plans for the building; he hoped it wasn't going to remain an overflow prayer space for very long. For years, he had had a vision of creating a multipurpose Islamic community center in New York City, something that offered art classes, exercise rooms, and a pool as well as a mosque. He often described it as a Muslim YMCA or a Muslim JCC. Imam Feisal almost built such a center in Lower Manhattan in 1999, but the financing fell through, and he saw the Park Street property as his second chance.

As news of the new prayer space spread, hundreds of Muslims began turning out to Park Street for Friday afternoon services. That fall, during a Ramadan break-fast at Gracie Mansion, Imam Feisal had a nice conversation with Mayor Bloomberg about his Islamic community center idea. And then, in December, the *New York Times* ran a front-page story on the new prayer space as well as on Imam Feisal's plans for a larger center. The article reported that Imam Feisal considered the location near Ground Zero to be part of the building's appeal. A community center and mosque "where a piece of the wreckage fell," Imam Feisal said, "sends the opposite statement to what happened on 9/11." He added, "We want to push back against the extremists." The article ran without a hitch, generating no negative comments.

But then the imam and his organizers presented the plan to Community Board 1, a downtown neighborhood advisory committee, in early May. The meeting itself went smoothly. Organizers outlined their basic concept, which they explained was still evolving but included plans to renovate the building and add another eight to ten stories. The imam's wife, Daisy Khan, also a leader in the interfaith and Islamic communities, had reached out to supporters in advance, including the United Jewish Federation of New York and the nonprofit September 11 Families for a Peaceful Tomorrow, and they voiced their enthusiasm. The Manhattan borough president Scott Stringer also liked the idea. A few people mentioned that some 9/11 families might find the location close to the WTC site upsetting, but otherwise the plan drew no concern. The board voted unanimously in favor of the center. The next day, a number of city papers reported on the meeting, some of which referred to plans for a "W.T.C. mosque." And that's when the uproar began.

Within days, hundreds of people had sent angry e-mails to the community board, and some victims' family members began to voice concerns that the center would bring unwanted politics to the site; meanwhile, some Tea Party leaders began to make inflammatory remarks. Community Board 1 held its next meeting a few weeks later, and both supporters and protesters filled the auditorium, but the protestors were more unruly. Some yelled about the construction of a "mega mosque" as others held signs that read, "Show respect for 3000." The community board voted in favor of the center again, 29–1, but the issue was no longer solely of interest to local tabloids. So the uproar grew louder.

To some degree, the controversy was reminiscent of the furor over the Freedom Center five years earlier: a summer uproar over an ill-defined center that tapped into simmering anger and fear, and generated the now-familiar refrain that an institution so political didn't belong at, or in this case near, sacred ground. The controversy over the Islamic center was bigger, though, and more complicated. While polls showed that a majority of New Yorkers believed it would be wrong for the city to bar the mosque from Park Street, polls also showed that a majority of New Yorkers believed it would be better for organizers to find a new spot a bit farther away. Being located two blocks away wasn't the same as being located on the sixteen-acre property; while the now-defunct Freedom Center had been planned for the WTC site, the Islamic center never was. Nonetheless, two blocks was meaningful to many people, including Imam Feisal, who recognized, in his early comments to the *Times*, the positive meaning of an Islamic community center "where a piece of the wreckage fell." Since days after the attacks, people had imagined different lines dividing the WTC site from the rest of the city, and they still did.

In early June, Jeff Jacoby, a conservative columnist at the *Boston Globe*, titled his op-ed "A Mosque at Ground Zero?" and quoted some "leading Muslim moderates" who opposed the center because they viewed it as too charged and insensitive. Jacoby closed the piece with these questions: "Will a mosque at ground zero make reconciliation more likely? Or will it needlessly rub salt in the unhealed wounds of 9/11?" Meanwhile, liberal commentators focused on the more fringe opposition to the center. A piece in *Salon*, headlined "Ground zero mosque touches off right-wing panic," reported on groups like Stop Islamization of America, headed by Pamela Geller, a New Yorker with no connection to the 9/11 attacks, who told CNN she believed the Park Street building should not house a mosque but a memorial to "the victims of hundreds of millions of years of jihadi wars, land enslavements, cultural annihilations and mass slaughter." Geller and her supporters, who gradually attracted more and more attention from the press, also described the project as a "victory mosque" that would celebrate America's defeat at Ground Zero.

Park51's organizers were completely unprepared for the backlash. Because Imam Feisal had a reputation as a moderate Islamic leader—he had worked with the FBI after 9/11—and because he had been leading Friday services at the building for months without incident, neither he nor his wife imagined the possibility of such attacks. They had no public relations team, no counter-messaging ready to go. Indeed, the organization was only beginning to get off the ground; they hadn't even started fund-raising for the center. Only after the controversy erupted, and became about something much bigger than an Islamic community center and mosque on Park Street, did the organizers hire a crisis relations firm and begin their own PR.

And had it not been for the political timing of the outcry, it's possible this might have been adequate. A few weeks of protests and news coverage followed by clarifications and outreach, and people gradually tuning out as they planned summer vacations. But the 2010 midterm elections were that fall, midterms that would announce the power of a new conservative movement, and so, as the summer progressed, more politicians engaged.

In July, a Republican candidate for governor of New York, Rick Lazio, demanded that Democratic gubernatorial candidate Andrew Cuomo, then the New York attorney general, investigate the finances of Imam Feisel's Cordoba Initiative. Cuomo promptly accused Lazio of religious intolerance, which prompted Lazio to accuse Cuomo of supporting a "sympathizer of terrorism." Then Sarah Palin and Newt Gingrich called upon Mayor Bloomberg to renounce the center; the Anti-Defamation League, which had condemned attacks against Imam Feisal, suddenly switched course and announced its own opposition to the Islamic center; and some democrats running for reelection began to voice concerns. In early September, Senate majority leader Harry Reid, in the midst of a tough campaign, said that he thought the organizers should find a new location. "It is time to bring people together, not a time for polarization, and I think it would be better off for everyone if it were built somewhere else," he said during a press conference.

But the politics of the midterms only partly explain why the Islamic center became a divisive issue. The question of the mosque brought together two ideals that many were struggling to fit together: the belief in individual rights and the belief that the WTC site was not a regular piece of the cityscape. When President Obama first commented on the issue, during an August Ramadan dinner at the White House, he spoke about the former, the country's long-held belief in rights. "I believe that Muslims have the same right to practice their religion as everyone else in this country," he said. "And that includes the right to build a place of worship and a community center on private property in Manhattan, in accordance with local laws and ordinances." After the comments drew a strong rebuke from Republicans, however, the president clarified his remarks the next day to recognize the latter, the country's strong belief in the land's special meaning. "I was not commenting, and I will not comment, on the wisdom of making the decision to put a mosque there," Obama said. "I was commenting very specifically on the right people have that dates back to our founding. That's what our country is about." Obama's attempt to recognize both ideals was so awkward that, a few hours after his clarification, he clarified again, adding that he was "not backing off in any way" from his original comments.

The strongest support for the Islamic center came from Mayor Bloomberg, who gave an emotional speech about the center in August, calling it "[as] important a test of the separation of church and state as we may see in our lifetimes." The mayor was joined by religious leaders of multiple faiths. "Whatever you may think of the proposed mosque and community center, lost in the heat of the debate has been a basic question: Should government attempt to deny private citizens the right to build a house of worship on private property based on their particular religion? That may happen in other countries, but we should never allow it to happen here," the mayor said. "The attack was an act of war, and our first responders defended not only our city, but our country and our constitution. We do not honor their lives by denying the very constitutional rights they died protecting. We honor their lives by defending those rights and the freedoms that the terrorists attacked."

Unlike the president and others before him, the mayor did not situate the two tenets of the controversy in conflict. Instead, he recognized individuals' rights and he recognized the meaning of 9/11 and Ground Zero, and then, most crucially, argued for the importance of respecting rights in the face of attacks on them. This is why Bloomberg's speech was important, and why it drew extended media coverage and debate. He made a case for building the community center near Ground

Zero not despite 9/11 but precisely because of it. The speech hardly quelled the outcry, however. By the end of summer, opposition to the Islamic center had grown angrier and larger, and hundreds of people were regularly protesting at and near the WTC site, most notably on September 11, 2010.

THE ANNIVERSARY PROTEST WASN'T SET TO BEGIN until Saturday, the eleventh, the first time the anniversary occurred on a weekend in five years, but people came out early. Late Friday afternoon, Marsha from Texas, wearing an American flag jacket, stood in front of 51 Park Street and belted out a rendition of "Let Freedom Ring," as her daughter filmed. "This is the site where they want to put the mosque, and everyone understands that they certainly have a right to do that, freedom to do that, but we just don't think it's a good thing to do as far as the feelings of everyone who was lost on 9/11," Marsha said. She and her daughter, who lived on Long Island, came to voice their opposition Friday because they thought Saturday was going to be too crazy. "You know, everyone respects everyone else's religion, but this is just adding fuel to the fire as far as we're concerned."

Around the corner, a man in a button-down shirt and tie was taping up sheets of paper printed with famous quotes on religious freedom, including those made by Thomas Jefferson and George Washington. He told me he lived in the Lower East Side, which prompted a woman listening in to interject, "That's where they should build the mosque, the Lower East Side." The confrontation heated up quickly. "We already have one," he told her. "Well, they should build this one there too," she said, walking away. He yelled after her, "Listen to the bigot! There's a bigot, in red, white, and blue! There's a bigot! You don't have to go far to find 'em in this city, which is the shame of this city, you don't have to go far to find the bigots." In the midst of this tirade, she shouted back, "You didn't lose someone on 9/11, asshole!"

That was Friday.

Saturday began with the anniversary service, which was calm and, as in years past, rather sparsely attended. Victims' families filled Zuccotti Park across the street from Ground Zero, while everyone else stood in the public square across from Zuccotti. Artists with memorial canvases filled one corner of the square and the Amish chorus group, with a table displaying free CDs, filled another. As always, bells chimed at 8:46 a.m., the moment the first plane flew into the North Tower, and then the reading of victims' names began.

Protesters were waiting until after the ceremony to begin voicing their opposition to the Islamic center, and congregating on the other side of the site too. The heart of the protests unfolded on West Broadway Street, around the corner from Zuccotti Park and closer to Park Street. Police had cordoned off parts of streets and sidewalks with metal barricades, and gradually, as morning turned into afternoon, more and more people squeezed into these bounded areas. Newspapers estimated that nearly three thousand people turned out to fight the mosque while another three thousand marched from City Hall to the Federal Building to support the mosque. But because most of the supporters departed after they marched, the pro-mosquers didn't have nearly the same presence as the anti-mosquers. Still, a few supporters mingled among the crowd on West Broadway, and participated in some of the day's more spectacular moments. Early in the afternoon, standing at the head of one cordoned-off area, a tall man in a green cap read aloud from the Koran. Midway through his reading, another man pushed his way to the front and lit a page of another Koran on fire. "Sir, why are you doing this?" a reporter yelled out, failing to elicit a response. Without seconds, half a dozen police officers swarmed the man with the burning pages and dragged him away, followed closely by a cluster of television cameras.

The protests had the feel of an angry carnival. There were antiabortion protestors and Tea Party supporters alongside the anti-mosquers, and there were more people than you might expect in costume. At least two women were dressed as the Statue of Liberty, one with a sign taped to her chest that read, "As a Christian, I believe in redemption. As an American, I believe in religious liberty." Also making his way through the crowd was a young guy dressed head to toe as a white bear with a sign around his neck that read, "Free Hugz." The bear told me he was "agnostic" on the question of the mosque and wanted to add some levity to the day; by early afternoon, he had hugged about fourteen people. Two large, muscled men with shaved heads, wearing American flag pants, carried a seven-foot-high cross that read, "In God We Trust The People"; they traveled from south Florida, they said, and opposed the mosque because this was sacred ground. A number of protesters brought yard chairs and coolers. One Florida family brought their twelve-year-old daughter. With her hair in a side ponytail, wearing oversized sunglasses, she held a large poster that read, "No Mosque at Ground Zero" underneath a hand-drawn picture of two airplanes flying into the Twin Towers. "It really gets me mad," she said, "because first they knocked down the Twin Towers, and now they just want to build a mosque and show it's a victory for them. It's not right."

Despite the array of causes and beliefs, practically everyone in attendance shared a few characteristics, or, more precisely, gadgets. Nearly everyone had a camera, which meant nearly everyone was on high alert for filmable moments. Some people even created their own. I watched one pro-mosquer strike up an argument with an anti-mosquer and then hold his cell phone out at a distance and film his own debate. One of the day's more endearing efforts was a series of flyers designed by high school students, taped on street poles and traffic lights. The sheets were completely blank except for two prompts, one on each side of the page. The left side read, "The Ground Zero mosque should not be built because:..." and the right side read, "The Islamic Community Center should be built because:..." I watched a few students collect the flyers later in the afternoon and express their frustration that so few people had responded. Everyone had been either too busy recording the scene or speaking into microphones to bother putting pen to paper.

To some degree, the cameras made it easier to dismiss the ugly things people were saying. Many voicing their opposition seemed drawn to the spectacle, and some were certainly performing for the cameras. But, then again, when thousands broke into a chant of "No Obama mosque!" the sentiment felt very sincere. One woman I spoke to, who came to support the mosque, commented on the dual nature of being at the protest. She said that when she took a step back and observed the debate, she found it interesting. When she stepped in and engaged, she found it upsetting.

Ultimately, the uproar did not succeed in defeating the project. After the midterm elections, the protests died down and plans for the community center and mosque moved forward. But the anti-mosque movement may have helped generate a rift among organizers. A few months after the anniversary protest, Imam Feisal announced that he was taking a reduced role in the project and that it was being led instead by the developer and cofounder of Soho Properties, Sharif el-Gamal. The rift stemmed in part from new statements by Imam Feisal that he was open to moving the location of the center in the name of "improving relationships with people." Mr. Gamal opposed any move and asked the imam to be a board member rather than a cofounder.

The uproar also helped obscure other news. That same summer, Congress decided not to pass a bill funding $7 billion in health care for sick 9/11 rescue workers. It was ugly politics all around. A majority of congressmen supported the bill, but Democrats used a special measure to bring it to the floor that required a two-thirds majority. The reason for the special measure was to prevent Republicans from adding an amendment that would have denied health benefits to rescue workers who were illegal immigrants; many Democrats disagreed with the amendment but didn't want to be seen supporting undocumented workers during an election season. So the 255–159 vote in favor of the bill fell short, with almost all Republicans voting against it, citing concerns over its cost, and almost all Democrats supporting it.

But that wasn't quite it; there was media spectacle here too. In early August, as the anti-mosque movement was heating up, a member of the House of Representatives, Democrat Anthony Weiner from New York (who later resigned amid controversy over unseemly text messages), gave an impassioned speech on the floor of the House railing against his Republican colleagues. In an op-ed titled "Why I Was Angry," Weiner wrote, "Instead of engaging in a real debate about how to address the challenges we face, Republicans have turned to obstruction, no matter the issue, and then cry foul after the fact. They claim to want an open legislative process with more consultation and debate, but the truth is they simply don't want to pass anything."

The speech didn't change their minds, but it generated buzz on YouTube and then caught the attention of *Daily Show* host Jon Stewart, a longtime friend of Weiner's, who played part of it on his show and became increasingly devoted to the cause of rescue workers' health care. Later that fall, Stewart devoted an entire show to a round-table discussion with rescue workers discussing their illnesses and was widely credited for bringing renewed public attention to the topic. Partly because of this public interest, Democrats brought the bill up for vote again in December 2010. This time, it passed the House but failed the Senate. Then, twelve days later, after Rudolph Giuliani and Mayor Bloomberg spoke out against Senate Republicans, the Senate voted again and passed a scaled-down version of the bill funding $4.3 billion in health care instead of $7.4 billion.

The Islamic center and mosque and the bill aiding rescue workers were very different projects, but the oppositions they generated were more related than they appeared. Those most opposed to the mosque often cited fears that it was a "victory mosque," that it would somehow signal the nation's defeat. And while politicians tended to cite costs in their opposition to the health bill, the result was a reluctance to assist heroic individuals who, years later, needed help. In different ways, both projects presented evidence of vulnerability, real or perceived. Both projects raised the possibility that national myths of strength and power were not as absolute as many may have liked them to be.

And, of course, both projects reminded everyone that the story of 9/11 remained hotly contested.

CHAPTER 15

THE MUSEUM

THE CONTROVERSY OVER THE ISLAMIC CENTER CAUGHT MANY off guard, but those least surprised by it may have been the staffers at the nascent 9/11 Memorial Museum. At the time of the debate, they were busy developing exhibits in consultation with experts and victims' families, and learning firsthand how differently people understood the 9/11 attacks. "9/11 means a whole lot of things besides just the day of 9/11," Michael Shulan, creative director of the museum, said. "It can mean a clash of cultures, it can be grief, it can be confusion, it could be betrayal, it could be our justification for military power, it can be all of those things. And in fact I think it is all of those things."

The 9/11 Memorial Museum was born in 2006, partly in response to the failure of the Freedom Center. After the center's demise, the Lower Manhattan Development Corporation worked with consultants to enlarge the underground area Michael Arad had conceived for an "interpretive center" and, working with the 9/11 Memorial Foundation, created a museum instead. (The LMDC briefly considered putting the museum in the first floors of the Freedom Tower because it was struggling to secure commercial tenants, but the match proved too awkward.) The distinction between "center" and "museum" mattered. A museum "comes with a set of expectations," said Jan Ramirez, a historian who began documenting 9/11 for the New-York Historical Society in 2001 and consulted on the interpretive center before becoming chief curator of the 9/11 Memorial Museum. While a center can really be anything, a museum maintains a permanent collection, which requires large off-site storage facilities as well as historians on staff to manage it and curate exhibits. Generally speaking, a museum is a more precise, more ambitious, and usually more expensive endeavor.

The institution isn't *simply* a museum, though. It is a memorial museum, dedicated to both educating people about what happened and commemorating the victims of the attacks. In this, it is not unlike the United States Holocaust Museum in Washington, D.C., or Yad Vashem in Jerusalem, or the Kigali Genocide Memorial Center in Rwanda. At Ground Zero, part of the underground space houses a memorial exhibit, displaying photographs of each victim of 9/11 and the 1993 bombing of the World Trade Center, and another part houses an historical exhibit, exploring the what, how, and why of the attacks.

The memorial museum, then, is like the antithesis of the Freedom Center, which hadn't planned to discuss 9/11 very much at all, much less memorialize its victims. To many 9/11 Memorial Museum staffers, this was the Freedom Center's fundamental misstep. "When you're at the actual site of an atrocity, I think you are obligated to focus on what happened at that place," said Alice Greenwald, who became director of the 9/11 Memorial Museum after nineteen years at the Holocaust Museum. The Freedom Center "didn't pay attention to where it was," she told me. "I don't think that, right out the gate, you can start making meaning out of it. You first have to attest to what happened."

Greenwald's years at the Holocaust Museum taught her the value of specificity, she said. Instead of attempting to tell a story of all genocides, the Holocaust Museum tells one very particular story, which it uses as a lens to extrapolate broader lessons. Greenwald aimed to achieve a similar balance at the 9/11 Memorial Museum, but she knew her prior experiences only partially prepared her for the job, because the Holocaust Museum isn't located at a site of violence. "Not only are we an historic site, we're an archaeological site," Greenwald said of the 9/11 Memorial Museum's location. "The museum embodies actual in situ remnants of what was here." Greenwald considers the museum's archaeology an incredible asset that helps dramatize the museum's story, but she knows that being at the WTC site also means being at a place where people were murdered. "It is a place where remains were recovered and not identified," she said. Architects designed the memorial museum to encompass the footprints of the Twin Towers at bedrock, below the memorial pools. The memorial exhibition sits within the South Tower footprint and the historical exhibition within the North Tower footprint.

Both the memorial and historical exhibitions have proved challenging to design, but the historical exhibition has raised particularly difficult questions, because this is where history and memory most conspicuously intermingle. Because it is a memorial museum, the historical exhibition has to remain consistent with the institution's overall memorial mood and, since the historical and memorial exhibitions are housed on the same level, directly under Michael Arad's memorial plaza, the history cannot veer too far from 9/11, lest it seem out of place. Designing the historical exhibition, in other words, meant honoring some built-in constraints that the Freedom Center did not have.

Working with a team of curators, educators, exhibition developers, and exhibition designers, Greenwald shaped the broad contours of the museum's historical narrative with creative director Michael Shulan, who isn't a historian or a museum expert but did create New York City's very first post-9/11 exhibition in two storefronts in SoHo, "here is new york: A Democracy of Photographs." After Shulan closed the SoHo show, he took his exhibition on the road, visiting locales around the world and talking with audiences about terrorism. The experiences dramatically shaped his curatorial approach, which Shulan explained via a story of his time in Russia. Shulan was being interviewed on a local Russian television station, when the translator told him that the interviewer was asking an offensive question. "I said, 'Let me guess,'" Shulan recounted. "'The question is, why should a bunch of Americans come to this place where there's terrorism all the time, and show pictures about this and tell us that what happened in New York is special?' I said, 'Tell them we don't come here as Americans, we don't come here to assert the primacy of our experience. This is a global story, it's an international problem, and you can [create an exhibition] too. And if you want to do it, we'll help you.'"

At the 9/11 Memorial Museum, Shulan wanted to create what he called "a non-didactic" museum that made space for every point of view. He didn't like the "museum voice," he said. "The visitors really need to feel that it is their story. Everyone has a stake, and therefore it needs to be an open museum." Greenwald believed in a "museum voice," at least some of the time, but she had hired Shulan for his unique approach and she generally agreed with it. Greenwald framed one of the museum's central tensions as one of authority. "How do you deal with the fact that everyone who comes in is a 9/11 expert?" She asked. "They're not coming to learn from you—they know it, at least, from their own sense of it."

Shulan and Greenwald's team decided to begin the historical exhibit with the day of the attacks, that is, the two planes flying into each tower, a plane crashing into the Pentagon, and a plane crashing in a field near Shanksville, Pennsylvania. It is the largest section of the exhibit, with over ten thousand square feet of floor space. Many of the iconic objects salvaged from Ground Zero and stored at Hangar 17 are in this section, including the dramatic, partially crushed fire truck from Ladder 3 and steel remnants that formed the facade of the Twin Towers. In addition to telling people what happened, however, Shulan believed it was important to replicate the mood of the day, particularly the experience of witnessing the attacks, since most people's experiences of 9/11 were as witnesses, whether via television or in person in New York and around Arlington, Virginia. The confusion, the shifting accounts of what was transpiring, the multiple ways in which people made sense of what was happening; instead of taming this uncertainty, Shulan hoped to build it into the story.

They achieved this mood in part by including news reports from the day and people's individual witness stories. But the museum could not, of course, express all points of view; it had to make choices. Chief curator Jan Ramirez recalled a few "feisty discussions," as she put it, in which senior staff wrangled over what should be included. One of the more contentious discussions, she said, concerned the famous photograph by Tom Franklin, of three firefighters raising an American flag in the rubble of the World Trade Center, evoking the classic image of the flag-raising at Iwo Jima during World War II. While many staff believed the photograph had to be included, some, including Shulan, believed the photograph was too kitschy.

But Ramirez and others felt strongly about including the photograph. "What are these guys doing? They are in this devastated zone and they are making meaning again," she said. "They have found a flag, they have seen a bent pole, they're going to put it back up. It's such an important moment. It's rallying the troops—we can't ignore it." It turned out that Tom Franklin wasn't the only photographer to capture the scene; the WTC site had not yet been closed off to the public, so a number of people were there with cameras, and, as Ramirez put it, "this was such an important moment that many photographers began sensing something was happening, and they came and caught different seconds." After multiple discussions, Ramirez and other staff proposed displaying a triptych, three different photographs from three different photographers, displaying multiple angles and moments of the flag-raising. Several images undercut the myth of "one iconic moment," Ramirez said, and suggest instead an event with multiple points of view, like the attacks more broadly. Shulan didn't like three photographs much more than he liked one, but he went along with it.

The staff consulted museum and history experts and victims' families to help them make informed decisions. This was another lesson from the failure of the Freedom Center as well as Greenwald's experience at the Holocaust Museum: victims' families needed to be included in the process. The museum's board of directors includes eleven family members, such as Debra Burlingame, who spearheaded the Freedom Center's removal, alongside stars like Robert De Niro, financiers like Frank Bisignano (the chief operating officer of JP Morgan), and public officials like John Cahill, Governor Pataki's former chief of staff. The Franklin photograph did not cause debate among representatives of victims' families; they agreed it should be included. But some other photographs proved highly contentious: those of the nineteen hijackers.

GREENWALD, SHULAN, AND THEIR TEAM KNEW they couldn't document only what happened on 9/11. "It wasn't a tsunami, it wasn't a natural disaster. There were human beings who were agents of this destruction." Greenwald said. "And if we're going to be honest about the story, we've got to talk about them." Some victims' families felt differently, however, because they feared that identifying the perpetrators could unintentionally commemorate them and their crimes. Indeed, some families believed the perpetrators wanted nothing more than to be recognized at the location of their so-called triumph. Still, Greenwald and Shulan believed the historical exhibition had to discuss who did this, in part to allay any doubts about the attackers' identities. "There was no conspiracy theory issue on our part," Greenwald said. "We know who did it and we are not fudging about it."

After visitors wind their way through a history of the day, they arrive at a break in the story and a brief discussion of Islamist extremism, the hijackers, and Al Qaeda, including why they targeted the Twin Towers, both in 1993 and 2001. Devoting a relatively small amount of floor space to this section was one way museum staffers made sure not to inadvertently commemorate or glorify the attackers. While the first part of the exhibition occupies ten thousand square feet, the part focusing specifically on Al Qaeda occupies less than eight hundred square feet. Some described it to me as more like a hallway than a full exhibition space. Staffers also decided to limit nearly all mention of the terrorists to this second part, to underscore their belief that the perpetrators are just one piece (and a minor piece) of the bigger story.

The most intense conflict concerned the perpetrators' photographs. Museum staffers and some victims' families believed that showing their faces was an important part of the museum's educational obligation. But other families didn't want to have to see the faces of the people who murdered their child or spouse or parent. And still other families worried about the symbolism of such display. Not too far away, in the South Tower footprint, the memorial exhibition displays the faces of all 2,983 victims of 9/11 and the 1993 World Trade Center bombing, and some families worried that displaying photographs of the perpetrators in the historical exhibition could end up suggesting they were part of the museum's broader commemorative project.

For months, museum staff met with families to discuss their concerns and brainstorm ways to responsibly display the photographs. When I spoke to museum staffers, in 2011, they had recently decided to include the images, and to make them very small. They planned to arrange them according to the four hijacked flights and at a shallow angle so that those who want can look and those who don't can pass on by. "You can't think of a less remarkable way to do it," said Katie Edgerton, an assistant curator who worked almost exclusively on this section of the exhibit. The hijackers' photographs also include FBI stickers from the criminal investigation that read, "evidence"—one more feature that differentiates these photographs from those in the memorial exhibition.

Logistically, photographs are one of the few *things* the museum can show here. The museum displays a few key objects, like a laptop owned by Ramzi Yousef, who orchestrated the 1993 bombing and is the nephew of 9/11 mastermind Khalid Sheikh Mohammed, but by and large it doesn't own many items that belonged to the perpetrators. As Edgerton put it, "We're not going to put in Osama bin Laden's slipper." Fewer artifacts is one more way this section looks and feels different from the rest of the exhibition and is figuratively as well as literally smaller. But the relative absence also draws more attention to what *is* displayed. And even small, unremarkable photographs are freighted with meaning, particularly at Ground Zero in the still-charged atmosphere of post-9/11 America. "You can't just say it was nineteen crazy guys who had a bad meal, so they decided to go kill somebody. They had ideas," Michael Shulan said. "One can't for a moment excuse what they did, but there is a process that took them to do this." Photographs turn the perpetrators from an abstraction into real people.

The museum produced a six-minute film about Islamist extremism to provide visitors with what Greenwald called "basic tools" to make sense of the perpetrators' actions. "We're giving you 'This is what unfolded,'" Greenwald said, emphasizing that the museum chronicles, but does not interpret, the stated reasons for the attacks. "Here's Osama bin Laden in a CNN interview in a cave in 1996, declaring war on the United States," Greenwald said, to illustrate the kind of information that appears in the historical exhibition. "Did we pay attention to that? No. We were living in another frame of reference. That is a fact. I'm not interpreting this, I'm just telling you."

The line between documenting and interpreting is, to be sure, a thin one, but museum staffers were adamant that they observe it, because they want to make sure no one accidently interprets their inclusion of bin Laden's statements as legitimating his ideology. "By laying out the facts, we avoid ambiguity," said Joe Daniels, president and CEO of the 9/11 Memorial, drawing a contrast between stating Al Qaeda's tactics, say, and trying to understand or explain those tactics.

As museum staffers' cautiousness suggests, broaching Al Qaeda's ideas, even calling them "ideas," has been an incredibly tricky prospect for public institutions and elected officials. In 2007, when Rudolph Giuliani was running for president, he engaged in a much-discussed exchange during a Republican primary debate with fellow aspirant Ron Paul. Paul said, "Have you ever read the reasons they attacked us? They attack us because we've been over there; we've been bombing Iraq for ten years." This comment prompted the moderator to ask Paul if he "was suggesting that we invited the 9/11 attack?" to which Paul responded, "I am suggesting that we listen to the people who attacked us and the reason they did it." Then Giuliani chimed in. "That's an extraordinary statement, as someone who lived through the attack of September 11, that we invited the attack because we were attack-ing Iraq. I don't think I've heard that before, and I've heard some pretty absurd explanations for September 11." Applause and cheers followed Giuliani's comment, and a few hours later, most pundits declared Giuliani the winner of the debate in large part because of this exchange.

One of the museum's approaches to its section on Al Qaeda is to "use their words to hang them," Edgerton said; that is, to let bin Laden and others speak for and indict themselves. But the Paul-Giuliani exchange reveals the dangers of this approach, which museum staffers appreci-ated as well. Playing uninterpreted clips of bin Laden subtly empowers the Al Qaeda leader; it accepts his reading of history. Partly for this reason, the six-minute film contextualizes bin Laden's statements and provides visitors with a broader, if introductory, historical framework. The museum worked with scholars of Middle Eastern history to docu-ment the relationships between Al Qaeda and the Soviet-Afghan War, for example, and to present the jihadist concept of "near enemy/far enemy," in which Al Qaeda advocates attacking "far enemies" like the United States to prompt them to withdraw support for "near enemies," like Egyptian president Anwar Sadat, who was assassinated by Islamist extremists in 1981.

There is only so much information a six-minute film can convey, however. Which is the point—the exhibition isn't about Al Qaeda. Nonetheless, the museum spent a great deal of time making sure they didn't show too much, or too little, about the group, a line that constantly evolved. Among the materials considered for exhibition were some of the hijackers' video suicide wills, in which they explain their actions in their own words. One of the wills, however, is different from the others. The hijacker who piloted Flight 11, which crashed into the North Tower, and the hijacker who piloted Flight 93, which crashed in Shanksville, Pennsylvania, recorded their video will together, and the two men are jokey and lighthearted. While the museum considered showing a clip or a still, it ultimately chose not to, because it decided that displaying the hijackers having fun while it documented their crimes was inappropriate. "You see him putting on a hat and then reading, then laughing, then him posing with a gun, and then putting the gun in another pose. It's very unchoreographed," Edgerton said. They were being playful.

Katie Edgerton was one of the younger members on the museum staff; she was in high school on 9/11, and, when we spoke in 2011, she was about to leave her job to pursue a masters degree in comparative media studies at MIT. She wanted to work at the museum because she didn't think that "as a society we knew what to make of [9/11] or knew how to talk about it," she said. But researching 9/11 has not provided simple answers; if anything, it has underscored how complicated the history remains.

Edgerton told me that her most lasting memories will be of the "little stories," like "the fact that thousands of golf balls survived the collapse of the Twin Towers." She continued, "You're left with these giant pieces of steel and these dented golf balls. It's weird, but it also tells you something about the people that worked in the buildings. Looking at the little golf ball, it's like, 'Oh my God.' I don't know what to say about that, but I feel something more powerfully looking at that golf ball than making a thesis about Osama bin Laden. In a sense, I think the dented golf ball is the counterpoint to his declaration of war. It's like, 'This is what's left.' "

THE THIRD AND FINAL PART OF THE HISTORICAL exhibition explores the days after the attacks, including the rescue and recovery operations at the World Trade Center site, and Americans' evolving responses to the day and its aftermath. By necessity, this is the historical exhibition's most open-ended section. "It was important for us to convey the sense of displacement," assistant curator Liz Mazucci said. "This was the next episode in the terrorist act itself. It's not distinct from the destruction of the buildings." She continued, "Part of the intention of the terrorist act was to leave people with this sense of anxiety and of something coming next."

Creative director Michael Shulan felt particularly close to and protective of this section, because it overlapped with his experiences downtown after the attacks. He wanted this section to reflect the kinds of spontaneous gatherings and debates that were happening in those early weeks and months. "Democracy is an imperfect system for working through differences between people," he said, "but it's a functioning society. And that's what this place has to do with the meaning of 9/11." Shulan wanted to create a museum "where this thing can be interrogated."

The potential content was limitless, but staff employed a few key criteria to guide decision making. Every event or moment had to be directly connected to 9/11. For example, rather than providing a brief history of the U.S. war in Afghanistan, the museum will document the war by explaining that it was a response to 9/11, and discuss, say, how soldiers wore 9/11 paraphernalia on their uniforms in remembrance of victims. Staff also aimed to show different sides of an issue. Mazucci mentioned the antiwar movement as an example. "You had a really healthy antiwar movement after 9/11, but a lot of people were staunch supporters of Bush's policies," she said, "so that's an easy one." The exhibition will display a number of ephemera from the aftermath, including a photograph of a rally in support of U.S. troops of Iraq and a flyer from an antiwar protest. "You're telling multiple stories and you're not choosing one over the other," she said.

Locating different lines—pro versus con, official versus grass-roots—helped curators structure the unwieldy narrative. But sometimes a clear line was difficult to find. One of the museum's most difficult decisions concerned an artifact from Hangar 17, the basalt-like mound discovered by the Port Authority's preservation team during recovery operations. Roughly three feet tall, the fifteen-ton mound contains per-haps four or five building stories compressed during the collapse of one of the towers and then subjected to intense heat from the ensuing fires. Bits of paper and edges of filing cabinets that weren't melted poke out on the surface. The museum refers to the artifact as "the composite," and believes it uniquely documents the power of the towers' collapse as well as the harsh conditions of rescue and recovery operations. But some family members have felt strongly that the composite shouldn't be displayed, because they believe it contains human remains.

The museum developed a policy about human remains early on: it will not display or collect human remains or show photographs of body parts. Some memorial museums have made different choices. The museum at Auschwitz exhibits human hair, and museums in Rwanda display the bones of victims of genocide. But at the WTC site, where remains have continued to be discovered long after the recovery period ended, the issue is incredibly delicate. The museum decided to display dust from the collapse of the towers, but only dust that has been tested and determined not to contain remains.

The museum hired specialists to perform forensic testing and analysis of two large composites and several smaller pieces that had broken off. All tests for microscopic traces of human DNA were negative. But the museum knew these tests were somewhat incomplete because scientists could test only the composites' outside surface; testing the interior risked destroying the artifacts. Consequently, the museum conducted additional research, analyzing the heat levels that had created the fused material. Scientists determined that, at heat levels in excess of two thousand degrees Fahrenheit, the possibility of there being human remains within the composites was exceedingly remote.

The museum also convened a planning meeting on the composite, one of a series of discussions the museum organized with involved constituencies and experts in museum planning and American history. At the meeting, museum staff told the audience of family members and experts that it understood the question of the composite as one of authenticity versus reverence for the dead. The museum also invited two family members of victims, both of whom had become activists after 9/11, to offer their contrasting viewpoints. 9/11 Memorial Foundation board member Debra Burlingame, whose brother was a pilot on the flight which crashed into the Pentagon, argued in favor of the composite's display. "We have an obligation to leave behind what we know," she said at the meeting. Diane Horning, founder of a group called WTC Families for a Proper Burial, whose son Matthew was a firefighter killed at the WTC, opposed the display of the composite because she believed it contains remains and should be buried. "The surviving families own the dead," she said, arguing that the museum should defer decisions on any object that may contain remains to family members.

Not surprisingly, neither the scientific testing nor the planning conversation changed the minds of those opposed to the composite's display. To them, Burlingame's testimony was compromised by the fact that her brother was killed at the Pentagon, not the World Trade

Center. And the issue tapped into their bigger concerns about how human remains have been, and continue to be, treated. Horning's WTC Families for a Proper Burial sued the city of New York in 2005 for its treatment of WTC debris at Fresh Kills Landfill (a judge dismissed the case in 2008). Similarly, Horning dislikes the decision to store unidentified human remains in an underground repository, overseen by the Office of Chief Medical Examiner, in a space adjacent to the public areas of the museum. Back in 2003, the LMDC consulted with a group of victims' families who wanted the unidentified remains to be at the bedrock of the World Trade Center site, but some, including Horning and Sally Regenhard, who founded the Skyscraper Safety Campaign, want them buried in a site visible from ground level. They have protested the underground repository, as well as the display of the composite, for years.

After the planning conversation, the museum conducted one more bit of research. In 2010, it hired a consulting agency to conduct focus groups on the composite and four other key artifacts, including the crushed fire truck from Ladder 3. The focus groups included randomly selected members of the public, first responders, recovery workers, downtown residents, and randomly selected 9/11 family members, all of whom strongly supported exhibition of the composite. The museum continued to deliberate after receiving the consulting agency's report, but it knew it had to make a decision. And so, eventually, it decided to include the composite as part of its discussion of rescue and recovery operations.

Endings presented a unique challenge for the museum. After all, while the story of 9/11 is unfinished, the historical exhibition cannot be. One of the last stops in the museum, outside the historical exhibition, tends to this paradox. It is a digital display of events connected to 9/11 and reported in the news, as determined by a specially designed computer program that identifies the most newsworthy events and issues and then plots them on a timeline ranging from 2001 to the present. The Museum calls it "Timescape," and when we spoke in 2011, Greenwald suggested it would likely pick up articles relating to the proposed Islamic center, since much of the reporting invoked the center's proximity to the WTC site. For a story without an ending, it was a novel solution. And, for staffers accustomed to endless deliberations and debates, it was a change of pace. They had a computer algorithm.

CHAPTER 16

A DEATH, THE DURSTS, AND AN ANNIVERSARY

AT 11:35 P.M. ON SUNDAY, MAY 1, 2011, PRESIDENT OBAMA interrupted the night's regular television programming. "Justice has been done," the president said. Special combat forces had killed Osama bin Laden. The leader of Al Qaeda was dead.

The news had actually begun to spread on social media about an hour before the president's speech. By 11 p.m., a dozen new posts about bin Laden were appearing on Facebook every second; he was trending on Twitter. By midnight, minutes after Obama signed off, hundreds had already flooded the streets around the White House, into Times Square, and around Ground Zero. Eventually, nearly one thousand people filled Vesey and Church streets bordering the site, climbing up traffic lights and in some instances trying to breach the construction fence around the sixteen-acre pit, only to be waved down by cops both monitoring and enjoying the celebration. People cheered, waved American flags, popped champagne, took swigs of beer, and sang "The Star-Spangled Banner."

The crowds at Ground Zero included people of all ages, but college students and twentysomethings were the most ubiquitous. They had their own memories of 9/11, mostly dating to elementary or middle school. They remembered sitting at their desks and listening to their teachers explain that terrorists had hijacked airplanes and flown them into buildings. They remembered watching the Twin Towers collapse on television. They were young at the time of the attacks, but they weren't *that* young. They knew bin Laden's work.

As the days passed, pundits assumed requisite positions. Some liberal writers cautioned against reading too much into the revelers' exuberance; they said that because the news hit as young people were leaving bars and looking for the next party, timing had as much to do with it as genuine feeling. Filmmaker Michael Moore chastised the American "frat boy" culture on display. "It's one thing to be happy that a criminal has been captured and dealt with," Moore wrote on his blog, not long after walking to Ground Zero that night. "It's another thing to throw a kegger celebrating his death at the site where the remains of his victims are still occasionally found." Writing in the UK's *Guardian*, Mona Eltahawy, who went to Ground Zero looking to, as she put it, "light candles," described the scene as "a parody of 'Team America,'" a film by the creators of *South Park* sending up American nationalism. "Now that we've parodied the parody," she wrote, "can the frat boys go home and can we return to the revolutions of the Middle East and north Africa that symbolically killed Bin Laden months ago?" While the crowds chanted "Fuck Osama," Moore and Eltahawy ended their critiques with a more restrained, but maybe not so different, refrain: "Good riddance, Osama," they wrote.

Meanwhile, conservative pundits used the killing to make a case for the Bush administration's controversial treatment of prisoners of the War on Terror. "Whence came the intelligence that led to

Abbottabad?" asked Charles Krauthammer in the *Washington Post*. "Many places, *including* from secret prisons in Romania and Poland; from terrorists seized and kidnapped, then subjected to interrogations, sometimes 'harsh' or 'enhanced'; from Gitmo detainees; from a huge bureaucratic apparatus of surveillance and eavesdropping. In other words, from a Global War on Terror infrastructure that critics, including Barack Obama himself, deplored as a tragic detour from American rectitude."

As details of the raid and killing emerged, Americans learned that bin Laden was unarmed when he was shot, raising questions about whether he could have been captured alive. Some wondered if the war with Al Qaeda was now over. Would troops in Afghanistan be coming home? Questions multiplied. Reporters called the 9/11 Memorial Museum to ask if, in light of the news, it was creating a new historical exhibition, and Director Alice Greenwald attempted to temper the frenzy. She told journalists that, while the museum would indeed integrate bin Laden's killing into the narrative, the news didn't necessitate large-scale changes. "We still have to tell what happened," Greenwald said. "The people who were murdered are still dead."

Later in the week, President Obama traveled to Ground Zero to meet with a group of victims' families and lay a wreath. Thousands of people descended upon the site for the president's visit; I went down too. The scene reminded me a little of the first year anniversary at Ground Zero, when people filled blocks and blocks and some stretches were so crowded it was difficult to move. The mood was lighter on this occasion, though, and instead of looking upon an empty skyline, people took photographs of the burgeoning 1 WTC/Freedom Tower. Its steel frame now rose up to the seventieth floor.

Margaret, from Ontario, was visiting her twentysomething son who lived a few blocks away on Wall Street. She told me that the whole family had rushed out to the site on Sunday night, and she was so thrilled about bin Laden's death that she and her husband extended their stay to attend the rally. "We got him!" she said triumphantly. Margaret was a bit peeved, though. Obama had announced right before his visit that he would not release the photographs of bin Laden's body. They risked enraging America's enemies, he said; it was akin to "spiking the football." But Margaret didn't buy it. "Americans paid billions of dollars to kill him, and they can't see him?" she asked. "We all saw the pictures of people jumping out of buildings on 9/11. What makes him so special that we can't see him?"

Three students from Pace University, located a few blocks from Ground Zero, also returned for Obama's visit after coming out Sunday night. Jamie said he disapproved of people's initial reaction. "Celebrating revenge? Where's the decency in that?" he asked. But his distaste hadn't been strong enough to keep him from joining the revelers. Kyle told me he thought college students turned out in such large numbers because social media spread the news first. Everyone was on their Facebook page, he said, when posts started appearing about bin Laden, at which point they headed outside. A few people were rowdy, he acknowledged, but he didn't think the crowd was too unruly. What he remembered was the singing and a moment of silence, and a round of applause that erupted when police officers walked through the crowd. "The emotion was amazing," he said.

A FEW WEEKS LATER, AT THE END OF May, news broke about 1 WTC/ Freedom Tower. It wasn't as consequential, of course, as Bin Laden's death, but for publishing insiders, downtown realtors, and the tower's owner, the Port Authority of New York and New Jersey, it came pretty close. Condé Nast, the prestigious publisher of magazines including the *New Yorker* and *Vanity Fair*, had just signed a deal to move its five thousand employees from Times Square to a new headquarters in the iconic skyscraper. The Freedom Tower, derided and mocked for years as the city's "white elephant," would soon be receiving Anna Wintour and guests in a fleet of black cars with tinted windows.

Port Authority executive director Chris Ward and 1 WTC architect David Childs had traveled to Times Square months earlier to make the pitch to the Newhouse family, which owns Condé Nast. Childs delivered a presentation on the building's state-of-the-art green technology and security systems, while Ward reviewed construction progress on the memorial plaza and the site's vehicle security center. As Ward tells it, the meeting's most critical moment came when someone asked the inevitable questions: Would they be safe? Would the building be targeted again? Ward was prepared. He reviewed the building's safety features, and then told everyone that *safe* was a relative term. "I said, 'You know, nothing in life now, post-9/11, will ever be safe.'" he told me. "I said, 'We live in a post-9/11 world and in some ways you're probably safer downtown on an hourly or daily basis, given all of the security that's there.'" Apparently, it was a good answer. Condé Nast agreed to lease one million square feet of brand-new, specially designed space at roughly $60 a foot, the same low rate it's been paying for its Times Square offices, constructed in 1999. As part of the deal, the Port Authority agreed to pay out the last five years of Condé's Times Square lease.

The Condé deal coincided with another big deal for the Port Authority. The Port Authority had decided to partner with a developer to help it lease the office space in 1 WTC/Freedom Tower, and after receiving bids from some of the city's most well-known firms, the Port Authority selected the Durst Organization, a storied, family-run outfit that helped develop Times Square, including 4 Times Square for Condé Nast. Chris Ward denied that the Durst deal set up the Condé Nast deal, even though the timing was uncanny. Condé first signaled its interest in the building a few weeks after the Port Authority selected Durst. The deal stipulated that Durst would pay the Port Authority $100 million for a roughly 10 percent stake in the building, and would oversee the tower's leasing and management. This meant that, regardless of the direct relationship between the Durst and Condé Nast deals, once Durst joined with the Port Authority, it was the developer's job to convince its prized tenant to move to 1 WTC.

For the Dursts, purchasing a stake in Freedom Tower echoed the organization's approach to Times Square: buy early, cheaply, and bring in high-profile tenants to increase property values. Currently in its third generation of ownership, the Dursts have developed large swathes of Midtown, and are well known for turning around bad neighborhoods. When they started developing areas around Times Square in the 1980s and '90s, it was the city's seedy red-light district; now it's the city's media hub.

Still, the Durst deal was surprising because a few years earlier Douglas Durst was one of the Freedom Tower's most outspoken critics. In 2007, a few weeks after Governor Pataki left office, Durst and Anthony Malkin, owner of the Empire State Building, took out full-page ads in the *New York Times* and the *Wall Street Journal*, among other city papers, calling for a halt on the building's construction. "We believe there is no reason to proceed with the commitments for the Freedom Tower," they wrote in an open letter. "We believe the Freedom Tower is a legacy of poor planning and decision-making by the Pataki Administration," it continued. "It is far too important an undertaking to be mired by inefficient planning, hasty design, or occupancy by government agencies paying sub-market rents." They signed the letter, "The Continuing Committee for a Reasonable World Trade Center," a riff on Durst's father's opposition to the Twin Towers forty years earlier and his creation of the Committee for a Reasonable World Trade Center.

Why did Durst and Malkin care? Durst said he was genuinely concerned about the impact of a poorly planned building on downtown's commercial market. He worried that Freedom Tower could be like the Twin Towers, he said, requiring huge government subsidies for years. There may have been other reasons. Writing in the *New York Sun*, reporter David Lombino pointed out that Durst and Malkin own the city's two most desirable locations for television and radio antennae, and when the Freedom Tower is completed, featuring the tallest antenna system in the region, the fees that Durst and Malkin are able to charge for their antennae will likely decrease. In any case, perhaps for multiple reasons, Durst derided the building and then, a few years later, changed his mind. Durst explained the about-face as a pragmatic business decision. The building was going forward, he said, and he figured he might as well make some money. Based upon current market projections, Durst is poised to net roughly $100 million from his ownership stake, plus millions more thanks to lowering the Port Authority's construction costs.

After Durst signed the deal and buzz swirled about Condé's interest, other companies started eyeing downtown too. *Newsweek/Daily Beast* moved to Lower Manhattan a few months after Durst signed with the Port Authority, and the New York *Daily News* and American Media also made plans to relocate below Canal Street. Realtors, sensing the momentum, quickly started marketing the area as the city's new publishing and design hub. A decade on, New York's commercial gods were finally giving the nod to Ground Zero.

While the Durst-Condé combo was an incredible coup for Port Authority executive director Chris Ward, who oversaw dramatic turns on both the memorial plaza and the site's signature tower, the deals may have been sweetest for Governor Pataki, who remained true to the skyscraper when almost no one else did. Now he could finally crow a bit. "There is no question in my mind that it will be an iconic property, and very, very desirable from a commercial standpoint, that achieves the symbolic goals that Daniel Libeskind and I had," he said of the Freedom Tower. "I just wished my firm went down there," he added. "There's nothing I'd rather like than working in that building." After he left public office, Pataki joined the New York City law firm Chadbourne & Parke, which considered moving its Midtown offices to the skyscraper but ultimately decided to stay put. At the firm, Pataki keeps on his windowsill a toaster-sized model of the three iterations of Freedom Tower. Standing in a row, from left to right, is the Libeskind design, the Childs design, and the NYPD-necessitated redesign. "There they are," Pataki said, gesturing fondly to the miniatures. "A, B, and C."

Larry Silverstein also keeps a model of Freedom Tower in the lobby of his headquarters—a reminder of his original ownership of the building. Silverstein said he regrets losing Freedom Tower, though he didn't use the word *regret*. Regret, he said, is something he doesn't do. (Was he disappointed to give up Freedom Tower? "Yes," he said.) "There's so much to do going forward," he said, "who the hell's got time to look back?"

At eighty-two, Silverstein still works every day, in a corner office in 7 WTC, next door to Ground Zero, with floor-to-ceiling windows and unobstructed views of the Hudson River and, in the foreground, the embryonic WTC site. Every day, he looks down upon the half-constructed parcel, his three emerging towers on the eastern side, and, in the middle, the memorial plaza. Many of the players have come and gone from their positions of influence, but Silverstein is still deep in the muck of the rebuilding, working with the Port Authority to finish developing his sites and looking for tenants for Towers 2 and 3, which he said he hopes will be constructed by 2017. The first of his skyscrapers, WTC 4, is on track to open in the fall of 2013, and will be partially occupied by the Port Authority (as part of their 2006 deal). Since he's still in the midst of it all—"Every day there's another set of issues; every day there's another crisis," he said—Silverstein remained more tight-lipped than some of his fellow stakeholders. He's also saving the best stories, he told me. "There's a book to read that lays this all out," he said. "I'm writing it."

Silverstein wouldn't explain why he has stuck with the rebuilding all these years, other than to say that he is the kind of person who determines a goal and then pursues it. And each person who came along and told him to get out—including, at one time or another, the insurers, the Port Authority, Mayor Bloomberg, and Governor Pataki—simply pissed him off and spurred him on. Nonetheless, the decade does seem to have taken a bit of a toll. "Did I do the right thing with the past twelve years of my life?" he asked. "Unquestionably. Would I do it again if I knew then what I know now?" Silverstein smiled and chuckled a bit. "I don't know…" he said, adding, more quietly, "It's so hard to know."

WHEN THE MEMORIAL PLAZA OPENED, AS PLANNED, on the ten-year anniversary, the traditional morning ceremony followed only a slightly altered script from anniversaries past. For each of the six moments of silence—when the four planes crashed and the two towers collapsed—Mayor Bloomberg selected short texts to be read by his distinguished guests. At 8:46 a.m., the time when the North Tower was hit, President Obama read Psalm 46. At 9:02 a.m., when the South Tower was hit, former President George W. Bush read Abraham Lincoln's "Letter to Lydia Bixby."

Written to a mother of five sons killed in the Civil War, the letter offers Lincoln's condolences. Its last sentence reads, "I pray that our Heavenly Father may assuage the anguish of your bereavement, and leave you only the cherished memory of the loved and lost, and the solemn pride that must be yours to have laid so costly a sacrifice upon the altar of freedom." An hour later, at 10:03 a.m., the time of the crash in Shanksville, Pennsylvania, Governor Pataki read "The Names," a poem by Billy Collins written in response to 9/11. Lastly, at 10:28 a.m., when the North Tower collapsed, Mayor Giuliani read Ecclesiastes 3:1–9. "For everything there is a season, and a time for every matter under heaven; a time to be born, and a time to die…"

Bloomberg announced a few weeks before the anniversary that there would be no speeches or original work to mark the event. He wanted to ensure, he said, that the day wasn't politicized. Even ten years later, a new narrative was risky. But even though the ceremony went smoothly, it was preceded by some conflict. In mid-August, the New York *Daily News* published a story highlighting that 9/11 first responders were not invited to the anniversary ceremony; space was being reserved for families of the nearly three thousand people killed, and the city planned to hold a special ceremony at the memorial for rescue workers on a different day. First responders have actually never been formally invited to anniversary ceremonies, but because there has always been available space, many firefighters and paramedics have attended. In 2011, however, space was limited, and rescue workers didn't make the cut. Some first responders protested the exclusion, saying it reminded them of their fights to obtain health care. First responder Bonnie Giebfried told CNN that she thought first responders weren't invited because their illnesses complicated official narratives of strength and resilience. If large numbers of sick rescue workers turned out for the ceremony, she said, "the promise 'we'll never forget' becomes a blatantly obvious lie—a public display that the government didn't do right by us." Not surprisingly, the protests didn't alter the city's plans.

The memorial received almost universally positive reviews from critics. Some were a bit muted. The *Los Angeles Times* architectural critic Christopher Hawthorne wrote that the design, with its two square pools, thirty-foot waterfalls, and a plaza dotted with trees, "has managed to preserve at least a kernel of genuine and affecting meaning." But some were ecstatic. Writing in the *New York Review of Books*, in a piece titled "A Masterpiece at Ground Zero," Martin Filler called Arad's design "a stupendous achievement" that reminded him of Maya's Lin's Vietnam Veterans Memorial. "Arad's inexorably powerful, enigmatically abstract pair of abyss-like pools, which demarcate the foundations of the lost Twin Towers, comes as a surprise to those of us who doubted that the chaotic and desultory reconstruction of Ground Zero could yield anything of lasting value," he wrote. "It is generally held that great architecture requires the participation of a great client, but just how this stunning result emerged from such a fraught and contentious process will take some time for critics and historians to sort out."

To master planner Daniel Libeskind, the answer to Filler's question was the process itself. "The reason this project will be good is precisely because it went through this baptism of fire," he said. "It's real, it's not like some investors got together, some architects, some politicians got together and did a project. It's because it really pushed itself through these interests." Sometimes, of course, politicians and investors did get together and make a deal, but Libeskind likes to focus on the half-full part of the glass. He loves to mention Winston Churchill's oft-quoted remark that "democracy is the worst form of government except all the others that have been tried." To give it his characteristic optimism, however, Libeskind interprets the quote and puts a few new words in Churchill's mouth: "In the end, I think, as Churchill said, 'there is no better system.'"

If Libeskind tends to be an idealistic pragmatist, memorial architect Michael Arad is just plain old pragmatic. "A lot of people worked hard, a lot of people were agents of the greater good," he said. But "some people were agents of their own self-interests on this, and it worked out." He continued, "I think we were incredibly lucky and I think we could have gone wrong at any moment. You have to feel proud of what happened here, as a New Yorker, but I think it should be pride leavened with the realization that it could have gone completely wrong."

Arad is pleased with the plaza, but he remained concerned about people's access. In 2011, Ground Zero was still very much a construction zone—indeed, construction bounded the memorial plaza on all sides—and it was still surrounded by chain-link fencing, now topped with barbed wire and draped with canvas panels that shrouded the view. Arad said his goal all along was "something that isn't set aside in this glass box and then ignored, but actually part of our day-to-day life." But achieving an integrated public space was going to take more time. There was only one access point to the memorial, a carefully monitored entrance on the site's western boundary, which required a free ticket reserved in advance, online. It wasn't a seamless part of the city yet.

I RESERVED A TICKET FOR THE MEMORIAL for early October 2011. Its entrance was a bit of a walk from the site's more heavily populated eastern boundary. From Vesey Street, I walked along Church Street, past the site itself, and past the fence's canvas panels, which advertised the memorial and soon-to-be-completed office towers. I also walked past Zuccotti Park, catty-corner to the WTC site, where the city had held past anniversary ceremonies. On this October afternoon, however, the square was being occupied.

A few hundred people filled the plaza as part of Occupy Wall Street, which had taken over the park in mid-September. I walked around the perimeter, taking a few photographs of the people inside making signs and food and, in some instances, simply taking up space. The encampment was basically across the street from Ground Zero, and their proximity to each other wasn't coincidental. Ten years before Occupy, Al Qaeda targeted the Twin Towers because they were symbols of American financial power, and now the Occupy movement was targeting a similar symbol around the corner—Wall Street. This was a peaceful protest, though. In addition to the signs and food, people were manning first-aid stations and libraries. And, even though Occupy was completely unrelated to the early outpourings around the WTC site, when people wrote on walls and hung homemade memorials on fence posts, it still reminded me of that time: people taking over sidewalks and streets to add their voices to the mix. On the park's northern edge, a guy in a black fleece and jeans sat in a cross-legged position, eyes closed, holding a sign that read, "Wake Up." The tradition of unkempt men displaying strange signs around the WTC site continued.

After passing by Zuccotti Park, and winding my way through a few more city blocks, I arrived at the security check for the memorial. The line moved relatively quickly; the 9/11 Memorial Foundation limited the number of tickets it distributed each day to make sure the plaza didn't become too rowdy. I placed my bag on a conveyer belt and walked through a scanner, but kept my shoes on. Then I exited the security building, walked a few more blocks guided by tarp-covered fencing, and, finally, stepped into the open plaza.

Hundreds of young, white oak trees surrounded benches and paved pathways. A few people sat on the benches and a few kids played on long patches of grass. The plaza floor is mostly concrete (specially constructed soil beds for the trees' roots lie underneath the floor), but this area where I entered, on the west side, is greener. The plaza stretched out before me, populated but not crowded, active but not bustling.

I walked immediately to the voids, as Arad calls them, which mark the footprints of the one-acre-square Twin Towers, and which are truly massive. Water streams over all sides, falling thirty feet before filling up the bottom of the square pools. Angled, waist-high granite parapets surround the voids and display the names of victims. They also serve as an ad hoc surface for people's homemade memorials. The angle is gentle enough that people can rest items on top of a particular name, or even squeeze a piece of thin fabric of a flag pole into the cut granite. That afternoon on the parapets there was one bouquet of red carnations and a blue arm patch that read, "Rescue 5, FDNY," and three miniature American flags.

Looming behind the voids, in the northwest corner, is Freedom Tower and its concrete base. The base will be covered with a reflective material, but that afternoon it was unadorned and muscular and looked very much like a bunker. An enormous American flag hung from the building's fortieth floor, just above the base, giving the mostly dark, glossy structure a bit of color. And from there, glass panels and steel rose up and up. Barely visible at the tip-top was a solitary construction crane, its mechanical arm stretched out over downtown.

Gazing up at Freedom Tower, standing on the rebuilt space, was sort of intoxicating. For ten years, there had simply been a hole and now there was *something*. There was structure. Above me, 1 WTC stretched up, and below me a concrete plaza lay atop soil beds, which lay above the roof of the underground memorial museum. In some spots, there was even a subway tunnel or two. At long last, Ground Zero felt orderly—even amid the continuing chaos. The new space still reflected the era's turmoil, of course, what with the winding security check, the looming bunker, and the fence topped with barbed wire—not to mention the people hoisting signs and taking up space just outside the site's boundaries. But now, for the first time in ten years, after the battles had been lost and won, there were other, bigger things to look at.

EPILOGUE

2011–

The rebuilding of the World Trade Center site was never beautiful. As the years passed, it became progressively more political and dysfunctional, much like the decade itself. But the completion of the memorial marked a turning point downtown, ushering in a sense of optimism and a belief that the project would indeed, eventually, get done. For the rebuilding, an end was in sight.

Not long after the memorial opened, 1 WTC/Freedom Tower hit a milestone: with 104 completed stories, it officially became the tallest building in North America. You could see the skyscraper from vantage points all over Manhattan. And construction on it had fallen only *slightly* behind; the Port Authority pushed its fall 2013 completion date back to the winter of 2014. Meanwhile, the Port Authority continued to work on its transit hub, designed by Santiago Calatrava. And, by the end of 2012, more than five million people had visited the memorial plaza, a number that would surely have been higher if it had been possible to simply walk onto it from the street.

Conflicts and uncertainty persisted, of course, and sometimes overshadowed the progress. The costs of the whole project, somewhere around the $15 billion mark, including roughly $4 billion for Freedom Tower and $4 billion for the transit hub, were understandably difficult for many to accept. When the Port Authority announced it was raising bridge and tunnel toll fares—and claimed the increase was to fund transportation projects, not the rebuilding, even though its budget allocated billions of dollars for the WTC site—many accused the Port Authority of building office space on the backs of commuters. In addition, the human costs of the attacks remained at the fore. As part of the ongoing construction work, crews continued to excavate new parts of the WTC site and, consequently, continued to find fragments that could be human remains. In early April 2013, more than 50 new fragments were found and sent to the office of the chief medical examiner for testing.

The underground memorial museum was delayed too. The Port Authority halted construction on it right after the ten year anniversary over a dispute with the 9/11 Memorial Foundation. At issue was whether the Port Authority or the foundation would pay $12 million to complete construction, but since New York Governor Andrew Cuomo ran half of the Port Authority and Mayor Bloomberg ran the 9/11 Memorial Foundation, the dispute doubled as a power struggle between the City and the State of New York. After a year of squabbling, the two sides finally struck a deal in September 2012. The foundation agreed to pay the remaining construction costs in exchange for official ownership of the eight-acre memorial and museum. The conflict postponed the museum's opening for over a year, until 2014.

And then, just after construction on the museum recommenced, Hurricane Sandy flooded New York City, further delaying the work and raising concerns about the prospects of an underground museum in a flood zone. Some of the exhibition's largest and most iconic artifacts, like the fire truck from Ladder 3 and the final column (both housed for years in Hangar 17), sat in flood water for days. They had been placed in the museum early because they were so large; the only way they could get in was through a special hole in the museum's roof, also the memorial plaza's floor, which had to be sealed before the tenth anniversary opening. Fortunately, the artifacts were wrapped in plastic and escaped permanent damage. But the hurricane raised questions about how to best protect the museum, as well as Lower Manhattan, in the future. As Governor Cuomo put it, it was the second "100 year flood" in two years. No one could plan for that and yet, somehow, people would have to. There would always be one more thing. And, a few months later, on the afternoon of April 15, 2013, there was—this time in Boston.

WHEN THE TWO BOMBS EXPLODED AT THE MARATHON, I was at home, as usual, sitting at my computer. My apartment was south of downtown Boston, a couple of miles from the finish line on Boylston Street, so the chaos felt a safe distance from me and my family. A few days later, however, when the entire city was ordered on "lockdown" after a midnight shootout in Watertown left one of the accused brothers dead and the other bleeding and hiding from police for what seemed like an eternity—but was, in fact, only twenty-four hours—the craziness felt much closer. Even though we lived a few miles from Watertown, we followed orders and stayed inside, scrolling through online photographs of a disturbingly empty city.

The Boston attack was different from 9/11: far fewer people were killed; instead of a global terrorist organization it was the work of two young brothers who had come to the United States a decade before; the weapons were not planes, but pressure cooker bombs. But, like 9/11, the target was an international symbol, a sporting event with athletes from scores of countries, being filmed by thousands. Within hours, images of the exploding finish line dominated screens around the world, and homemade memorials dotted downtown.

Soon, talk proliferated of resilience and unity, heroism and justice. "We come together to pray, and mourn, and measure our loss,"

President Obama said at an interfaith memorial service near the site of the bombings. "But we also come together today to reclaim that state of grace, to reaffirm that the spirit of this city is undaunted, and the spirit of this country shall remain undimmed." Joe Daniels, the President of the 9/11 Memorial, sent out an e-mail titled, "We Stand United with Boston." "The 9/11 Memorial is a constant reminder not only of what we have endured as a result of terrorism," he wrote, "but also of our ability to come together with limitless compassion." This was one of the legacies of 9/11: familiar, uncomplicated words that Americans could draw upon to renew some sense of normalcy. *Boston Strong. United We Stand. America the Re-build-iful.*

I NEVER DID FORGET MY FAVORITE REFRAIN. As the years passed, the words stayed with me, but not without a shift in meaning. The refrain gradually came to mean something grittier, more pragmatic, even cynical, in keeping with the new spirit of the times. "*That's* America the Re-Build-iful," I would say to myself after another redesign or another round of arbitration or another awkward compromise moved the rebuilding one inch forward while depleting more goodwill. That, alas, is how things get done. "America the Re-Build-iful" acquired an edge.

But the refrain's original idealism *was* still there, buried underneath the layers of cynicism, and that's the other reason the words stayed with me. The rebuilding wasn't, after all, a story only of dysfunction and messiness. It was also a story of public engagement and expression (also always messy), as well as persistence, compromise, and luck. It was a story of how things worked, and how things didn't work, at the turn of twenty-first-century America.

NOTES

CHAPTER 1: PEOPLE COME

3   Mark L., telephone conversation with author, June 17, 2002.

6   Numerous books document urban rebuilding efforts, including Edward Linenthal, *The Unfinished Bombing: Oklahoma City in American Memory* (Oxford: Oxford University Press, 2001); Andreas Huyssen, *Present Pasts, Urban Palimpsests and the Politics of Memory* (Stanford: Stanford University Press, 2003); and Lisa Yoneyama, *Hiroshima Traces: Time, Space, and the Dialectics of Memory* (Berkeley: University of California Press, 1999).

7   Andrew Sullivan, "Rebuild It," *The Daily Dish*, Atlantic.com, September 14, 2001.

7   Crispin Sartwell, "Rebuilding after the Disaster: New Towers or New Flowers?" *Philadelphia Inquirer*, September 24, 2001.

8   David Friend, *Watching the World Change* (New York: Farrar Straus Giroux, 2006), 32.

9   Associated Press photographers captured numerous responses to 9/11 around the world. The mentioned events: (1) Berlin WW3: Jan Bauer, September 11, 2001; (2) Islamabad street: John McConnico, September 21, 2001; (3) European moment of silence: Noemi Bruzak, September 14, 2001; (4) Rome street rally: Corrado Giambalvo, September 20, 2001; (5) Chilean Students: Santiago Llanquin, September 22, 2001.

9   President George W. Bush, "Joint Address to Congress and the Nation," September 20, 2001.

11   Sam, author interview at WTC site, February 9, 2002.

12   Steve, Amy; author interviews at the WTC site, November 18, 2001.

12   Lev and Naomi, author interview at the WTC site, February 10, 2002.

13   Paul Grondahl, "Scrolls of Sorrow Find Home," *Times Union*, September 10, 2003.

14   Miles Richardson, "The Gift of Presence: The Act of Leaving Artifacts at Shrines, Memorials and Other Tragedies," in *Textures of Place: Exploring Humanist Geographies*, ed. P. C. Adams, S. D. Hoelscher, and K. E. Till (Minneapolis: University of Minnesota Press, 2001), 257–72.

15   Mark L., telephone conversation with author, June 17, 2002.

16   Michael Shulan, author interview, May 25, 2010. Susan Sontag also discusses the exhibit, and specifically its blurry lines between professional and amateur photographers, in *Regarding the Pain of Others* (New York: Picador, 2003), 27–29.

CHAPTER 2: THE LEASEHOLDER AND THE LANDOWNER

17   Port Authority press release, "Governor Pataki, Acting Governor DiFrancesco Laud Historic Port Authority Agreement to Privatize World Trade Center," July 24, 2001, Press Release Number: 101–2001.

18   "A Discussion with Larry Silverstein about the 9/11 Memorial," *The Charlie Rose Show*, February 27, 2003, PBS; Robin Finn, "Public Lives; Undaunted and Planning the Next Great Skyline," *New York Times*, February 15, 2002; Budd Mishkin, "One On 1: Developer Larry Silverstein," NY1, July 31, 2006.

19   Biographical information on Larry Silverstein comes from James Glanz and Eric Lipton, *City in the Sky: The Rise and Fall of the World Trade Center* (New York: Times Books, Henry Holt and Company, 2004).

20   Paul Goldberger makes a similar point about the negative effect of Larry Silverstein's early decisions in his book *Up From Zero* (New York: Random House 2004), 40–41.

20   Associated Press, "World Trade Center Landlord Envisages Four New Towers in Aftermath," September 22, 2001.

21   Tracy, author interview at the WTC site, January 23, 2002.

22   George Pataki, author interview, February 14, 2013.

23   Marshall Berman, *All That Is Solid Melts into Air: The Experience of Modernity* (New York: Penguin Books, 1982), 305.

23   Eric Darton details the Port Authority's creation in *Divided We Stand: A Biography of New York's World Trade Center* (New York: Basic Books, 1999), 41–43.

24   The earliest ideas for the WTC are chronicled in James Glanz and Eric Lipton, *City in the Sky: The Rise and Fall of the World Trade Center* (New York: Times Books, Henry Holt and Company, 2004); and Angus Kress Gillespie, *Twin Towers: The Life of New York City's World Trade Center* (New Jersey: Rutgers University Press, 1999).

24   Lower Manhattan Association Records, as recorded by James Glanz and Eric Lipton, *City in the Sky: The Rise and Fall of the World Trade Center* (New York: Times Books, Henry Holt and Company, 2004), 33.

26   Eric Darton chronicles the destruction of Radio Row in *Divided We Stand* (New York: Basic Books, 1999), 62–68.

27   Ada Louise Huxtable, "Who's Afraid of the Big, Bad Buildings?," *New York Times*, May 29, 1966.

28   Philippe Petit's walk is chronicled in, among others, the documentary *Man on Wire*, directed by James Marsh (2008).

28   Office for Special Planning Report, as quoted in Eric Darton, *Divided We Stand* (New York: Basic Books, 1999), 205.

CHAPTER 3: ARCHITECTS

31   Rick Bell, author interview, April 19, 2002.

33   Jane Jacobs, *The Death and Life of Great American Cities* (New York: Vintage, 1992).

33   Author notes, New York New Visions meeting, Van Alen Institute, New York, November, 27, 2001.

34   "Memorials Process Team Briefing Book: Findings from Outreach, Temporary Memorials & Research Working Groups," New York New Visions, March 2002.

34   Tina Chui, author interview, December 7, 2001.
35   Monica Iken, author interview, September 26, 2002.
36   Tina Chui, author interview, December 7, 2001.
36   Author notes, New York New Visions meeting, Van Alen Institute, New York, November 16, 2001.
37   "Nous sommes tous américains," *Le Monde*, September 13, 2001; "Ground Zero, Madrid," *New York Times*, March 12, 2004.
38   Kevin Kennon, author interview, July 3, 2003.
40–41 The viewing platform's creation was reported by John Leland, "Letting the View Speak for Itself," *New York Times*, January 3, 2002; and by Robin Finn, "Instead of a Fancy Restaurant, Raw Wood," *New York Times*, January 9, 2002.
41   Rudolph Giuliani, "Farewell Address," December 27, 2001.
42   David Rockwell and Kurt Anderson, "David Rockwell Builds at Ground Zero," TED Talk, filmed February 2002, posted June 2007.

CHAPTER 4: THE VIEWING PLATFORM

45   George Pataki, author interview, February 14, 2013.
46   Slide courtesy of Marilyn Jordan Taylor.
47   LMDC advisory councils, http://www.renewnyc.com/aboutus/advisory/index.asp.
48   Resident, author interview, February 24, 2002.
49   Neil, Tom, and Susan, author interview at the WTC site, January 23, 2002.
53   Monica Iken, author interview, September 23, 2002.
53   Letter published in "As Public Yearns to See Ground Zero, Survivors Call a Viewing Stand Ghoulish," *New York Times*, January 13, 2002.
53   Dean E. Murphy, "As Public Yearns to See Ground Zero, Survivors Call a Viewing Stand Ghoulish," *New York Times*, January 13, 2002.
54   Deyan Sudjic, "Can Anyone Do Justice to Ground Zero," *Guardian*, January 27, 2002.
55   Michael Wilson, "How to Say Enough Gracefully; Trinity Church Ponders Future of a Sept. 11 Memorial," *New York Times*, October 11, 2002.
56   Craig Williams, author interview at the WTC site, July 31, 2002.

CHAPTER 5: THE FENCE

59   Adam Nagourney, "Ground Zero: The Site. Mayor Gets A Bigger Say On Rebuilding," *New York Times*, March 7, 2002. A photograph of the proposed wall accompanied the article, with the following caption: "A 30-foot-high wall made of wood may be erected around the site of the World Trade Center, shown in a picture taken on Tuesday. A state official said yesterday that it was intended to block a disconcerting view."
59   Rick Bell, author interview, September 17, 2002.
60   Diana Balmori, author interview, January 8, 2003; The New York New Visions design was also chronicled in multiple newspapers, including Katia Hetter, "WTC Wall Will Have Removable Panels," *New York Newsday*, April 19, 2002; and Edward Wyatt, "Viewing Wall Proposed at Trade Center Site," *New York Times*, April 18, 2002.
61   Mark Wagner, author interview, June 24, 2004.

61 Robert Frost, "Mending Wall," 1914.

62 Mark Wagner, author interview, August 4, 2004.

63 Author notes on viewing fence, October 2002.

64 Carol Willis, phone conversation with author, April 19, 2004.

65 Mark Wagner, author interview, August 4, 2004.

66 Family from Scotland, author interview at the WTC site, October 3, 2002.

68 Author notes on viewing fence, July 2002. This change was also chronicled in "Defaced Panels Removed at Ground Zero," *New York Times*, July 6, 2003; and Glenn Collins, "Look Up, and Trade Center's Story is Readable Again," *New York Times*, September 13, 2003.

69 Father and child, author interview at WTC site, July 7, 2003.

CHAPTER 6: THE PEOPLE VERSUS THE PORT AUTHORITY

72 Author notes, "Listening Session," Pace University, organized by the Lower Manhattan Development Corporation, May 23, 2002.

73 Lou Tomson, as quoted in Paul Goldberger, *Up From Zero* (New York: Random House 2004), 98.

74–77 Author notes and interviews, "Listening to the City," July 20, 2002. The results of the hearing were also published in "Listening to the City, Report of Proceedings," by the Civic Alliance to Rebuild Downtown New York, August 2002.

78 Leslie Eaton, "Visions of Ground Zero: The Plans; New York Embraces Commerce, as It Always Has," *New York Times*, July 21, 2002.

78 Herbert Muschamp, "An Appraisal, Marginal Role for Architecture at Ground Zero," *New York Times*, May 23, 2002.

79 George Pataki, author interview, February 14, 2013.

80 Robert Yaro, as quoted in Paul Goldberger, *Up From Zero* (New York: Random House 2004), 180.

81 Design Studies, Lower Manhattan Development Corporation, December 2002.

83 Herbert Muschamp, "Balancing Reason and Emotion in Twin Towers Void," *New York Times*, February 7, 2003.

85 Janno Lieber, author interview, September 21, 2012.

86 Alex Garvin, author interview, August 12, 2010.

86 George Pataki, author interview, February 14, 2013.

86 The possibility of a land swap was discussed in Paul Goldberger, *Up From Zero* (New York: Random House, 2004), 128–30; and Philip Nobel, *Sixteen Acres: Architecture and the Outrageous Struggle for the Future of Ground Zero* (New York: Metropolitan Books, 2005), 127–28.

87 George Pataki, author interview, February 14, 2013.

CHAPTER 7: LADY LIBERTY AND THE FREEDOM TOWER

92 Libeskind interview published in "Jewish Museum Berlin: Architect Daniel Libeskind" (Berlin: G+B Arts International, 2000).

92 Daniel Libeskind, author interview, September 27, 2012.

94   George Pataki, author interview, February 14, 2013.

94   Daniel Libeskind, introductory text, "Memory Foundations," 2002.

95   Daniel Libeskind, author interview, September 27, 2012.

95   Larry Silverstein, as quoted in Deborah Sontag, "The Hole in the City's Heart," *New York Times*, September 11, 2006.

96   "A Discussion with Larry Silverstein about the 9/11 Memorial," *The Charlie Rose Show*, February 27, 2003, PBS.

97   The SOM break-in was chronicled in Philip Nobel, *Sixteen Acres* (New York: Metropolitan Books, 2005), 225.

98   Paul Goldberger chronicled the changes that David Childs made to Daniel Libeskind's design in *Up From Zero* (New York: Random House 2004), 194–99.

99   Libeskind and Silverstein, as quoted in Paul Goldberger, *Up From Zero* (New York: Random House 2004), 200.

100 The story of the cornerstone was chronicled by Deborah Sontag, "The Hole in the City's Heart," *New York Times*, September 11, 2006.

101 The story of the complaints by the NYPD was chronicled by Deborah Sontag, "The Hole in the City's Heart," *New York Times*, September 11, 2006.

102 John Cahill, author interview, February 14, 2013.

102 George Pataki, author interview, February 14, 2013.

102 John Cahill, author interview, February 14, 2013.

103 T. J. Gottsdeigner, as quoted in Glenn Collins, "A Freedom Tower Restarted from Scratch," *New York Times*, July 10, 2005.

103 The *Times* provided a nice graphic to compare Childs's original and Childs's redesign, http://www.nytimes.com/imagepages/2005/06/29/nyregion/20050630_appraisal_GRAPHIC.html.

103 Nicolai Ouroussoff, "A Tower of Impregnability, the Sort Politicians Love," *New York Times*, June 30, 2005.

103 Janno Leiber, author interview, September 21, 2012.

104 Nicolai Ouroussoff, "A Tower of Impregnability, the Sort Politicians Love," *New York Times*, June 30, 2005.

CHAPTER 8: FAMILIES

105 Janno Leiber, author interview, September 21, 2012.

106 Ada Louise Huxtable, "Don't Blame the Architects," *Wall Street Journal*, January 7, 2003.

106 Michael Bloomberg, as quoted in Edward Wyatt, "Less is More, Mayor Suggests on World Trade Center Site," *New York Times*, June 13, 2002; and Edward Wyatt, "Remark on Memorial Puts Bloomberg on the Defensive," *New York Times*, June 14, 2002.

107–111 Meetings and interviews with Philadelphia Families Group, 2003–2004.

111 Gary Smiley, author interview, October 21, 2002.

113 Carol S. Fullerton, Robert J. Ursano, and Leming Wang, "Acute Stress Disorder, Posttraumatic Stress Disorder, and Depression in Disaster or Rescue Workers," *American Journal of Psychiatry* 161(2004): 1370–76.

CHAPTER 9: THE MEMORIAL

117   Daniel Libeskind, author interview, September 27, 2012.

118   World Trade Center Site Memorial Competition Guidelines, Lower Manhattan Development Corporation, 2003, p. 10.

118   Michael Arad, author interview, September 24, 2012.

118   Michael Arad's battles were chronicled in Joe Hagan, "The Breaking of Michael Arad," *New York*, May 14, 2006.

119   Michael Arad, author interview, September 24, 2012.

120   Libeskind, as quoted in Joe Hagan, "The Breaking of Michael Arad," *New York*, May 14, 2006.

121   Michael Arad, author interview, September 24, 2012.

122   The story of Maya's Lin early career is told in the documentary "A Strong, Clear Vision," directed by Freida Lee Mock (1994).

125   Michael Arad, author interview, September 24, 2012.

126   I visited Hangar 17 in August 2004, when I was given a tour by Mark Wagner.

127   Mark Wagner, author interview, August 4, 2004.

127   In the spring of 2004, Wagner received a second, larger shipment of almost six hundred pieces of steel that the New York City Department of Design and Construction (DDC) had collected as part of its effort (along with FEMA) to study the buildings' collapse. This second collection, after extensive measuring, photographing, and cataloguing, joined the primary collection of steel inside the hangar.

129   Arad's visit to Hangar 17 is mentioned by Deborah Sontag, "The Hole in the City's Heart," *New York Times*, September 11, 2006.

CHAPTER 10: THE FREEDOM CENTER

132   Report on the Memorial Center and Cultural Complex at the World Trade Center Site; Lower Manhattan Development Corporation, February 10, 2004, p. 10.

132   Robin Pogrebin, "Freedom Center is Still a Somewhat Vague Notion," *New York Times*, June 24, 2004.

132   Richard Tofel, author interview, September 11, 2008.

133   President George W. Bush, "Second Inaugural Address," January 5, 2005.

134   Nicolai Ouroussoff, "A Temple of Contemplation and Conflict," *New York Times*, May 26, 2006.

134   Debra Burlingame, "The Great Ground Zero Heist," *Wall Street Journal*, June 7, 2005.

135   Michelle Malkin, "The Desecration of Ground Zero," *National Ledger*, June 8, 2005.

135   Richard Tofel, "A Fitting Place at Ground Zero," *Wall Street Journal*, June 9, 2005.

135   Richard Tofel, author interview, September 11, 2008.

135   Debra Burlingame, author interview, February 22, 2012.

139   Takebackthememorial.org, August 2005.

139   Letter to the Editor, "Honoring the Dead at Ground Zero," *New York Times*, September 28, 2005, p. A17.

140 Patrick Healy, "Pataki Warns Cultural Groups for Museum at Ground Zero," *New York Times*, June 25, 2005.

140 Editorial, "Keeping Ground Zero Free," *New York Times*, July 12, 2005.

140 Debra Burlingame, author interview, February 12, 2012.

140 Burlingame recounted the interaction between Gardner and Clinton to me during our February 2012 interview.

141 Manny Fernandez, "Clinton Says She Opposes Freedom Center," *New York Times*, September 24, 2005; David Dunlap, "Governor Bars Freedom Center at Ground Zero," *New York Times*, September 28, 2005.

141 Richard Tofel, author interview, September 11, 2008.

141 George Pataki, author interview, February 14, 2013.

142 Richard Tofel, author interview, September 11, 2008.

143 Debra Burlingame, author interview, February 22, 2012.

CHAPTER 11: THINGS FALL BEHIND

146 Seth Pinsky, author interview, January 19, 2012.

147 Janno Lieber, author interview, September 21, 2012.

147 Seth Pinsky, author interview, January 19, 2012.

148 Janno Lieber, author interview, September 21, 2012.

149 Charles Gargano, as quoted in Charles V. Bagli, "Negotiations Break Down for Trade Center Plan," *New York Times*, March 15, 2006.

149 Janno Lieber, author interview, September 21, 2012.

150 Seth Pinsky, author interview, January 19, 2012.

151 George Pataki, author interview, February 14, 2012.

151 Janno Lieber, author interview, September 21, 2012.

151 George Pataki, author interview, February 14, 2012.

152 Memorial costs and report: Charles V. Bagli and David W. Dunlap, "Memorial Cost at Ground Zero Nears $1 Billion," *New York Times*, May 5, 2006.

154 Author notes and interviews, September 11, 2008.

155 Wearechange.com/about.

159 Sarah Palin, press conference, World Trade Center site, September 25, 2008.

CHAPTER 12: ANTI-MONUMENTALISM

163 Chris Ward, author interview, September 19, 2012.

164 Ibid.

164 Ibid.

164 Ibid.

165 Ibid.

165 Ibid.

165 Governor Pataki quoted in David Dunlap, "Farewell to 'Freedom' for a While," *New York Times*, March 3, 2008.

166 Douglas Feiden, " 'Freedom' out at WTC: Port Authority says The Freedom Tower is now 1 World Trade Center," *Daily News*, March 27, 2009.

166 Parenthesis, David Dunlap, "The 'Freedom Tower' Name Roars Back," *New York Times*, March 27, 2009.

166 Comments in response to "The 'Freedom Tower' Name Roars Back," *New York Times*, March 27, 2009, http://cityroom.blogs.nytimes. com/2009/03/27/the-freedom-tower-name-roars-back/.

167 Chris Ward, author interview, September 19, 2012.

167 Governor Pataki quoted in Associated Press, "Freedom Tower in NYC Gets Name Change," March 27, 2009.

168 Daniel Libeskind, author interview, September 27, 2012.

168 Chris Ward, "Remarks by Port Authority Executive Director Christopher O. Ward on the World Trade Center Assessment." Press Release, Port Authority of New York and New Jersey, July 1, 2008, Press Release Number: 68–2008.

169 Chris Ward, author interview, September 19, 2012.

169 Josh Wallack, author interview, January 20, 2012.

170 Michael Arad, author interview, September 24, 2012.

171 Port Authority Report: "Port Authority Issues Report Outlining Road Map for Rebuilding of World Trade Center Site," October 2, 2008, Press Release Number: 107–2008.

171 Chris Ward, author interview, September 19, 2012.

172 Ibid.

173 Josh Wallack, author interview, January 20, 2012.

173 Chris Ward, author interview, September 19, 2012.

173 Janno Lieber, author interview, September 21, 2012.

174 Chris Ward, author interview, September 19, 2012.

175 "In the Matter of the Arbitration between 2 World Trade Center LLC, 3 World Trade Center LLC, 4 World Trade Center LLC, and the Port Authority of New York and New Jersey: Decision, Interim Award, and Supplemental Order," January 26, 2010. (Document made available by the *New York Times*.)

175 Janno Lieber, author interview, September 21, 2012.

175 "In the Matter of the Arbitration between 2 World Trade Center LLC, 3 World Trade Center LLC, 4 World Trade Center LLC, and the Port Authority of New York and New Jersey: Decision, Interim Award, and Supplemental Order," January 26, 2010. (Document made available by the *New York Times*.)

176 "Joint Statement on World Trade Center Development Plan," March 25, 2010, Press Release Number: 15–2010.

176 Chris Ward, author interview, September 19, 2012.

176 Ibid.

CHAPTER 13: THE MEMORIAL AND THE MAYOR

179 Josh Wallack, author interview, January 20, 2012.

181 Bloomberg's comments published in Deborah Sontag, "The Hole in the City's Heart," *New York Times*, September 11, 2006.

182 Letter to the Editor, *New York Times*, October 11, 2006.

183 Memorial donations documented in David Dunlap, "$350 Million Raised to Date for 9/11 Memorial," *New York Times*, April 9, 2008.

183 Michael Arad, author interview, September 24, 2012.

183 Ibid.

185 Ibid.

186 Ibid.

186 Ibid.
187 Ibid.
188 Ibid.
188 Ibid.
188 Michael Eisner, as quoted in Joe Hagan, "The Breaking of Michael Arad," *New York* (magazine), May 14, 2006.
190 Frank Sciame, "World Trade Center Memorial: Draft Recommendations and Analysis," prepared for the Lower Manhattan Development Corporation, June 20, 2006.
190 Michael Arad, author interview, September 24, 2012.

CHAPTER 14: THE ISLAMIC CENTER

194 Imam Feisal, quoted in Ralph Blumenthal and Sharaf Mowjood, "Muslim Prayers and Renewal Near Ground Zero," *New York Times*, December 8, 2009.
195 Anne Barnard, "For Muslim Center Sponsors, Early Missteps Fueled Storm," *New York Times*, August 11, 2010.
195 Associated Press, "NYC Community Board OKs Ground Zero Mosque Plans," May 25, 2010.
196 Jeff Jacoby, "A Mosque at Ground Zero?" *Boston Globe*, June 6, 2010.
196 Gabriel Winant, "Ground Zero Mosque Touches Off Right-Wing Panic," *Salon*, May 27, 2010.
197 Caroline May, "Rick Lazio and Andrew Cuomo fight over Ground Zero mosque," *The Daily Caller*, August 8, 2010.
197 Harry Reid, quoted in Carl Hulse, "G.O.P Seizes on Islamic Center Near Ground Zero as Election Issue," *New York Times*, August 17, 2010.
197 President Obama, quoted in Sheryl Gay Stolberg, "Obama Says Mosque Remarks Were About Rights," *New York Times*, August 15, 2010.
198 Michael Barbaro, "Bloomberg's Fierce Defense of Muslim Center Has Deep Roots," *New York Times*, August 13, 2010.
199 Author field notes from protests at the World Trade Center site, September 10, 2010, and September 11, 2010.
200 The numbers for the protests were cited in Joe Walker, Douglas Montero, Amber Sutherland, and Kathianne Boniello, "Thousands Rally For, Against Mosque on Tragic Day," *New York Post*, September 11, 2010.
201 Field notes from protests at the World Trade Center site, September 11, 2010.
203 Anthony Weiner, "Why I Was Angry," *New York Times*, August 3, 2010.

CHAPTER 15: THE MUSEUM

205 Michael Shulan, author interview, May 19, 2011.
206 Jan Ramirez, author interview, May 20, 2011.
206 Alice Greenwald, author interview, May 19, 2011.
207 Ibid.
208 Michael Shulan, author interview, May 19, 2011.
208 Ibid.
208 Alice Greenwald, author interview, May 19, 2011.
209 Jan Ramirez, author interview, May 20, 2011.
209 Michael Shulan, author interview, May 19, 2011.

209 Jan Ramirez, author interview, May 20, 2011.

210 Alice Greenwald, author interview, May 19, 2011.

211 Katie Edgerton, author interview, May 20, 2011.

212 Ibid.

212 Michael Shulan, author interview, May 19, 2011.

212 Alice Greenwald, author interview, May 19, 2011.

212 Joe Daniels, author interview, March 26, 2013.

213 Ron Paul and Rudolph Giuliani, Republican Primary Debate, South Carolina, May 15, 2007, http://www.youtube.com/watch?v=AD7dnFDdwu0.

213 Katie Edgerton, author interview, May 20, 2011.

214 Ibid.

214 Ibid.

215 Liz Mazucci, author interview, May 19, 2011.

215 Michael Shulan, author interview, May 19, 2011.

216 Liz Mazucci, author interview, May 19, 2011.

217 Debra Burlingame, as quoted in "Museum Planning Conversation Series Report, 2006–2008," National September 11 Memorial Museum.

217 Diane Horning, as quoted in "Museum Planning Conversation Series Report, 2006–2008," National September 11 Memorial Museum.

218 "Focus Group Report for 9/11 Memorial and Museum Research on Museum," Landor Consulting, February 14, 2010.

CHAPTER 16: A DEATH, THE DURSTS, AND AN ANNIVERSARY

222 Michael Moore, "Some Final Thoughts on the Death of Osama bin Laden," May 12, 2011, http://www.michaelmoore.com/words/mike-friends -blog/some-final-thoughts-on-death-of-osama-bin-laden.

222 Mona Eltahawy, "No Dignity at Ground Zero," Guardian, May 2, 2011.

223 Charles Krauthammer, "Evil Does Not Die of Natural Causes," Washington Post, May 5, 2011.

223 Alice Greenwald, author interview, May 19, 2011.

224 Author field notes, World Trade Center site, May 5, 2011.

225 Chris Ward, author interview, September 19, 2012.

226 Douglas Durst and Anthony Malkin, "An Open Letter to the Port Authority of NY & NJ and Governor Eliot Spitzer Recommending a Reconsideration of the Development Plan for the Freedom Tower," Wall Street Journal, February 23, 2007.

226 David Lombino, "Durst and Malkin Could Lose Big If Tower Is Built," New York Sun, March 2, 2007.

227 Durst spoke about his ownership stake in Andrew Rice, "The Saving of Ground Zero," Bloomberg Businessweek, August 3, 2011.

227 George Pataki, author interview, February 14, 2013.

228 Larry Silverstein, author interview, March 15, 2013.

228 Ibid.

229 Ibid.

230 Bonnie Giebfried, as quoted in Jeff Stein, "First Responders Decry Exclusion from 9/11 Ceremony," CNN, August 16, 2011.

230 Christopher Hawthorne, "Feeling the Void," Los Angeles Times, August 12, 2011.

230 Martin Filler, "A Masterpiece at Ground Zero," *New York Review of Books*, October 27, 2011.

231 Daniel Libeskind, author interview, September 24, 2012.

231 Michael Arad, author interview, September 21, 2012.

EPILOGUE: 2011—

236 Joe Nocera speaks out against the Port Authority's toll increases in "9/11's White Elephant," *New York Times*, August 19, 2011.

238 President Barack Obama, "Speech for Victims of the Boston Bombing," April 18, 2013.

238 Joe Daniels, "We Stand United With Boston," e-mail message, April 18, 2013.

SELECTED BIBLIOGRAPHY

Berman, Marshall. *All That is Solid Melts Into Air: The Experience of Modernity*. New York: Penguin Books, 1982.

Darton, Eric. *Divided We Stand: A Biography of New York's World Trade Center*. New York: Basic Books, 1999.

Friend, David. *Watching the World Change: The Stories Behind the Images of 9/11*. New York: Farrar Straus Giroux, 2006.

Gillespie, Angus Kress. *Twin Towers: The Life of New York City's World Trade Center*. New Brunswick, New Jersey: Rutgers University Press, 1999.

Glanz, James and Eric Lipton. *City in the Sky: The Rise and Fall of the World Trade Center*. New York: Times Books, Henry Holt and Company, 2004.

Goldberger, Paul. *Up From Zero: Politics, Architecture, and the Rebuilding of New York*. New York: Random House, 2004.

Huyssen, Andreas. *Present Pasts: Urban Palimpsests and the Politics of Memory*. Stanford: Stanford University Press, 2003.

Jacobs, Jane. *The Death and Life of Great American Cities*. New York: Vintage Books Edition, 1992.

Libeskind, Daniel. *Jewish Museum Berlin*. Berlin: G+B Arts International, 2000.

Linenthal, Edward. *The Unfinished Bombing: Oklahoma City in American Memory*. New York: Oxford University Press, 2001.

Low, Setha. *On the Plaza: The Politics of Public Space and Culture*. Austin: University of Texas Press, 2000.

Mock, Freida Lee. *Maya Lin: A Strong, Clear Vision*. 1994, documentary.

Nobel, Philip. *Sixteen Acres: Architecture and the Outrageous Struggle for the Future of Ground Zero*. New York: Metropolitan Books, 2005.

Richardson, Miles. "The Gift of Presence: The Act of Leaving Artifacts at Shrines, Memorials and Other Tragedies," in *Textures of Place: Exploring Humanist Geographies*. Edited by Paul Adams, Steven Hoelscher and Karen E. Till, 257–272. Minneapolis: University of Minnesota Press, 2001.

Sassen, Saskia. *Cities in a World Economy*, 4th ed. New York: Sage, 2011.

Sontag, Susan. *Regarding the Pain of Others*. New York: Picador, 2003.

Stephens, Suzanne, with Ian Luna and Ron Broadhurst. *Imagining Ground Zero: Official and Unofficial Proposals for the World Trade Center Site*. New York: Rizzoli International Publications, Inc, 2004.

Sturken, Marita. *Tangled Memories: The Vietnam War, the AIDS Epidemic, and the Politics of Remembering*. Berkeley: University of California Press, 1997.

Tilley, Christopher. *A Phenomenology of Landscape: Places, Paths, and Monuments*. Oxford: Berg Press, 1994.

Trouillot, Michel-Rolph. *Silencing the Past: Power and the Production of History*. Boston: Beacon Press, 1995.

Yoneyama, Lisa. *Hiroshima Traces: Time, Space, and the Dialectics of Memory*. Berkeley: University of California Press, 1999.

Young, James E., *The Art of Memory: Holocaust Memorial in History*. New York: Prestel-Verlag, 1994.

INDEX